Elementary
Mandarin
Chinese

*The Complete Language Course
for Beginning Learners*

CORNELIUS C. KUBLER, Ph.D

TUTTLE Publishing

Tokyo | Rutland, Vermont | Singapore

Published by Tuttle Publishing, an imprint of Periplus Editions (HK) Ltd.

www.tuttlepublishing.com

Assistance received from the following in the filming of conversations is gratefully acknowledged:
Lesson 5, Part 1: The Mandarin Training Center, National Taiwan Normal University, Taipei. Lesson 6, Part 1: Shangrila Hotel, Beijing; Part 2: Hilton Hotel, Taipei. Lesson 8, Unit 2: Beijing West Railway Station, Beijing. Lesson 9, Part 1: The Mandarin Training Center, National Taiwan Normal University, Taipei; Part 2: Jianquan Clinic, Taipei. Lesson 10, Part 1: Swisshotel, Beijing. Lesson 12, Part 1: Yuelong Restaurant, Beijing. Lesson 17, Part 2: Fortune Garden Restaurant, North Adams, Massachusetts.

ISBN 978-0-8048-5124-4

Distributed by

North America, Latin America & Europe
Tuttle Publishing
364 Innovation Drive, North Clarendon,
VT 05759-9436 U.S.A.
Tel: 1 (802) 773-8930; Fax: 1 (802) 773-6993
info@tuttlepublishing.com
www.tuttlepublishing.com

Asia Pacific
Berkeley Books Pte. Ltd.
3 Kallang Sector #04-01, Singapore 349278
Tel: (65) 6741-2178; Fax: (65) 6741-2179
inquiries@periplus.com.sg
www.periplus.com

22 21 20 19   10 9 8 7 6 5 4 3 2 1

Printed in Singapore   1909MP

ABOUT TUTTLE
"Books to Span the East and West"

Our core mission at Tuttle Publishing is to create books which bring people together one page at a time. Tuttle was founded in 1832 in the small New England town of Rutland, Vermont (USA). Our fundamental values remain as strong today as they were then—to publish best-in-class books informing the English-speaking world about the countries and peoples of Asia. The world has become a smaller place today and Asia's economic, cultural and political influence has expanded, yet the need for meaningful dialogue and information about this diverse region has never been greater. Since 1948, Tuttle has been a leader in publishing books on the cultures, arts, cuisines, languages and literatures of Asia. Our authors and photographers have won numerous awards and Tuttle has published thousands of books on subjects ranging from martial arts to paper crafts. We welcome you to explore the wealth of information available on Asia at www.tuttlepublishing.com.

Free Bonus Material may also be Downloaded.

How to Download the Bonus Material of this Book.

1. You must have an internet connection.
2. Type the URL below into to your web browser.

https://www.tuttlepublishing.com/Elementary-Mandarin-Chinese-Testbook

For support email us at
info@tuttlepublishing.com.

Contents

Preface

This book, which is a concise, streamlined, combined version of the author's *Basic Mandarin Chinese: Speaking & Listening* and *Basic Mandarin Chinese: Reading & Writing* (Tuttle Publishing 2017), will help learners establish a strong foundation in listening, speaking, reading, and writing Mandarin Chinese.

The book was designed for a beginning level course in Mandarin Chinese that meets three hours a week for one academic year. In addition to time in class, students will need to prepare approximately two to three hours for each class hour. This textbook book should be used with the accompanying *Elementary Mandarin Chinese Workbook* (Tuttle Publishing 2019), which is available separately, and with the accompanying audio files, which can be downloaded directly from the Tuttle Publishing website.

In a college or university environment, it is recommended that this textbook be taught at the rate of approximately one lesson per week. Each lesson is divided into two parts, so Part One could be taken up on the first class day each week and Part Two on the second day, with the third day being used for review, testing, and supplemental activities. Since it would take 24 weeks to go through the materials at this rate but most institutions schedule 25-35 weeks of instruction per academic year, this would still leave some time for other activities, or else allow for a somewhat slower rate of progress through the materials, if preferred. The exact schedule and rate of progress will, of course, need to be determined based on local conditions.

With the exception of two introductory lessons and two review lessons, each part of each lesson in this book includes a conversation, lists of new and supplementary vocabulary, questions on the conversation, general questions, notes on the conversation, and a section specifically on reading (which in turn consists of new characters and words, sentences, conversations, narratives, and notes). Since Pinyin is included everywhere except in the reading exercises, the book is usable even by learners who wish to focus on speaking and listening.

I wish to acknowledge here the following, who have been particularly helpful in the preparation and publication of these materials: Nancy Goh, Jerling G. Kubler, Qunhu Li, Eric Oey, Amory Shih, Yang Wang, and Jun Yang.

Cornelius C. Kubler
Williamstown, Massachusetts

LESSON 1

Orientation to the Study of Chinese

The first task facing you as you set about learning Chinese is to become familiar with the pronunciation system. There are two aspects to this: (1) being able to recognize the sounds of Chinese when someone else produces them and (2) being able to produce the sounds of Chinese yourself. Since the pronunciation you develop during your first few weeks of learning Chinese is likely to stay with you for the rest of your Chinese-speaking days—and will to a large degree determine whether or not people understand you and what effect your speech has on them, it's crucial that you do all you can now to acquire the best pronunciation possible.

Transcription Systems for Chinese

As you're no doubt already aware, Chinese is ordinarily written in Chinese characters. However, since the characters take time to learn and don't provide information on pronunciation in a systematic way, it's more efficient to begin the study of Chinese via a transcription system. The Pinyin system is the transcription system we'll be using in this text.

The written symbols of Pinyin are basically the same as those of the Roman alphabet except that the letter v isn't used. Be aware that Pinyin doesn't record all the details of Chinese sounds; it can only be a rough reminder of the real sounds, which must exist in your heads based on frequent hearing of live or recorded sounds. It's very important that you practice in class with your instructor, and at home with the accompanying audio recordings, just as much as possible.

The Sounds of Mandarin

The basic unit of Mandarin pronunciation is the syllable. A typical Mandarin syllable is composed of three parts: an initial sound, a final sound, and a tone. For example, in the syllable **mà** "scold," **m** is the initial, **a** is the final, and ` represents the tone. Some syllables lack an initial and some syllables, when they're unstressed, have no tone; but every syllable must have a final. In Pinyin the same letter may have two or more different pronunciations depending on what letters come before or after. For example, the **i** in the syllable **xi** sounds different from the **i** in the syllable **zi**, or the **u** in **gu** sounds different from the **u** in **ju**. Therefore, it's best to learn Mandarin pronunciation via syllables rather than focusing on individual letters.

The initials and finals of Mandarin are listed below in the traditional order with instructions on how to produce them and a comparison with the closest English sounds. There is also a pronunciation exercise for each initial and final, which includes several examples of syllables containing the sounds being practiced. The pronunciation exercises are included in the accompanying audio recordings, which are available online for free. Later, this section can serve as a reference if you should forget which Mandarin sound a Pinyin symbol stands for and don't have access to a native speaker or the audio recordings.

How to Learn Chinese Pronunciation

In class, listen attentively to your teachers, carefully observing their lip, tongue, and mouth movements. Mimic your instructors loudly and actively, trying to sound as "Chinese" as possible. Drill enthusiastically and be receptive to correction. You'll want to work on both producing sounds correctly and recognizing them accurately.

For out-of-class study, read the descriptions of the sounds and the suggestions for producing them below. Work intensively with the audio recordings that accompany this section. Listen carefully, then repeat during the pause provided after each item. The first few times work with your book open, then practice with your book closed. Be sure to repeat out loud. When reading Pinyin transcription, always remember the symbols you see before you represent Chinese sounds, not English sounds. In the same way that French, German, and Spanish are written with the Roman alphabet but are not pronounced the same as English, Pinyin stands for Chinese sounds, many of which are very different from English. So beware of the natural tendency to give English pronunciations to the Pinyin symbols. Trust your ears, not your eyes!

Pronunciation Exercises

INITIALS

B   Like the **p** in English **spy** or **spa**. It differs from English **b** as in **by** in that English **b** is voiced (that is, your Adam's apple is buzzing while you say it) while Mandarin **b** is voiceless. Hint: If you're having problems, first say **spa**, then hiss the **s** on **spa** like this: **sssspa**. Then, remove the **s**.

 Pronunciation Exercise A-1

1. **bā** "eight"	3. **bāo** "pack"	5. **bān** "move"	7. **bāng** "help"
2. **bī** "force"	4. **bēi** "cup of"	6. **bēn** "run"	8. **bīng** "soldier"

P   Like the **p** in English **pie** but with a stronger puff of breath. Similar to **p** plus the following **h** in English **hop high**.

 Pronunciation Exercise A-2

1. **pā** "lie"	3. **pāi** "pat"	5. **Pān** (surname)	7. **piān** "essay"
2. **pū** "spread"	4. **piāo** "float"	6. **pēn** "squirt"	8. **pēng** "simmer"

M   Like the **m** in English **my**.

 Pronunciation Exercise A-3

1. **mā** "mom"	3. **māo** "cat"	5. **mōu** "moo"	7. **mēng** "cheat"
2. **mō** "grope"	4. **miāo** "meow"	6. **mēn** "stuffy"	

F   Like the **f** in English **fight**.

 Pronunciation Exercise A-4

1. **fā** "issue"	3. **fēi** "fly"	5. **fēn** "divide"	7. **fēng** "wind"
2. **fū** "husband"	4. **fān** "overturn"	6. **fāng** "square"	

D   Like the **t** in English **steam**. It differs from English **d** as in **day** in that English **d** is voiced while Mandarin **d** is voiceless. Mandarin **d** is produced by most speakers with the tip of the tongue in a slightly more forward position than in English. Hiss the **s** on **stew** like this: **sssstew**. Then divide that into **ssss-tew**. Finally, omit the **sss-** altogether. The end result should be close to Mandarin **du**.

Pronunciation Exercise A-5

1. **dā** "get on"   3. **dāi** "stay"   5. **diē** "dad"   7. **duān** "hold"
2. **dī** "low"   4. **dāo** "knife"   6. **duō** "much"   8. **dēng** "lamp"

T   Like the **t** in **tea** but with a stronger puff of breath. Mandarin **t** is produced by most speakers with the tip of the tongue in a slightly more forward position than in English. Similar to the **t** plus the following **h** in English **can't he**.

Pronunciation Exercise A-6

1. **tā** "she/he"   3. **tiē** "stick"   5. **tiān** "day"   7. **tāng** "soup"
2. **tī** "kick"   4. **tuī** "push"   6. **tūn** "swallow"   8. **tīng** "listen"

N   Like the **n** in English **neat**. Mandarin **n** is produced by most speakers with the tip of the tongue in a slightly more forward position than in English.

Pronunciation Exercise A-7

1. **Nā** (surname)   3. **niū** "girl"   5. **nāng** "murmur"
2. **niē** "pinch"   4. **niān** "pick up"

L   Like the **l** in English **leaf** but tenser (like French, German, or Spanish **l**). Mandarin **l** is produced by most speakers with the tip of the tongue in a slightly more forward position than in English.

Pronunciation Exercise A-8

1. **lā** "pull"   3. **lēi** "tighten"   5. **lōu** "gather up"
2. **lāo** "fish for" 4. **liū** "sneak out" 6. **luō** "talkative"

G   Like the **k** in English **sky**. It differs from English **g** as in **go** in that English **g** is voiced while Mandarin **g** is voiceless. First say **sky**, then hiss the **s** on **sky** like this: **ssssky**. Finally, remove the **s**. The end result should be close to Mandarin **gai**.

Pronunciation Exercise A-9

1. **gē** "brother"   3. **gāo** "tall"   5. **guō** "pot"   7. **gāng** "just"
2. **gāi** "should"   4. **guāi** "well-behaved" 6. **guān** "officer" 8. **gēng** "plough"

K   Like the **k** in English **kite** but with a stronger puff of breath. Similar to the **ck** plus the following **h** in English **black hole**.

Pronunciation Exercise A-10

1. **kē** "harsh"   3. **kāi** "open"   5. **kuī** "lose"   7. **kuān** "wide"
2. **kū** "cry"   4. **kuā** "boast"   6. **kān** "print"   8. **kōng** "empty"

H   Initial **h** sounds like the **h** in English **hand** but is pronounced with more friction so that it sounds rougher, like German **ch** in **Loch** "hole" or Spanish **j** in **mujer** "woman."

Pronunciation Exercise A-11

1. **Hā** (surname)　　3. **hēi** "black"　　5. **huī** "ashes"　　7. **hēng** "hum"
2. **hē** "drink"　　　4. **huā** "flower"　　6. **hūn** "faint"　　8. **huāng** "panic"

J　Like the **j** in English **jeep** but unvoiced and with the middle part of the tongue pressed tightly against the roof of the mouth. There is more friction in Mandarin than in English. Though the lips are always rounded in English, they are rounded in Mandarin only in front of **u**, being spread before the other vowels. Say the Biblical pronoun **ye**, then pronounce **j** as in **jeep** at the same time as **ye**, all the while pressing your tongue tightly against the roof of your mouth.

 Pronunciation Exercise A-12

1. **jī** "chicken"　　5. **jiān** "shoulder"
2. **jū** "dwell"　　　6. **juān** "donate"
3. **jiā** "home"　　　7. **jūn** "army"
4. **jiē** "street"　　　8. **jiāng** "ginger"

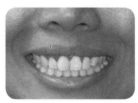

This shows the correct mouth position for the syllable **ji**, but the position of the lips and the teeth is the same for **qi**, **xi**, and **yi**.

Q　Like the **ch** in English **cheap** but with a stronger puff of breath and with the middle part of the tongue pressed tightly against the roof of the mouth. There is a greater amount of friction in Mandarin than in English, and while the lips are always rounded in English, they are rounded in Mandarin only in front of **u**, being *spread* before the other vowels. First say the Biblical pronoun **ye**, then pronounce **ch** as in **cheap** at the same time as **ye**, all the while pressing your tongue tightly against the roof of your mouth.

 Pronunciation Exercise A-13

1. **qī** "seven"　　3. **qiāo** "knock"　　5. **quē** "lack"　　7. **qiān** "thousand"
2. **qū** "district"　　4. **qiē** "slice"　　6. **qīn** "kiss"　　8. **qiāng** "rifle"

X　Between the **s** in English **see** and the **sh** in English **she**, with the middle part of the tongue pressed tightly against the roof of the mouth. There is a greater amount of friction in Mandarin than in English. While the lips are always rounded in English, they are rounded in Mandarin only in front of **u**, being spread in front of the other vowels. First say English **kiss Hugh**, then divide this into **ki-ssHugh**, finally dropping off the **ki** and **ugh** entirely. You should be left with a fairly authentic **x**.

 Pronunciation Exercise A-14

1. **xī** "west"　　3. **xiē** "some"　　5. **xīn** "new"　　7. **xīng** "putrid"
2. **xū** "weak"　　4. **xiā** "shrimp"　　6. **xiān** "first"　　8. **xiōng** "mean"

ZH　Like the **j** in English **jerk** but stronger, unvoiced, and with the tongue curled further back. Draw the tip of the tongue back and up to the roof of the mouth. While the lips are always rounded in English, they are rounded in Mandarin only in front of **u** and **o**, being spread before the other vowels.

 Pronunciation Exercise A-15

1. **zhī** "juice"　　3. **zhuā** "catch"　　5. **zhēn** "really"　　7. **Zhāng** (surname)
2. **zhū** "pig"　　　4. **zhuī** "chase"　　6. **zhuān** "brick"　　8. **zhōng** "clock"

CH　Like the **ch** in English **chirp** but with a stronger puff of breath and with the tongue curled further back. Draw the tip of the tongue back and up to the roof of the mouth. While the lips are always rounded in English, they are rounded in Mandarin only in front of **u** and **o**, being *spread* before the other vowels.

 Pronunciation Exercise A-16

1. **chē** "car"   3. **chū** "out"   5. **chōu** "draw"   7. **chuān** "wear"
2. **chī** "eat"   4. **chāo** "copy"   6. **chuī** "blow"   8. **chēng** "call"

SH   Like the **sh** in English **shrew** but with the tongue curled further back. Draw the tip of the tongue back and up to the roof of the mouth. There is a greater amount of friction in Mandarin than in English, and while the lips are always rounded in English, they are rounded in Mandarin only in front of **u** and **o**, being spread before the other vowels.

 Pronunciation Exercise A-17

1. **shā** "kill"   3. **shāo** "burn"   5. **shān** "mountain"   7. **shēng** "give birth"
2. **shū** "book"   4. **shuā** "brush"   6. **shēn** "deep"   8. **shuāng** "frost"

R   Like the **r** in American English **shrew** but with the tongue tip curled a little further back and with more friction, so that it sounds almost like the **s** in English **measure** or the **z** in English **azure**. While English **r** is always accompanied by lip rounding, Mandarin **r** has lip rounding only when preceding **o** and **u**; in front of **a**, **e**, and **i** there is no lip rounding and the lips are spread.

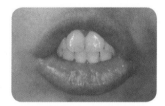

This shows the correct mouth position for the syllable **ri**, but the position of the lips and the teeth is the same for **zhi**, **chi**, and **shi**.

 Pronunciation Exercise A-18

1. **rāng** "shout"   2. **rēng** "throw"

Z   Like the **ds** in English **beds** but stronger and unvoiced. Mandarin **z** is produced by most speakers with the tongue tip in a slightly more forward position than in English. Say English **that zoo**, then divide this into **tha-tzoo**, and finally omit the **tha** entirely. The end result should be close to Mandarin **zu**.

 Pronunciation Exercise A-19

1. **zī** "capital"   3. **zāo** "bad"   5. **zūn** "respect"   7. **zāng** "dirty"
2. **zū** "rent"   4. **Zōu** (surname)   6. **zuān** "bore"   8. **Zēng** (surname)

C   Like the **ts** in English **cats** but with a strong puff of breath immediately following. Mandarin **c** is produced by most speakers with the tip of the tongue in a slightly more forward position than in English. Say English **it's high** several times, then divide that into **i-tshigh**, and finally omit the **i-** entirely. The end result should be close to Mandarin **cai**.

 Pronunciation Exercise A-20

1. **cā** "wipe"   3. **cāi** "guess"   5. **cān** "meal"   7. **cāng** "cabin"
2. **cū** "coarse"   4. **cuī** "hurry"   6. **cūn** "village"   8. **cōng** "scallion"

S   Like the **s** in English **sigh** but stronger and more hissing. Mandarin **s** is produced by most speakers with the tip of the tongue in a slightly more forward position than in English. To attain the correct tongue position, pronounce **s** as in English **months**.

 Pronunciation Exercise A-21

1. **sā** "let go"   3. **sōu** "search"   5. **sān** "three"   7. **sēng** "monk"
2. **Sū** (surname)   4. **suī** "though"   6. **suān** "sour"   8. **sōng** "loose"

W
Like the **w** in English **wide**. The lips are not so tightly rounded as in English and are not pushed forward. When Mandarin **w** precedes **u**, it is often barely pronounced so that, as spoken by many people, **wu** sounds the same as **u**.

Pronunciation Exercise A-22

1. **wā** "dig"	3. **wāi** "crooked"	5. **wān** "bend"	7. **Wáng** (surname)
2. **wū** "room"	4. **wēi** "danger"	6. **wēn** "lukewarm"	8. **Wēng** (surname)

Y
Initial **y** sounds like the **y** in English **yet**. When initial **y** precedes **i** or **u**, it is often barely pronounced so that, as spoken by many people, **yi** sounds the same as **i**.

Pronunciation Exercise A-23

1. **yī** "one"	3. **yā** "press"	5. **yuē** "invite"	7. **yīng** "cherry"
2. **yū** "silt"	4. **yāo** "waist"	6. **yān** "smoke"	8. **yāng** "seedling"

FINALS

I
(a) After **c**, **ch**, **r**, **s**, **sh**, **z**, and **zh**, **i** has no sound of its own but indicates the holding and voicing of the preceding consonant sound. These sounds should be pronounced without your tongue or lips changing position from the beginning to the end of the sound and with a good deal of tension in the throat.

(b) Everywhere else, **i** sounds like the **ee** of English **see**, but with the tongue tenser and with the lips spread flat. Mandarin **i** is a pure vowel, the tongue remaining steady throughout the production of the sound, not relaxing half-way through and adding a **y**-sound, as in English **see**.

Pronunciation Exercise A-24

(a) after **c**, **ch**, **r**, **s**, **sh**, **z**, and **zh**

1. **cī** "flaw"	3. **sī** "silk"	5. **zī** "money"
2. **chī** "eat"	4. **shī** "moist"	6. **zhī** (measure for pens)

(b) elsewhere

1. **bī** "press"	3. **jī** "chicken"	5. **qī** "seven"	7. **xī** "west"
2. **dī** "low"	4. **pī** "drape"	6. **tī** "kick"	8. **yī** "one"

U
(a) After **j**, **q**, **x**, and **y**, the final **u** is pronounced like French **u** as in **tu** "you" or German **ü** as in **über** "over," made by rounding your lips while saying **ee** as in English **seat**. Say **eee** as in English **seat**. Without moving your tongue, move your lips from the spread position to a rounded, pursed position, then back to the spread position, giving the sequence **yi yu yi**. Then try to isolate the **yu** sound. Once you've learned how to make this sound, it won't be necessary to purse your lips quite so much—indeed, some speakers make this sound with only partly rounded lips.

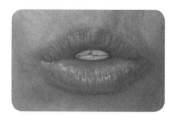
This shows the correct mouth position for the syllable **yu**, but the position of the lips and the teeth is the same for **ju**, **qu**, and **xu**.

(b) Everywhere else, **u** is pronounced like the **oo** of English **ooze** but tenser, with the lips rounded, and with the entire tongue higher and further back than in English. Mandarin **u** is a pure vowel, the tongue remaining absolutely steady throughout the production of the sound, not relaxing half-way through and moving toward a **w**-sound, as it does in English **shoe**.

Pronunciation Exercise A-25

(a) after **j**, **q**, **x**, and **y**

1. **jū** "arrest" 2. **qū** "district" 3. **xū** "weak" 4. **yū** "mud"

(b) elsewhere

1. **cū** "coarse" 3. **kū** "cry" 5. **shū** "book" 7. **zū** "rent"
2. **chū** "go out" 4. **pū** "spread" 6. **wū** "room" 8. **zhū** "pig"

Ü Like French **u** as in **tu** "you" or German **ü** as in **über** "over," made by rounding your lips while saying **ee** as in English **seat**. Say **eee** as in English **seat**. Without moving your tongue, move your lips from the spread position to a rounded, pursed position, then back to the spread position, giving the sequence **yi yu yi**. Then try to isolate the **yu** sound. Once you've learned how to make this sound, it won't be necessary to purse your lips quite so much—indeed, some speakers make this sound with only partly rounded lips. This final occurs only after **l** and **n**.

Pronunciation Exercise A-26

1. **lǜ** "green" 2. **nǚ** "female"

A Like the **a** in English **spa** but tenser, with the lower jaw well down and the mouth wide open.

Pronunciation Exercise A-27

1. **bā** "eight" 3. **fā** "issue" 5. **mā** "mom" 7. **tā** "he"
2. **cā** "rub" 4. **lā** "pull" 6. **shā** "kill" 8. **zhā** "sediment"

IA Like the **ya** of English **yacht** but tenser.

Pronunciation Exercise A-28

1. **jiā** "home" 2. **qiā** "pinch" 3. **xiā** "shrimp"

UA Like the **wa** of English **wash** but tenser and with the mouth open wider than in English. The emphasis is on the **a**-part of the final, with the **u**-part being quite short in duration.

Pronunciation Exercise A-29

1. **guā** "melon" 3. **kuā** "brag" 5. **zhuā** "catch"
2. **huā** "flower" 4. **shuā** "brush"

O This final occurs after the initials **b**, **p**, **m**, and **f**, where it stands for the final **uo**. The pronunciation of this final is between the **woe** of English **woe** and the **wa** of English **war**.

Pronunciation Exercise A-30

1. **bō** "dial" 2. **mō** "grope" 3. **pō** "slope" 4. **wō** "nest"

UO Between the **woe** of English **woe** and the **wa** of English **war**. Begin with **u**, move to **o**, then end with the Mandarin **e**-sound without closing your lips again. Be careful to distinguish the final **uo** from the final **ou**!

Pronunciation Exercise A-31

1. **cuō** "rub" 3. **duō** "much" 5. **suō** "shrink" 7. **tuō** "drag"
2. **chuō** "jab" 4. **guō** "pot" 6. **shuō** "speak" 8. **zhuō** "catch"

E   (a) After **y**, like the **e** in English **yet** but held longer.

(b) Everywhere else, somewhat like the **u** in English **bud**. The pronunciations of **u** in Southern American English **up**, or of **ir** in British English **bird**, are even closer. The back of the tongue is held high and then, as the vowel is pronounced, the tongue relaxes and moves down to a more central position. Say **oo** as in **wood** but with lips spread and jaw lowered a little. Your mouth should be half open when making this sound, which should come from deep down in your throat.

 Pronunciation Exercise A-32

(a) after **y**
1. **yē** "choke"

(b) elsewhere
1. **chē** "car"	3. **hē** "drink"	5. **shē** "extravagant"
2. **gē** "older brother"	4. **Kē** (surname)	6. **zhē** "cover"

IE   Like the **ye** of English **yet** but held longer, or like saying rapidly the name of the English letter **E** plus **ye** as in **yet**. Be careful not to add a **y**-sound after the **ie**.

 Pronunciation Exercise A-33

1. **biē** "turtle"	3. **jiē** "street"	5. **piē** "cast away"	7. **tiē** "stick"
2. **diē** "dad"	4. **niē** "pinch"	6. **qiē** "cut"	8. **xiē** "some"

UE   Like French **u** as in **tu** "you" or German **ü** as in **über** "over," followed immediately by **e** as in English **met**. The emphasis of the syllable is on the **e** rather than the **u**. First say **ee** as in English **keep** while rounding your lips, then open your lips very slightly to say **e** as in English **met**.

 Pronunciation Exercise A-34

1. **juē** "pout"	2. **quē** "lack"	3. **Xuē** (surname)	4. **yuē** "about"

ÜE   Like French **u** as in **tu** "you" or German **ü** as in **über** "over," followed immediately by **e** as in English **met**. The emphasis of the syllable is on the **e** rather than the **u**. First say **ee** as in English **keep** while rounding your lips, then open your lips very slightly to say **e** as in English **met**. This final occurs only after **l** and **n**.

 Pronunciation Exercise A-35

1. **lüè** "plunder"   2. **nüè** "malaria"

AI   Like the **y** in English **my** but shorter and tenser. Unlike English, where the a-sound is emphasized over the **i**-sound, in Mandarin the **a** and **i** are given equal prominence. To produce this sound, repeat the names of the two English letters of the alphabet **I** and **E** rapidly, one immediately after the other.

 Pronunciation Exercise A-36

1. **āi** "be close"	3. **dāi** "foolish"	5. **kāi** "open"	7. **wāi** "crooked"
2. **cāi** "guess"	4. **gāi** "should"	6. **pāi** "pat"	8. **zhāi** "pick"

UAI   Like the **wy** in English **Wyoming**, but shorter and tenser. In Mandarin, unlike English, the **u**, **a**, and **i** are all given equal prominence. To make this sound, pronounce very rapidly English

oo-Y-E (where **oo** sounds like the **oo** in **too**, and **Y** and **E** are the names of the English letters of the alphabet).

Pronunciation Exercise A-37

1. **guāi** "well-behaved" 2. **chuāi** "carry"   3. **shuāi** "fall"

EI   Like the **ei** in English **sleigh** but shorter and tenser. Unlike English, where the e is emphasized over the **i**, in Mandarin the **e** and **i** are given equal prominence. To produce this sound correctly, repeat the names of these two letters of the English alphabet rapidly, one immediately after the other: **A E**.

Pronunciation Exercise A-38

1. **bēi** "cup of"   3. **hēi** "black"   5. **wēi** "danger"
2. **fēi** "fly"   4. **pēi** "embryo"

UI   For most speakers like the English word **way** but shorter and tenser. For some speakers, in syllables in tones one and two, this final sounds somewhere between English **way** and English **we**.

Pronunciation Exercise A-39

1. **cuī** "hasten"   3. **duī** "heap"   5. **huī** "ashes"   7. **tuī** "push"
2. **chuī** "blow"   4. **guī** "return"   6. **kuī** "lack"   8. **zhuī** "chase"

AO   This sound falls midway between the **ow** of English **cow** and the **aw** of English **caw**. Unlike English, where the **a** is emphasized over the **o**, in Mandarin the **a** and **o** are given equal prominence.

Pronunciation Exercise A-40

1. **āo** "concave"   3. **chāo** "copy"   5. **gāo** "high"   7. **māo** "cat"
2. **bāo** "wrap"   4. **dāo** "knife"   6. **lāo** "fish for"   8. **shāo** "burn"

IAO   Like the **yow** of English **yowl** but shorter and tenser. In Mandarin, unlike English, the **i**, **a**, and **o** are all given equal prominence.

Pronunciation Exercise A-41

1. **biāo** "mark"   3. **jiāo** "hand over"   5. **piāo** "float"   7. **tiāo** "choose"
2. **Diāo** (surname)   4. **miāo** (cat's meow) 6. **qiāo** "knock"   8. **xiāo** "flute"

OU   Like the **o** in English **go** but shorter and tenser. Unlike English, where the **o**-sound is given prominence over the **u**-sound, in Mandarin the **o** and **u** are given equal prominence. Be careful to distinguish the final **ou** from the final **uo**!

Pronunciation Exercise A-42

1. **chōu** "take"   3. **gōu** "hook"   5. **sōu** "search"   7. **tōu** "steal"
2. **dōu** "all"   4. **Ōu** "Europe"   6. **shōu** "receive"   8. **zhōu** "state"

IU   Starts out like English **yo** as in **yo-yo**, then ends up like the **oo** in English **too**. For some speakers, in syllables in tones one and two, this final sounds more like English **you**, while in syllables in tones three and four it sounds more like **yo** as in **yo-yo**.

Pronunciation Exercise A-43

1. **diū** "throw"   3. **liū** "sneak out"   5. **qiū** "autumn"
2. **jiū** "turtle dove"   4. **niū** "maiden"   6. **xiū** "rest"

AN   (a) After **y**, for most speakers, Mandarin **an** sounds like the **en** in English **Yen** (Japanese monetary unit) but shorter and tenser.

(b) Everywhere else, **an** sounds somewhat like the **awn** in English **pawn**, but shorter and tenser. Be careful not to pronounce **an** like English **an** in **pan**!

Pronunciation Exercise A-44

(a) after **y**
1. **yān** "smoke"

(b) elsewhere
1. **ān** "at ease"   3. **fān** "overturn"   5. **sān** "three"   7. **tān** "covet"
2. **bān** "class"   4. **gān** "dry"   6. **shān** "mountain" 8. **zhān** "moisten"

IAN   Like the English word **Yen** (Japanese monetary unit) but shorter and tenser.

Pronunciation Exercise A-45

1. **biān** "edge"   3. **jiān** "sharp"   5. **piān** "essay"   7. **tiān** "day"
2. **diān** "bump"   4. **niān** "pick"   6. **qiān** "thousand" 8. **xiān** "first"

UAN   (a) After **j**, **q**, **x**, and **y**, the final **uan** is pronounced by most speakers like French **u** as in **tu** "you" or German **ü** as in **über** "over," followed immediately by the **wen** of English **went**. The emphasis is on the **an**-part of the syllable.

(b) Everywhere else, **uan** is pronounced somewhat like the **wan** of English **want**, but shorter and tenser. Again, the emphasis is on the **an**-part of the syllable.

Pronunciation Exercise A-46

(a) after **j**, **q**, **x**, and **y**
1. **juān** "donate"   2. **quān** "circle"   3. **xuān** "proclaim"   4. **yuān** "injustice"

(b) elsewhere
1. **chuān** "wear"   3. **guān** "close"   5. **suān** "sour"   7. **zuān** "bore"
2. **duān** "carry"   4. **kuān** "wide"   6. **shuān** "tie up"   8. **zhuān** "brick"

EN   Somewhat like the **en** in English **chicken**.

Pronunciation Exercise A-47

1. **ēn** "mercy"   3. **gēn** "and"   5. **pēn** "squirt"   7. **wēn** "warm"
2. **fēn** "divide"   4. **mēn** "stuffy"   6. **shēn** "deep"   8. **zhēn** "real"

IN   Between the **in** of English **sin** and the **een** of English **seen**, but tenser and with the lips spread more than in English.

Pronunciation Exercise A-48

1. **bīn** "guest"   3. **pīn** "spell"   5. **xīn** "new"
2. **jīn** "catty"   4. **qīn** "kiss"   6. **yīn** "sound"

UN (a) After **j**, **q**, **x**, and **y**, **un** is pronounced like French **u** as in **tu** "you" or German **ü** as in **über** "over," plus **win** as in English **win**.

(b) Everywhere else, **un** is pronounced somewhat like the **w** of English **won**, the **oo** of English **book**, plus the **n** of English **sun**.

 Pronunciation Exercise A-49

(a) after **j**, **q**, **x**, and **y**
1. **jūn** "army"   2. **qūn** "loiter"   3. **xūn** "smoke"   4. **yūn** "dizzy"

(b) elsewhere
1. **cūn** "village"   3. **dūn** "squat"   5. **kūn** "female"   7. **tūn** "swallow"
2. **chūn** "spring"   4. **hūn** "faint"   6. **Sūn** (surname)   8. **zūn** "statue"

ANG Between the **ong** in English **song** and the **ung** in English **sung**. The tongue begins slightly further back and the vowel is longer than for **an**. The ng-sound should not be pronounced with too much force; it's lighter than in English. Don't pronounce Mandarin **ang** like English **ang** as in **sang**! Also, be careful to pronounce the **ng** as in English **hung** and not as in English **hunger**, where there is an additional **g**-sound.

 Pronunciation Exercise A-50

1. **bāng** "help"   3. **gāng** "just"   5. **tāng** "soup"   7. **zāng** "dirty"
2. **fāng** "square"   4. **rāng** "shout"   6. **Wāng** (surname)   8. **Zhāng** (surname)

IANG Somewhat like the English word **young**. The ng-sound should not be pronounced with too much force; it is lighter than in English. Be careful not to pronounce the **ng** as in English **younger**, where there is an additional **g**-sound.

 Pronunciation Exercise A-51

1. **jiāng** "ginger"   2. **qiāng** "rifle"   3. **xiāng** "box of"

UANG Somewhat like the **w** of English **won** plus the **ong** in English **song**, but shorter and tenser and with the mouth open wider. The emphasis should be on the **ang**-part of the syllable. Also, the **ng**-sound should not be pronounced with too much force; it is lighter than in English. Be careful to pronounce the **ng** as in English **long** and not as in English **longer**, where there is an additional **g**-sound.

 Pronunciation Exercise A-52

1. **chuāng** "window"   3. **huāng** "panic"   5. **shuāng** "frost"
2. **guāng** "only"   4. **kuāng** "basket"   6. **zhuāng** "pretend"

ENG Somewhat like the **ung** in English **lung**. The ng-sound should not be pronounced with too much force; it's lighter than in English. Be careful to pronounce the **ng** as in English **hung** and not as in English **hunger**, where there is an additional **g**-sound.

 Pronunciation Exercise A-53

1. **chēng** "call"   3. **fēng** "wind"   5. **hēng** "hum"   7. **rēng** "throw"
2. **dēng** "lamp"   4. **gēng** "plough"   6. **kēng** "pit"   8. **shēng** "give birth"

ING Somewhat like the **ing** of English **sing**. The ng-sound should not be pronounced with too much force; it is lighter than in English. Consonants before the **i** are often pronounced with a slight **y**-sound after them, so that **bing** "soldier" sounds almost as if it were pronounced **bying**. Be careful to pronounce the **ng** as in English **sing** and not as in English **finger**, where there is an additional **g**-sound.

 Pronunciation Exercise A-54

1. **bīng** "ice"   3. **jīng** "skillful"   5. **qīng** "light"   7. **xīng** "putrid"
2. **dīng** "nail"   4. **pīng** "ping-pong"   6. **tīng** "listen"   8. **yīng** "should"

ONG   Somewhat like the **oo** of English **book** plus the **ng** of English **rung**. The **ng**-sound should not be pronounced with too much force but more lightly than in English. Be careful not to make this final rhyme with the **ong** in English **song** and be careful to pronounce the **ng** as in English **sing** and not as in English **finger**, where there is an additional **g**-sound.

 Pronunciation Exercise A-55

1. **chōng** "rush"   3. **gōng** "work"   5. **kōng** "empty"   7. **tōng** "penetrate"
2. **dōng** "east"   4. **hōng** "dry"   6. **sōng** "loose"   8. **zhōng** "middle"

IONG   Somewhat like the **y** of English **you**, the **oo** of English **book**, plus the **ng** of English **rung**. The **ng**-sound should not be pronounced with too much force; it is lighter than in English. Be careful to pronounce the **ng** as in English **sing** and not as in English **finger**, where there is an additional **g**-sound.

 Pronunciation Exercise A-56

1. **jiōng** "bolt"   2. **xiōng** "mean"

ER   Between English **are** and **err**, but with the tongue curled even further back. For some speakers, the pronunciation may be different depending on the tone, sounding more like English **are** in tones two and four, and more like English **err** in Tone Three.

 Pronunciation Exercise A-57

1. **ér** "and"   2. **ěr** "ear"   3. **èr** "two"

Tones

Every regularly stressed syllable in Mandarin is pronounced in one of four different tones. The tone of a Chinese syllable is as much a part of the syllable as are the consonants and vowels. Two syllables with the same initials and finals but with different tones are likely to have completely different meanings. For example, take the three verbs **wèn** "ask," **wén** "smell," and **wěn** "kiss." Learners of Chinese who mispronounce **Wǒ wèn nǐ** "I ask you" as **Wǒ wén nǐ** "I smell you" or **Wǒ wěn nǐ** "I kiss you" are apt to leave a rather curious impression on their Chinese interlocutors!

The tone system of Mandarin consists not of fixed notes on a scale but rather of relationships between tones. The actual pitch of each of the four tones varies considerably depending on such factors as the speakers' voice range, sex, age, emotional state, and physical condition. What matters is relative pitch, that is, the pitch of the four tones in relation to each other in the speech of a particular speaker. In Pinyin transcription, tones are indicated with diacritical marks over the main vowel of a syllable, for example: **mā má mǎ mà**. The tone marks are iconic, meaning they are a "picture" of what they represent (since the high and level line ˉ represents the high and level Tone One, the high rising line ′ represents the high rising Tone Two and so on). The rules for determining on which vowel the tone mark is placed are as follows:

(1) If there is only one vowel in a syllable, it's the main vowel and the tone mark is placed over it.

(2) If there is more than one vowel, the first vowel in the syllable is considered the main vowel, except when **i**, **u**, or **ü** is the first vowel, in which case the second vowel is considered the main vowel.

(3) When a tone mark is placed over the vowel **i**, the dot over the **i** is dropped, for example: ī í ǐ ì.

The four tones of Mandarin are described below and are illustrated in the diagrams below. In those diagrams, the vertical dimension stands for pitch, with the top of each diagram slightly above the normal pitch range in English and the bottom slightly below. The horizontal dimension stands for duration, with the thickness of the tone curve representing loudness. When practicing tones and speaking Chinese, you are encouraged to widen your voice range! Try to make the highs higher and the lows lower than in your normal English voice range.

THE FOUR TONES OF MANDARIN

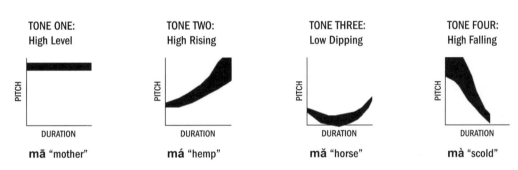

TONE ONE: High Level — **mā** "mother"
TONE TWO: High Rising — **má** "hemp"
TONE THREE: Low Dipping — **mǎ** "horse"
TONE FOUR: High Falling — **mà** "scold"

TONE ONE: HIGH LEVEL

Tone One has a steady high pitch and is average in length. It is pronounced at or near the top of your comfortable speaking voice range. Be sure to maintain the high level pitch from the beginning to the end of the syllable, without wavering until you are finished. Tone One is indicated by a straight line over the main vowel of the syllable: ¯. Be sure to make Tone One high enough, and be sure to keep it level. Native English speakers tend to relax and drop their voice at the end of this tone, making it sound similar to Tone Four.

 Pronunciation Exercise A-58

1. **bāo** "wrap"	3. **mā** "mother"	5. **qiān** "thousand"	7. **yī** "one"
2. **gāng** "just"	4. **Ōu** "Europe"	6. **shān** "mountain"	8. **Zhāng** (surname)

TONE TWO: HIGH RISING

Tone Two begins at about the middle of the voice range and rises rapidly to the top. It's average in length and increases in loudness as it rises. Tone Two is indicated by a rising mark on the main vowel of the syllable: ´. Don't start Tone Two too low, and be sure to emphasize the climb up.

 Pronunciation Exercise A-59

1. **bái** "white"	3. **máng** "busy"	5. **néng** "can"	7. **shí** "ten"
2. **báo** "thin"	4. **nán** "difficult"	6. **shéi** "who"	8. **wán** "finish"

TONE THREE: LOW DIPPING

Tone Three starts low, dips even lower to the bottom of the voice range, where it stays for a while, and then rises quickly above the middle of the pitch range. Speakers from Taiwan and some other parts of China often omit the the final rise. The low part of this tone is emphasized, both in length and in pitch. Tone Three has greater than average length. Tone Three is indicated by a falling and rising mark over the main vowel of the syllable: ˇ . Be sure to make Tone Three low enough. Don't try too hard to produce the initial dip; just start as low as you can and the dip will take care of itself.

 Pronunciation Exercise A-60

1. **gǒu** "dog"   3. **jǐn** "tight"   5. **nǐ** "you"   7. **wǎn** "bowl"
2. **hǎo** "good"   4. **mǎ** "horse"   6. **qǐng** "invite"   8. **zhǎng** "grow"

TONE FOUR: HIGH FALLING

Tone Four starts at the top of the voice range and falls sharply to the bottom, diminishing in loudness as it falls. It has shorter than average length. Tone Four is indicated by a falling mark over the main vowel of the syllable: ˋ . Be sure to start Tone Four high enough and let it fall all the way down. In English, we often use this intonation in imperatives such as "Quick!" or when emphatically answering a ridiculous question with "No!"

 Pronunciation Exercise A-61

1. **bào** "newspaper"   3. **gèng** "even more"   5. **shì** "be"   7. **xìn** "letter"
2. **èr** "two"   4. **mà** "scold"   6. **wàn** "10,000"   8. **xìng** "surname"

NEUTRAL TONE

In normal Mandarin conversation there is a fairly large number of unstressed syllables which are spoken in a weak and hurried manner without a discernible tone of their own. Such syllables, which bear no tone mark, are commonly referred to as being in the "neutral tone." Although neutral tone syllables have no tone, they do have pitch. The pitch of neutral tone syllables is influenced mainly by the tone of the preceding syllable, so it's important to notice the pitch of neutral tone syllables relative to the preceding tone.

Neutral tones are to some extent used in all dialects of Mandarin but are especially common in the speech of Beijing and other parts of North China. Speakers from southern China tend to use fewer neutral tones, especially as concerns the second syllable of two-syllable words. For your Chinese to sound fluent and natural, it's important for you to pay attention to and imitate the neutral tones in your instructor's speech and the speech on the accompanying recordings. You should learn neutral tone syllables as you learn the word or sentence in which they occur.

 Pronunciation Exercise A-62: Tone One + Neutral Tone

1. **māma** "mom"   3. **shuōzhe** "talking"   5. **wūzi** "room"
2. **shūle** "has lost"   4. **tāde** "hers"   6. **xiānsheng** "mister"

 Pronunciation Exercise A-63: Tone Two + Neutral Tone

1. **bízi** "nose"   3. **niánji** "age"   5. **shéide** "whose?"
2. **láile** "has come"   4. **péngyou** "friend"   6. **Wáng jia** "the Wangs"

 Pronunciation Exercise A-64: Tone Three + Neutral Tone

1. **hǎode** "O.K."   3. **liǎngge** "two of them"   5. **yǐzi** "chair"
2. **hǎo ma** "O.K.?"   4. **wǒmen** "we"   6. **zǒule** "has gone"

 Pronunciation Exercise A-65: Tone Four + Neutral Tone

1. **lèile** "has become tired"   3. **qù ba** "let's go"   5. **shìde** "yes"
2. **mèimei** "younger sister"   4. **sìge** "four of them"   6. **zhànzhe** "standing"

TONE CHANGES

When certain tones occur directly before certain other tones, their tones change in fairly predictable ways. Although this may seem difficult and confusing at first, you'll get used to these changes within a few weeks and they'll soon become automatic for you. There are three major tone changes:

1. When a Tone Three syllable occurs directly before a syllable in Tone One, Tone Two, Tone Four or before most neutral tones, it loses its final rise and remains low throughout. The changed tone is then called a Half Tone Three.

     Pronunciation Exercise A-66: Half Tone Three

    1. **mǎi + shū → mǎi shū** "buy books"
    2. **mǎi + xié → mǎi xié** "buy shoes"
    3. **mǎi + cài → mǎi cài** "buy groceries"
    4. **mǎi + le → mǎile** "has bought"

2. When a Tone Three syllable occurs directly before another Tone Three syllable, the first Tone Three syllable changes to Tone Two. It is then called a Raised Tone Three.

     Pronunciation Exercise A-67: Raised Tone Three

    1. **hěn + lǎo → hěn lǎo** "very old"
    2. **gǎn + jǐn → gǎnjǐn** "quickly"
    3. **mǎi + bǐ → mǎi bǐ** "buy pens"
    4. **nǐ + hǎo → nǐ hǎo** "how are you"

3. In the speech of many speakers, when two Tone Four syllables follow each other in close succession, the first receives lighter stress than the second. The tone of the first Tone Four syllable often does not fall all the way to the bottom of the pitch range but only to the middle. It is then called a Half Tone Four.

     Pronunciation Exercise A-68: Half Tone Four

    1. **dà + gài → dàgài** "probably"
    2. **guì + xìng → guìxìng** "what's your last name?"
    3. **tài + kuài → tài kuài** "too fast"
    4. **zài + jiàn → zàijiàn** "goodbye"

The (r) Suffix

In the dialect of Beijing and to a lesser extent in standard Mandarin, some words end in a suffixed (**r**) which is attached to the ends of the finals listed previously. The (**r**) suffix may cause modifications in the vowels and consonants of those finals. The (**r**) suffix sounds like the **-r** at the end of the Mandarin final **-er**, or much like the English word **are**. To pronounce the (**r**) suffix, draw back the tongue, at the same time turning the tip of the tongue upwards.

In general, the (**r**) suffix is more common in informal conversation than in formal speech or writing. It is also more common in Beijing and other parts of North China than in the rest of the country. Learn words with the (**r**) suffix as they come up in the course and imitate carefully the usage of your teacher and that of the speakers in the accompanying materials. Now practice pronouncing the examples of the (**r**) suffix given below:

 Pronunciation Exercise A-69

1. **nà** "that" → **nàr** "there"
2. **xiǎodāo → xiǎodāor** "small knife"
3. **kàn yixia → kàn yixiar** "take a look"
4. **niǎo → niǎor** "bird"
5. **dǎqiú → dǎqiúr** "play ball"
6. **shānpō → shānpōr** "mountain slope"
7. **xiǎotōu → xiǎotōur** "thief"
8. **huà** "paint" → **huàr** "painting"
9. **xiǎoshuō → xiǎoshuōr** "novel"
10. **báitù → báitùr** "white rabbit"

Pronunciation Exercise A-70

1. **jīnjú** → **jīnjúr** "kumquat"
2. **yǒuqù** → **yǒuqùr** "interesting"
3. **yú** → **yúr** "fish"
4. **xiǎojī** → **xiǎojīr** "chick"
5. **xiǎomǐ** → **xiǎomǐr** "millet"
6. **pí** → **pír** "skin (of fruit)"

 Pronunciation Exercise A-71

1. **cì** → **cìr** "thorn"
2. **jùchǐ** → **jùchǐr** "tooth of a saw"
3. **ròusī** → **ròusīr** "meat shreds"
4. **méi shì** → **méi shìr** "never mind"
5. **guāzǐ** → **guāzǐr** "watermelon seed"
6. **guǒzhī** → **guǒzhīr** "fruit juice"

 Pronunciation Exercise A-72

1. **gài** "to cover" → **gàir** "a cover"
2. **yíkuài** "one dollar" → **yíkuàir** "together"
3. **xiāngwèi** → **xiāngwèir** "fragrant odor"
4. **qìshuǐ** → **qìshuǐr** "soda"
5. **duōbàn** → **duōbànr** "for the most part"
6. **yìdiǎn** → **yìdiǎnr** "a little"
7. **huāpén** → **huāpénr** "flower pot"
8. **fànguǎn** → **fànguǎnr** "restaurant"

 Pronunciation Exercise A-73

1. **méi jìn** → **méi jìnr** "have no energy"
2. **sòngxìn** "deliver a letter" → **sòngxìnr** "deliver a message"
3. **huāqún** → **huāqúnr** "colored skirt"
4. **méi zhǔn** → **méi zhǔnr** "can't say for sure"

 Pronunciation Exercise A-74

1. **huāpíng** → **huāpíngr** "vase"
2. **xiàngyàng** → **xiàngyàngr** "decent"
3. **dàshēng** → **dàshēngr** "in a loud voice"
4. **yǒukòng** → **yǒukòngr** "have free time"

Reading Part One

New Characters and Words

1.	一	**yī**	one
2.	二	**èr**	two
3.	三	**sān**	three
4.	四	**sì**	four
5.	五	**wǔ**	five
6.	王	**Wáng**	Wang (surname)

Reading Exercises

A. SINGLE DIGITS

1. 三
2. 一
3. 五
4. 二
5. 四
6. 一
7. 三
8. 二
9. 四
10. 五

B. TELEPHONE NUMBERS

1. 三二一二五
2. 一一四二
3. 三五一三四
4. 五二一一一
5. 三三二四三

6. 五五四三
7. 四四二一五三四二
8. 一一三五一二三四
9. 三五二三四四一四
10. 二五二三四二三一

C. SURNAMES

1. 王

Notes for Reading Part One

B1. In formal writing, as on business cards or letterheads, telephone numbers may be indicated using the Chinese numerals, as here. However, telephone numbers are also commonly written with Arabic numerals, as in English, but often without the use of any hyphens, for example, as 42235151 rather than 4223-5151. The lack of hyphens doesn't seem to bother Chinese people, who are used to reading and memorizing long number sequences.

B7. Telephone numbers in the larger cities of China are eight digits in length. In smaller cities and the countryside, telephone numbers may consist of fewer than eight digits. Mobile phone numbers usually have eleven digits.

Reading Part Two

New Characters and Words

7.	六	**liù**	six
8.	七	**qī**	seven
9.	八	**bā**	eight
10.	九	**jiǔ**	nine
11.	十	**shí**	ten
12.	林	**Lín**	Lin (surname)

Reading Exercises

A. SINGLE DIGITS

1. 十
2. 七
3. 六
4. 九
5. 八

6. 六
7. 七
8. 十
9. 九
10. 八

Automobile license plate from Taipei

B. TELEPHONE NUMBERS

一、三九五九四一三九

二、八六一二四

三、七一九二六八七九

四、五七八九二六

五、九六八四一八七三

六、二二八五六七八五

C. MISCELLANEOUS NUMBERS

一、一三五

二、二四六

三、一二三四五

四、五四三二一

五、六七八九十

六、十九八七六

七、一二三四五六七八九十

八、十九八七六五四三二一

九、二四六八十

十、一三五七九

The characters at the top are in written Cantonese, which is quite different from written Mandarin

D. SURNAMES

一、林

二、王

Notes for Reading Part Two

B1. While Chinese, like Latin, was originally written without any punctuation marks, and later in its history only with a kind of period (。) that served as an all-purpose punctuation mark, it has over the last 150 years adopted the punctuation system of Western languages, though there exist a few differences in usage. China has also created several punctuation marks that don't exist in Western languages. One of these is a kind of inverted comma called the 顿号 **dùnhào** that looks like this: 、 One use of the **dùnhào** is after numbers, for example: 一、二、三、

C1. 一三五 could either represent the numbers 1 3 5 or stand for the first, third, and fifth days of the week, much like the English abbreviation "MWF."

C2. 二四六 could either represent the numbers 2 4 6 or stand for the second, fourth, and sixth days of the week, like English "T Th Sat."

Reading Part Three

New Characters and Words

13.	大	**dà**	big, large, great
14.	山	**shān**	mountain
15.	明	**míng**	bright (can't be used alone)
16.	北	**běi**	north
17.	京	**jīng**	capital (can't be used alone)
	北京	**Běijīng**	Beijing (city name)
18.	台	**tái**	terrace; (abbreviation for Taiwan)
	台北	**Táiběi**	Taipei (city name)
	台山	**Táishān**	Taishan (county name)

Reading Exercises

A. PERSONAL NAMES

一、 王大山
二、 林京
三、 王明山
四、 林明明
五、 王林
六、 王明大
七、 林台山
八、 王明
九、 王山明
十、 林大明

B. PLACE NAMES

一、 台山
二、 北京
三、 台北

Notes for Reading Part Three

A5.   Some characters can occur both as surnames and in given names. For example, the character 林 is a common surname but can also occur in a one or two-syllable given name.

Kiosk in Hong Kong selling telephone calling cards and other items

Reading Part Four

New Characters and Words

19.	何	**Hé**	He (surname)
20.	李	**Lǐ**	Li (surname)
21.	文	**Wén**	Wen (surname)
22.	生	**shēng**	be born, give birth to
23.	中	**zhōng**	middle, among
	台中	**Táizhōng**	Taichung (city name)
24.	小	**xiǎo**	be small, little, young

Reading Exercises

A. TWO-CHARACTER PERSONAL NAMES

一、何文   五、林山

二、李京   六、王生

三、王文   七、文山

四、李明   八、林中

B. THREE-CHARACTER PERSONAL NAMES

一、李大一   六、文大中

二、林台生   七、何小山

三、王小文   八、李大林

四、何明明   九、林明生

五、王京生   十、李小明

C. PLACE NAMES

一、台山   三、台中

二、北京   四、台北

Notes for Reading Part Four

B2.   When choosing personal names, Chinese people sometimes choose names that describe some aspect of a person. Consider the name 林台生; the character 台 can stand for Taiwan and 生 means "be born." Thus, 林台生 could mean "a person with the family name 林 who was born in Taiwan."

B5.   Look carefully at the name 王京生. Keeping in mind note B2 above and the fact that the literal meaning of the character 京 is "capital" (which refers to 北京), what do you think 王京生 might mean?

Common Classroom Expressions

To help you learn Chinese as efficiently as possible, it's important to immerse yourself in as "Chinese" an atmosphere as you can. Therefore, as much as possible each class should be conducted in Chinese only. To facilitate this, your instructors will frequently be using the Chinese classroom expressions below. While it will be helpful for you to repeat each one several times after your instructor and after the accompanying audio recordings, for now your primary task is to learn to *understand* these expressions when you hear them; you needn't learn how to use them yourself just yet. Don't worry too much about what the individual words mean but rather try to understand the meaning of each expression as a whole.

1. 早！   **Zǎo!**   Good morning!
2. 你好！   **Nǐ hǎo!**   How are you?
3. 你们好！   **Nǐmen hǎo!**   How are you?
4. 我们上课吧。   **Wǒmen shàngkè ba.**   Let's begin class.
5. 你们听我说。   **Nǐmen tīng wǒ shuō.**   You all listen to me say it.
6. 你们跟我说。   **Nǐmen gēn wǒ shuō.**   You all repeat after me.
7. 好，我们下课了。   **Hǎo, wǒmen xiàkèle.**   All right, we end class now.
8. 好。   **Hǎo.**   Good.
9. 很好。   **Hěn hǎo.**   Very good.
10. 请你再说一遍。   **Qǐng nǐ zài shuō yíbiàn.**   Please say it again.
11. 明天见。   **Míngtiān jiàn.**   See you tomorrow.
12. 再见。   **Zàijiàn.**   Goodbye.
13. 第几声？   **Dìjǐshēng?**   Which tone?
14. 第一声。   **Dìyīshēng.**   First tone.
15. 第二声。   **Dì'èrshēng.**   Second tone.
16. 第三声。   **Dìsānshēng.**   Third tone.
17. 第四声。   **Dìsìshēng.**   Fourth tone.
18. 轻声。   **Qīngshēng.**   Neutral tone.
19. 请注意你的声调。   **Qǐng zhùyì nǐde shēngdiào.**   Please pay attention to your tones.
20. 对。   **Duì.**   Correct.

21. 不对。	Bú duì.	Not correct.
22. 请你大声一点儿。	Qǐng nǐ dà shēng yidianr.	Please a little louder.
23. 请你快一点儿。	Qǐng nǐ kuài yidianr.	Please a little faster.
24. 请你慢一点儿。	Qǐng nǐ màn yidianr.	Please a little slower.
25. 请你问她（他）。	Qǐng nǐ wèn tā.	Please you ask her/him.
26. 请回答我的问题。	Qǐng huídá wǒde wèntí.	Please answer my question(s).
27. 我们现在听写。	Wǒmen xiànzài tīngxiě.	We'll now take a dictation quiz.
28. 我们现在考试。	Wǒmen xiànzài kǎoshì.	We'll now take a test.
29. 我们明天考试。	Wǒmen míngtiān kǎoshì.	We'll take a test tomorrow.
30. 请你们把功课给我。	Qǐng nǐmen bǎ gōngkè gěi wǒ.	Please you all give me your homework.
31. 请你们把考卷给我。	Qǐng nǐmen bǎ kǎojuàn gěi wǒ.	Please you all give me your test papers.
32. 请你们说中文，别说英文！	Qǐng nǐmen shuō Zhōngwén, bié shuō Yīngwén!	Please you all speak Chinese, don't speak English!

Notes on the Classroom Expressions

1. In the first classroom expression above, **zǎo** literally means "be early." **Zǎo** has become a conventionalized greeting which can be used on first seeing someone in the morning any time until about 10:00 A.M. If someone says **Zǎo** to you, you would typically reply by saying **Zǎo** to them. So a conversational exchange, repeated countless times every morning in China is:

    Speaker A: **Zǎo!**
    Speaker B: **Zǎo!**

2-3. The basic structure of classroom expressions 2 and 3 is "You're good." Presumably, a preceding expression like "I hope that..." has been deleted. In any case, the functional meaning is that of a greeting, similar to English "How are you?"

5. This sentence literally means "You (plural) listen (to) me say (something)."

6. **Gēn** is a verb with the basic meaning "follow," so this sentence literally means "You (plural) follow me (in) saying."

7. **Hǎo** here means "it's all right." **Xiàkè** is a verb that can be translated "get out of class" or "finish class." The **le** at the end of this sentence indicates there has been a change (that is, "before we were in class but now class is over").

8-9. In these two expressions, **hǎo** has its basic meaning of "be good" or "it's good."

10. **Qǐng** literally means "request politely." It often occurs at the beginning of sentences indicating requests, much like English "please." **Nǐ** means "you" (singular). **Zài shuō yíbiàn** literally means "again say one time."

12. **Zàijiàn** "goodbye" literally means "again see."

13.   **Dìjǐshēng?** literally means "number what tone?"

16.   **Qīng** literally means "be light (not heavy)" and refers to the very light stress given neutral tone syllables.

18.   Both **shēngdiào** and **shēng**, which was introduced in line 13, mean "tone," but while **shēngdiào** can be said by itself, **shēng** is usually said only in combination with other syllables.

22-24.   The basic structure of all these sentences is **Qǐng nǐ...yidianr** "(I) request that you a little more...."

25.   **Tā** is the third person singular pronoun, meaning "he," "she," "her," "him" (and occasionally "it"). You've by now encountered the following personal pronouns:

wǒ "I, me"	**wǒmen** "we, us"
nǐ "you" (singular)	**nǐmen** "you" (plural)
tā "he, she; her, him"	

Do you see how the pluralizing suffix **-men** converts pronouns from singular to plural? How do you think you would say "they" in Chinese? (Answer: **tāmen**)

30.   **Qǐng nǐmen bǎ gōngkè gěi wǒ** literally means "Please you all take (the) homework (and) give (it to) me."

31.   **Qǐng nǐmen bǎ kǎojuàn gěi wǒ** literally means "Please you all take (the) test paper (and) give (it to) me."

Reading Part One

New Characters and Words

25.	上	**shàng**	above
26.	海	**hǎi**	ocean, sea
	上海	**Shànghǎi**	Shanghai
27.	广	**guǎng**	broad (can't be used alone)
28.	州	**zhōu**	state, district (can't be used alone)
	广州	**Guǎngzhōu**	Guangzhou (city name)
29.	东	**dōng**	east
	广东	**Guǎngdōng**	Guangdong (province)
	山东	**Shāndōng**	Shandong (province)
	台东	**Táidōng**	Taitung (city name)
	东京	**Dōngjīng**	Tokyo (city name)
30.	人	**rén**	person
	北京人	**Běijīng rén**	person from Beijing
	广东人	**Guǎngdōng rén**	person from Guangdong
	上海人	**Shànghǎi rén**	person from Shanghai

Reading Exercises

A. PERSONAL NAMES

一、 林广海

二、 王文

三、 李东山

四、 何海文

五、 文明明

B. PLACE NAMES

一、 上海

二、 广州

三、 广东

四、 山东

五、 东京

六、 台东

C. PEOPLE AND THEIR PLACES OF ORIGIN

一、 北京人

二、 广东人

三、 台北人

四、 上海人

五、 台中人

六、 台东人

七、 东京人

八、 广州人

九、 山东人

十、 台山人

Notes on Reading Part One

C1. Since Chinese nouns usually don't explicitly indicate singular or plural, an expression like 北京人 could mean either "a person from Beijing" or "people from Beijing." The context usually makes the meaning clear.

Restaurant sign in Macau (large characters read from right to left)

Reading Part Two

New Characters and Words

31.	成	**chéng**	become
32.	都	**dū**	large city, capital; Du (surname)
	成都	**Chéngdū**	Chengdu (city name)
	京都	**Jīngdū**	Kyoto (city name)
33.	天	**tiān**	sky, heaven
34.	津	**jīn**	(abbreviation for Tianjin)
	天津	**Tiānjīn**	Tianjin (city name)
35.	西	**xī**	west
	广西	**Guǎngxī**	Guangxi (province)
	山西	**Shānxī**	Shanxi (province)
36.	路	**lù**	road; Lu (surname)
	上海路	**Shànghǎi Lù**	Shanghai Road
	成都西路	**Chéngdū Xī Lù**	Chengdu West Road
	天津东路	**Tiānjīn Dōng Lù**	Tianjin East Road

Reading Exercises

A. PERSONAL NAMES

一、路广天　　　　四、文明成

二、李成　　　　　五、王海

三、林天生　　　　六、都明海

B. PLACE NAMES

一、成都　　　四、广西　　　七、山东

二、上海　　　五、天津　　　八、京都

三、广东　　　六、广州　　　九、东京

C. PEOPLE AND THEIR PLACES OF ORIGIN

一、台中人　　　四、山西人　　　七、成都人

二、台东人　　　五、天津人　　　八、北京人

三、广西人　　　六、台北人　　　九、台山人

D. NAMES OF ROADS

一、 北京路
二、 上海路
三、 广州路
四、 山西东路
五、 成都西路
六、 天津东路
七、 广西西路
八、 台中路
九、 山东西路
十、 台山东路

Notes on Reading Part Two

D1.   As in the West, Chinese roads are sometimes named after famous cities, provinces, or people.

READING PART THREE

New Characters and Words

37.	安	ān	peace (can't occur alone)
	西安	Xī'ān	Xian (city name)
38.	川	chuān	river (can't occur alone)
	四川	Sìchuān	Sichuan (province)
39.	香	xiāng	fragrant
	香山	Xiāng Shān	Fragrant Hills (suburb of Beijing)
40.	港	gǎng	harbor
	香港	Xiānggǎng	Hong Kong
41.	南	nán	south
	南京	Nánjīng	Nanjing (city name)
	台南	Táinán	Tainan (city name)
	海南	Hǎinán	Hainan (province)
	中山南路	Zhōngshān Nán Lù	Zhongshan South Road
42.	街	jiē	street
	大街	dàjiē	main street, avenue
	西安街	Xī'ān Jiē	Xian Street
	香港街	Xiānggǎng Jiē	Hong Kong Street
	天津大街	Tiānjīn Dàjiē	Tianjin Avenue

Reading Exercises

A. PERSONAL NAMES

一、 安小明　　　　四、 林小川
二、 李南　　　　　五、 南山
三、 何安天　　　　六、 王海香

B. PLACE NAMES

一、 成都　　　四、 西安　　　七、 山东
二、 台南　　　五、 天津　　　八、 南京
三、 广东　　　六、 香山　　　九、 香港

C. PEOPLE AND THEIR PLACES OF ORIGIN

一、 南京人　　　四、 山西人　　　七、 成都人
二、 台东人　　　五、 四川人　　　八、 台南人
三、 广西人　　　六、 香港人　　　九、 台北人

D. NAMES OF STREETS AND ROADS

一、 四川街　　　四、 山西东街　　　七、 香港街
二、 中山南路　　五、 南京东路　　　八、 上海街
三、 广州街　　　六、 天津大街　　　九、 山东西街

Notes on Reading Part Three

D2.　　中山 here refers to Dr. Sun Yatsen (1866–1925), the founder of the Republic of China.

Reading Part Four

New Characters and Words

43. 河	hé	river
河南	Hé'nán	Henan (province)
河北	Héběi	Hebei (province)
44. 湖	hú	lake
湖南	Hú'nán	Hunan (province)
湖北	Húběi	Hubei (province)
五大湖	Wǔ Dà Hú	Great Lakes ("five great lakes")
45. 湾	wān	bay
台湾	Táiwān	Taiwan
46. 金	jīn	gold, metal
金	Jīn	Jin (surname)
金山	Jīnshān	(district in Shanghai; town in Taiwan)
47. 市	shì	city
北京市	Běijīng Shì	Beijing City
广州市	Guǎngzhōu Shì	Guangzhou City
台北市	Táiběi Shì	Taipei City
48. 省	shěng	province
河南省	Hé'nán Shěng	Henan Province
河北省	Héběi Shěng	Hebei Province
湖南省	Hú'nán Shěng	Hunan Province
湖北省	Húběi Shěng	Hubei Province
山西省	Shānxī Shěng	Shanxi Province
四川省	Sìchuān Shěng	Sichuan Province

Reading Exercises

A. PERSONAL NAMES

一、 王金海

二、 金广

三、 林安河

四、 李南川

五、 李天湖

B. PLACE NAMES

一、台湾省台东市　　　六、四川省成都市
二、上海市　　　　　　七、河北省
三、广西省　　　　　　八、河南省
四、北京市　　　　　　九、湖北省
五、广东省广州市　　　十、湖南省

C. PEOPLE AND THEIR PLACES OF ORIGIN

一、河北人　　　　　　六、香港人
二、河南省人　　　　　七、成都市人
三、台湾省台北市人　　八、北京市人
四、山西人　　　　　　九、天津市人
五、四川人　　　　　　十、西安市人

D. NAMES OF STREETS AND ROADS

一、天津街　　　　　　六、四川大街
二、台南路　　　　　　七、香港街
三、广州街　　　　　　八、河南街
四、湖北街　　　　　　九、台湾东路
五、河北路　　　　　　十、湖南东街

Notes on Reading Part Four

B1.　When mentioning a series of categories, the Chinese language alway proceeds from larger or more general to smaller or more specific. That is why, in this item and several others in parts B and C of this lesson, the province is mentioned before the city. This is also why, as we've already seen, Chinese people's surnames are mentioned before their given names.

The name of a famous street in Beijing

LESSON 3
Greetings

PART ONE

Conversation 🎧

Situation: Wang Jingsheng, a Chinese student, and Alex Crane, an American student, pass each other on the campus of Capital University of Economics and Business in Beijing.

1. **WANG:** 柯雷恩，你好！
   Kē Léi'ēn, nǐ hǎo!
   Hi, Alex!

2. **CRANE:** 王京生，你好！
   Wáng Jīngshēng, nǐ hǎo!
   Hi, Jingsheng!

3. **WANG:** 你到哪儿去啊？
   Nǐ dào nǎr qù a?
   Where are you going?

4. **CRANE:** 我去图书馆。你呢？
   Wǒ qù túshūguǎn. Nǐ ne?
   I'm going to the library. How about you?

5. **WANG:** 我回宿舍。
   Wǒ huí sùshè.
   I'm going back to the dorm.

New Vocabulary

柯雷恩	Kē Léi'ēn	(transliteration of the English name "Crane")
你好!	Nǐ hǎo!	"How are you?"
王京生	Wáng Jīngshēng	(Chinese name)
你	nǐ	you
到	dào	to
哪儿	nǎr	where
去	qù	go
啊	a	(softens the sentence)
我	wǒ	I, me
图书馆	túshūguǎn	library
呢	ne	and how about, what about
回	huí	return to
宿舍	sùshè	dormitory

Supplementary Vocabulary

食堂	shítáng	cafeteria, dining hall
办一点儿事	bàn yìdiǎnr shì	take care of some things
也	yě	also, too

Questions on the Conversation

1. 柯雷恩到哪儿去? Kē Léi'ēn dào nǎr qù?
2. 王京生到哪儿去? Wáng Jīngshēng dào nǎr qù?

General Questions

1. 你下了课到哪儿去? Nǐ xiàle kè dào nǎr qù?
2. 你下了课去图书馆吗? Nǐ xiàle kè qù túshūguǎn ma?
3. 你下了课去食堂吗? Nǐ xiàle kè qù shítáng ma?
4. 你下了课回宿舍吗? Nǐ xiàle kè huí sùshè ma?
5. 我下了课去办一点儿事。你下了课也去办一点儿事吗?
   Wǒ xiàle kè qù bàn yìdiǎnr shì. Nǐ xiàle kè yě qù bàn yìdiǎnr shì ma?

Notes on the Conversation

Greetings

The pattern **Name + Greeting** is very common in Chinese, for example, **Kē Léi'ēn, nǐ hǎo!** "Ke Leien, how are you?" A greeting may also simply consist of a person's name: **Wáng Jīngshēng!** "Wang Jingsheng!" A common response to the pattern **Name + Greeting** is to say the name of the other person followed by the same greeting.

Chinese names

Wáng Jīngshēng is a typical Chinese name. **Wáng** is the surname or family name, which in Chinese always comes first, while **Jīngshēng** is the given name, which in Chinese always comes *after* the surname.

How to say "go to a place"

The pattern **dào...qù** "go to..." is commonly used for asking or stating where someone is going. **Dào** literally means "arrive" or "to" and **qù** literally means "go." Between the **dào** and the **qù** is placed a question word indicating place such as **nǎr** "where" or a place word like **túshūguǎn** "library." The basic pattern is: SUBJECT + **DÀO** + PLACE + **QÙ**. For example, **Wáng Jīngshēng dào nǎr qù?** "Where is Jingsheng Wang going?"

Question word questions

One common way of forming a question in Chinese is by using a question word such as **nǎr** "where." For example, **Nǐ dào nǎr qù?** "Where are you going?" (literally, "You to where go?").

The final particle <u>a</u> to soften questions, greetings, and exclamations

The particle **a** at the end of a question, greeting, or exclamation makes the phrase or sentence softer, less abrupt, and more conversational. The difference between **Nǐ dào nǎr qù?** and **Nǐ dào nǎr qù a?** might be compared to English "Where are you going?" in an interrogation vs. "And where might you be going?" in a casual conversation among good friends.

Chinese greetings

Inquiring where another person is going is one common type of greeting in Chinese. To a Chinese person, this isn't being "nosy" but just a way of making casual conversation, indicating interest and concern for the other person and that communication lines are open. A precise reply to such a question isn't necessary, in the same way that English "How are you?" does not require a detailed answer. If you don't wish to tell the questioner where you're going, you could answer with a vague response like **Wǒ qù bàn yìdiǎnr shìr** "I'm going to take care of a little something" (see Supplementary Vocabulary, page 35).

How to indicate that you are going to a certain place

One common way to state where you are going is simply to use the verb **qù** "go" followed immediately by a place word, such as **túshūguǎn** "library" or **shítáng** "cafeteria." The pattern is: SUBJECT + **QÙ** + PLACE WORD, for example, **Wǒ qù túshūguǎn.** "I'm going to the library."

The final particle <u>ne</u> to abbreviate questions

One function of the final particle **ne** is to abbreviate questions when a question which has previously been asked is repeated with a new subject or topic, but the rest of the question remains the same. Look at this example:

Speaker A: **Nĭ dào năr qù a?** "Where are you going?"

Speaker B: **Wŏ qù túshūguăn. Nĭ ne?** "I'm going to the library. And you?"

In Speaker B's response, the **ne** stands for **dào năr qù**. The effect of the particle **ne** here is like English "And how about you?" or "What about you?"

Reading

New Characters and Words

49.	你	**nĭ**	you
50.	好	**hăo**	be good
	你好	**nĭ hăo**	"how are you?," "hi"
51.	我	**wŏ**	I, me
52.	也	**yĕ**	also, too
53.	去	**qù**	go, go to
54.	呢	**ne**	and what about, and how about

A. SENTENCES

一、何大山，你好！文中生，你好！
二、我去山东，你去山西。
三、李小山去河北，王大文去河南。
四、你去南京，我也去南京，李大明也去南京。
五、去，去，去，去北京！
六、何台生去台北，王大明呢？
七、王京生去台山，林台生也去台山。
八、你去广东，我也去广东。
九、何大海，你去香港，我也去。
十、我去北京，王大海也去北京。

B. CONVERSATIONS

一、
王京生：我去北京，也去香山。你呢？
文小山：我去天津。

二、
李京生：北京好！

王台生：台北好！

何大海：北京好，台北也好。

C. NARRATIVES

一、何大海去西安，李中山也去西安。林文生去台中，也去台北。我
　　去北京，也去上海。你呢？

二、王安湖去东京。东京好！金明去上海。上海也好。李京去香港，
　　我也去香港。何小文，你呢？

Notes

A2.　Some Chinese punctuation marks are similar to English but others are different. Notice the "Chinese period" at the end of this sentence. The Chinese period is called 句号 **jùhào**. Instead of a dot as in English, a Chinese period is a small circle, like this: 。 In horizontal writing, the Chinese period is placed to the bottom right of the last character of the sentence. It occupies the same amount of space as any other character.

A5.　Verbs, such as the 去 in this sentence, are sometimes repeated for emphasis.

A6.　Note the name 何台生. 台 could here stand for 台湾, and 生 could mean "be born," so 台生 could be an abbreviated way to indicate "born in Taiwan."

A7.　Considering the information in the previous note, where do you think 王京生 was probably born?

A8.　This sentence has two possible interpretations. In addition to "You go to Guangdong, and I also go to Guangdong," it could also be interpreted as "If you go to Guangdong, then I'll also go to Guangdong." Although there are in Chinese explicit words for "if," be aware that "if" must sometimes be inferred from the context and be supplied in the English translation.

B2.　好 here functions as a stative verb meaning "be good." Thus, 北京好 means "Beijing is good" or "Beijing is better." 台北好 works the same way.

Typical street scene in Hong Kong

PART TWO

Conversation

Situation: Michael Smith meets his Chinese friend Zhao Guocai on the street in Beijing. The two men haven't seen each other for a while. Smith is in a bit of a hurry, as he has an appointment in a few minutes.

1. **SMITH:**   赵国材，你好啊！
   Zhào Guócái, nǐ hǎo a!
   Zhao Guocai, how are you?

2. **ZHAO:**   你好！好久不见了。怎么样啊？
   Nǐ hǎo! Hǎo jiǔ bú jiànle. Zěmmeyàng a?
   How are you? Haven't seen you for a long time. How have you been?

3. **SMITH:**   还行。你爱人、孩子都好吗？
   Hái xíng. Nǐ àiren, háizi dōu hǎo ma?
   Pretty good. Are your wife and child both well?

4. **ZHAO:**   他们都很好，谢谢。
   Tāmen dōu hěn hǎo, xièxie.
   They're both fine, thanks.

5. **SMITH:**   我有一点儿事，先走了。再见！
   Wǒ yǒu yìdiǎnr shì, xiān zǒule. Zàijiàn!
   I have something I have to do, I'll be going now (first). Goodbye!

6. **ZHAO:**   再见！
   Zàijiàn!
   Bye!

New Vocabulary

赵国材	**Zhào Guócái**	(Chinese name)
好久不见了	**hǎo jiǔ bú jiànle**	"long time no see"
怎么样	**zěmmeyàng**	how?, in what way?
还	**hái**	still
行	**xíng**	be all right, O.K.
爱人	**àiren**	spouse, husband, wife
孩子	**háizi**	child, children
都	**dōu**	all, both
好	**hǎo**	be good
吗	**ma**	(indicates questions)
他们	**tāmen**	they, them
很	**hěn**	very
谢谢	**xièxie**	"thank you"
有	**yǒu**	have
先	**xiān**	first, before someone else
走	**zǒu**	leave, depart
了	**le**	(indicates changed status)
再见	**zàijiàn**	"goodbye"

Supplementary Vocabulary

爸爸	**bàba**	dad
妈妈	**māma**	mom
他	**tā**	he, him
她	**tā**	she, her
忙	**máng**	be busy
累	**lèi**	be tired, fatigued

Questions on the Conversation

1. Smith怎么样啊？ **Smith zěmmeyàng a?**

2. 赵国材的爱人好吗？ **Zhào Guócáide àiren hǎo ma?**

3. 赵国材的孩子怎么样啊？ **Zhào Guócáide háizi zěmmeyàng a?**

4. 赵国材的爱人、孩子怎么样啊？ **Zhào Guócáide àiren, háizi zěmmeyàng a?**

5. Smith很忙吗？ **Smith hěn máng ma?**

6. Smith有一点儿事吗？ **Smith yǒu yìdiǎnr shì ma?**

7. 赵国材先走了吗？ **Zhào Guócái xiān zǒule ma?**

8. Smith先走了吗？ **Smith xiān zǒule ma?**

General Questions

1. 你好！ **Nǐ hǎo!**

2. 你怎么样啊？ **Nǐ zěmmeyàng a?**

3. 你好！好久不见了！ **Nǐ hǎo! Hǎo jiǔ bú jiànle!**

4. 我有一点儿事儿，先走了。 **Wǒ yǒu yìdiǎnr shìr, xiān zǒule.**

5. 你好吗？ **Nǐ hǎo ma?**

6. 你忙吗？ **Nǐ máng ma?**

7. 你现在忙吗？ **Nǐ xiànzài máng ma?**

8. 你明天忙吗？ **Nǐ míngtiān máng ma?**

9. 你累吗？ **Nǐ lèi ma?**

10. 你还行吗？ **Nǐ hái xíng ma?**

11. 你爸爸好吗？ **Nǐ bàba hǎo ma?**

12. 你妈妈好吗？ **Nǐ māma hǎo ma?**

13. 你爸爸、妈妈都好吗？ **Nǐ bàba, māma dōu hǎo ma?**

Notes on the Conversation

Pronouns before nouns with possessive meanings

Look at **nǐ àiren** "your spouse." When pronouns like **wǒ**, **nǐ**, and **tā** occur before words that are close-ly related to the person being referred to by the pronoun (like family members), the pronouns can acquire a possessive meaning. Here are two more examples: **wǒ bàba** "my dad," **tā māma** "her mom."

....

The adverb dōu

Dōu can be translated into English as "all" or "both"; the context usually makes the meaning clear. Since **dōu** is an adverb, it must always precede a verb or other adverb and can never precede a noun like English "all." So while **Háizi dōu hěn hǎo** "The children are all (or both) fine" is good Chinese, you could NOT say ***Dōu háizi hěn hǎo** to mean "All the children are very good."

....

Ma to transform statements into questions

One of the most common ways of forming a question in Chinese is by adding the final particle **ma** to the end of a statement. Take the statement **Tāmen qù shítáng** "They're going to the dining hall." By adding **ma** to the end of that statement, we can transform the statement into a question: **Tāmen qù shítáng ma?** "Are they going to the dining hall?" Be careful not to confuse **Ma** Questions with Question Word Questions. If a question already contains a question word such as **nǎr** or **zěmmeyàng**, then **ma** isn't added.

....

Order of adverbs

You've now learned the adverbs **dōu** "all, both," **hěn** "very," and **yě** "also." Remember that adverbs can occur only before verbs or before other adverbs. When two or more of these adverbs occur together, the normal order is: first **yě**, then **dōu**, and finally **hěn**. To help you remember the correct order, memorize this sentence: **Tāmen yě dōu hěn hǎo** "They also are all very well."

Stative verb sentences

Look at the sentence **Tāmen hěn hǎo** "They're very good." This is an example of a Stative Verb Sentence. Stative Verb Sentences consist of a subject or topic, an adverb like **hěn**, and a stative verb like **hǎo** "be good." Here are some more examples of Stative Verb Sentences: **Wǒ hěn lèi** "I am very tired," **Wǒ bàba, māma dōu hěn máng** "My mom and dad are both very busy." Keep in mind that Chinese stative verbs correspond to English adjectives plus the verb "to be." When using a Chinese stative verb, there is no need to add an extra verb "to be," since the "to be" is built into the Chinese stative verb.

Reading

New Characters and Words

55.	他	tā	he, him
56.	她	tā	she, her
57.	们	men	(plural marker for pronouns)
	他们	tāmen	they, them (males only, or males and females)
	她们	tāmen	they, them (females only)
58.	很	hěn	very
59.	忙	máng	be busy
60.	吗	ma	(particle that indicates questions)

A. SENTENCES

一、 北京很好，香港、台北也都很好。

二、 我很忙，他们也很忙。你呢？你忙吗？

三、 我很好。李小明、何台生他们也都很好。

四、 金中、何大生他们都去上海吗？

五、 王明，你好！你去天津吗？

六、 她们去台山。他呢？他也去台山吗？

七、 我去东京，文文去京都。他们呢？

八、 我去上海，他们也都去上海。

九、 广东人去广西，广西人去广东！

十、 王大海去台北，我也去台北。你呢？你也去台北吗？

B. CONVERSATIONS

一、

王大中：林小文，你好！
林小文：王大中，你好！
王大中：你忙吗？
林小文：很忙。你呢？
王大中：我也很忙。

二、

何京生：林一明，你好！
林一明：何京生，你好！我去山西。你呢？
何京生：我去山东。
林一明：她们呢？
何京生：她们也去山东。

C. NARRATIVES

一、李文、王京生他们去南京。我也去南京。金明明也去南京。李
文、王京生他们都很忙。我也很忙。金明明也很忙。你呢？你也
去南京吗？你也很忙吗？

二、林文生去河北，也去河南。他很忙。李京去湖北，也去湖南，她
也很忙。我去广东，也去广西。我也很忙。

Notes

A1A. Another use of the 顿号 dùnhào (、) is to separate items in a series, somewhat like the English conjunction "and." Thus, 香港、台北也都很好 could mean "Hong Kong and Taipei would also both be fine."

A1B. Notice that the character 都 can represent two different words with two different pronunciations. Pronounced dū (as in 成都 Chéngdū) it means "city," but pronounced dōu it is an adverb meaning "all, both."

A3. After a listing of names in a series, the appropriate plural pronoun is often added so as to sum up and clarify or emphasize the group of people concerned. Thus, in this sentence, 李小明、何台生他们 means "Li Xiaoming and He Taisheng, they...." Normally, the "they" would be omitted in an English translation.

LESSON 4
Meeting People

PART ONE

Conversation 🎧

Situation: Brian Kao, who is studying martial arts in Beijing, runs into his Chinese friend, He Zhiming.

1. **KAO:**　欸，老何！
Èi, Lǎo Hé!
Hey, Old He!

2. **HE:**　小高！
Xiǎo Gāo!
Little Gao!

3. **KAO:**　最近怎么样啊？
Zuìjìn zěmmeyàng a?
How've you been lately?

4. **HE:**　还可以。你呢？
Hái kéyi. Nǐ ne?
Pretty good. How about you?

5. **KAO:**　还是老样子。你工作忙不忙？
Hái shi lǎo yàngzi. Nǐ gōngzuò máng bu máng?
Still the same as before. Is your work keeping you busy?

6. **HE:**   不太忙。你学习怎么样？
             Bú tài máng. Nǐ xuéxí zěmmeyàng?
             Not too busy. How are your studies going?

7. **KAO:**   挺紧张的。
              Tǐng jǐnzhāngde.
              Very intense.

New Vocabulary 🎧

欸	**èi**	"hey, hi"
老	**lǎo**	be old (of people)
小	**xiǎo**	be small, little, young
最近	**zuìjìn**	recently
可以	**kéyi**	be O.K.
是	**shì**	be
样子	**yàngzi**	way, appearance
工作	**gōngzuò**	work
不	**bù**	not
太	**tài**	too, excessively
学习	**xuéxí**	study, studies
挺	**tǐng**	quite, very
挺……的	**tǐng...-de**	very, quite
紧张	**jǐnzhāng**	be intense, nervous

Supplementary Vocabulary 🎧

中文	**Zhōngwén**	written Chinese, Chinese
难	**nán**	be difficult, hard
容易	**róngyi**	be easy
困	**kùn**	be sleepy
高	**gāo**	be tall, high
矮	**ǎi**	be short (not tall)

Questions on the Conversation

1. 老何最近怎么样？ **Lǎo Hé zuìjìn zěmmeyàng?**
2. 小高呢？ **Xiǎo Gāo ne?**
3. 老何的工作怎么样？ **Lǎo Héde gōngzuò zěmmeyàng?**
4. 小高的学习怎么样？ **Xiǎo Gāode xuéxí zěmmeyàng?**

General Questions

1. 你最近怎么样？ **Nǐ zuìjìn zěmmeyàng?**
2. 你学习怎么样？ **Nǐ xuéxí zěmmeyàng?**
3. 你学习忙不忙？ **Nǐ xuéxí máng bù máng?**
4. 你最近学习紧张不紧张？ **Nǐ zuìjìn xuéxí jǐnzhāng bù jǐnzhāng?**
5. 我最近很忙，你最近也很忙吗？ **Wǒ zuìjìn hěn máng, nǐ zuìjìn yě hěn máng ma?**
6. 我最近很累，你最近也很累吗？ **Wǒ zuìjìn hěn lèi, nǐ zuìjìn yě hěn lèi ma?**
7. 我最近很困，你呢？ **Wǒ zuìjìn hěn kùn, nǐ ne?**
8. 你工作吗？ **Nǐ gōngzuò ma?**
9. 你爸爸工作忙不忙？ **Nǐ bàba gōngzuò máng bù máng?**
10. 你妈妈工作紧张不紧张？ **Nǐ māma gōngzuò jǐnzhāng bù jǐnzhāng?**
11. 你爸爸、妈妈还是老样子吗？ **Nǐ bàba, māma hái shi lǎo yàngzi ma?**
12. 中文难不难？ **Zhōngwén nán bù nán?**
13. 中文挺容易吗？ **Zhōngwén tǐng róngyi ma?**
14. 中文的声调难不难？ **Zhōngwénde shēngdiào nán bù nán?**
15. SAT考试难不难？ **SAT kǎoshì nán bù nán?**

Notes on the Conversation

Lǎo and Xiǎo before surnames

Lǎo is a stative verb meaning "be old" (usually of people, not things). Unlike English "old," **lǎo** ordinarily has favorable connotations, indicating wisdom and experience. **Xiǎo** is also a stative verb, meaning "be small, little, young." **Lǎo** and **Xiǎo** followed by a monosyllabic surname are commonly used together in informal, colloquial conversation to address people or to refer to them. For example, **Lǎo Lǐ** "Old Li," **Xiǎo Gāo** "Little Gao." **Lǎo** is used for people who are older than oneself while **Xiǎo** is used for people who are younger than or about the same age as oneself. These terms are especially common in China, where they are used for women as well as men; in other Chinese-speaking areas they are used less often, and usually for men only. It is best for nonnative speakers not to use these terms until invited to do so. In this text, we'll translate **Lǎo** as "Old" and **Xiǎo** as "Little," though in English the best translation of **Lǎo** or **Xiǎo** plus surname would often be the given name of the person.

Stative verbs before nouns as adjectives

One-syllable stative verbs can stand directly before nouns to describe them. In this sentence, the stative verb **lǎo** "be old" stands before the noun **yàngzi** "way" to describe it, creating the phrase **lǎo yàngzi** "old way." Here are some more examples of stative verbs before nouns functioning as adjectives: **hǎo māma** "good mother," **hǎo gōngzuò** "good job," **xiǎo shìr** "small matter." The stative verb and noun could then be inserted together into a sentence, as in **Tā shi hǎo māma** "She is a good mother." Be careful to distinguish stative verb + noun constructions like **hǎo māma** "good mother" from noun + stative verb constructions like **Māma hěn hǎo** "Mom is good."

Bù to negate verbs

With the exception of the verb **yǒu** "have," all other verbs in Chinese are negated by placing the adverb **bù** "not" before the verb. Here are the affirmative and negative forms of several verbs you've had:

AFFIRMATIVE	NEGATIVE
hǎo "be good"	**bù hǎo** "not be good"
xíng "be O.K."	**bù xíng** "not be O.K."
zǒu "leave	**bù zǒu** "not leave"
huí sùshè "go back to the dormitory"	**bù huí sùshè** "not go back to the dormitory"

Affirmative-Negative Questions

A common way to create a question in Chinese is to give the affirmative and negative forms of the verb one after another and let the person who is asked choose one of the two alternatives as the answer. For example, **Nǐ gōngzuò bu gōngzuò?** "Do you work?" (literally, "You work not work?"). In affirmative-negative questions, the **bù** is often pronounced in the neutral tone as **bu**. The answer to the above question would be either **(Wǒ) gōngzuò** "I work" or **(Wǒ) bù gōngzuò** "I don't work." Here are some more examples of this pattern: **Nǐ máng bu máng?** "Are you busy?," **Zhōngwén nán bu nán?** "Is Chinese hard?," **Xiǎo Wáng qù bu qù?** "Is Little Wang going?" Note that adverbs like **dōu** "all, both," **yě** "also," or **hěn** "very" are not compatible with Affirmative-Negative Questions, so you could never ask a question like ***Tāmen dōu qù bu qù?** to mean "Are they all going?" Instead, you would just say **Tāmen qù bu qù?** "Are they going?" If the speaker felt it were important to keep the sense of **dōu**, then he or she could use a **Ma** Question and ask **Tāmen dōu qù ma?** "Are they all going?"

Three basic question types

You've now been introduced to three basic question types of Chinese, which you should be sure to distinguish carefully:

1. *Question Word Questions*:   **Nǐ dào nǎr qù?**
2. **Ma** *Questions*:   **Nǐ àiren, háizi dōu hǎo ma?**
3. *Affirmative-Negative Questions*:   **Nǐ gōngzuò máng bu máng?**

Topic-Comment construction

The question **Nǐ gōngzuò máng bu máng?** is an example of a Topic-Comment construction, a very common sentence type in Chinese. The first topic is **nǐ** "you" and the first comment is **gōngzuò máng bu máng** "work is busy or not busy?." The noun **gōngzuò** can be analyzed as a second topic that is embedded within the first comment, with **máng bu máng** being a second comment. A literal rendering of the whole sentence might be: "As far as you are concerned (topic no. 1), regarding your work (topic no. 2), is it busy or not busy?"

Tone change of <u>bù</u> to <u>bú</u> before Tone Four syllables

Look carefully at the sentence **Bú tài máng** "Not too busy." The adverb **bù** "not" is normally a Tone Four syllable. However, when it stands directly before another Tone Four syllable, **bù** changes from Tone Four to Tone Two. That is to say, **bù + tài → bú tài** "not very." Here are some more examples of this tone change: **bù + qù → bú qù** "not go," **bù + lèi → bú lèi** "not be tired," **bù + bàn → bú bàn** "not take care of."

The pattern tǐng...-de to mean "very"

The pattern **tǐng...-de** can surround stative verbs to indicate "quite, very." **Tǐng...-de** has about the same meaning as **hěn** "very" but is more colloquial and less formal. **Tǐng** is also sometimes used alone without a following **-de** with the same meaning, so you could simply say **tǐng jǐnzhāng** "very intense." Here are some more examples with this pattern: **tǐng hǎode** "quite good," **tǐng lèide** "quite tired," **tǐng róngyide** "very easy."

Reading

New Characters and Words

61.	老	**lǎo**	be old; (surname)
	老王	**Lǎo Wáng**	Old Wang
62.	高	**gāo**	be tall, high; (surname)
	老高	**Lǎo Gāo**	Old Gao
63.	不	**bù**	not
	不忙	**bù máng**	not busy
	不高	**bù gāo**	not tall
64.	太	**tài**	excessively, too
	太忙	**tài máng**	too busy
	不太高	**bú tài gāo**	not too tall
65.	难	**nán**	be difficult, hard
66.	谢	**xiè**	thank; (surname)
	谢谢	**xièxie**	"thank you"

A. SENTENCES

一、老高，谢谢！小何，谢谢！

二、林文生很高吗？

三、小何很高，你也很高。

四、林一明，香山好不好？去香山难不难？

五、你不去台湾吗？我也不去台湾。

六、她们太忙，她们不去。你呢？你去不去？

七、她很老，她们都很老。
八、小明太小吗？他不小！
九、中文难不难？
十、王大海不太忙。

B. CONVERSATIONS

一、
小何：老王，你好！
老王：小何，你好！
小何：你忙不忙？
老王：我很忙。
小何：你去不去北京？
老王：我太忙，不去。你去不去？
小何：我也不去。

二、
王大山：林京生！
林京生：王大山！
王大山：你好吗？
林京生：我很好，谢谢！你呢？
王大山：我很忙。我去西安，你去不去？
林京生：我也去西安。去西安难不难？
王大山：去西安不太难。
林京生：很好，很好。

C. NARRATIVES

一、小金，去天津街难不难？不太难吗？好。去上海路难不难？很难吗？
好，我去天津街，不去上海路。小金，你很好，谢谢！

二、北京人很高吗？北京人很高。山东人呢？山东人也很高。上海人高不
高？上海人不太高。广东人、台湾人呢？广东人、台湾人也都不太高。

Notes

B2.   Note that the first two lines of this conversation consist of nothing other than each speaker's
name: 林京生！ 王大山！ Calling out someone's name in this manner is a common type
of informal greeting.

C2.   This description of the relative heights of Chinese people from different regions is greatly
simplified due to vocabulary limitations.

PART TWO

Conversation 🎧

Situation: Jean Smith visits Li Xianfen at her home in downtown Taipei. Mrs. Smith and Mrs. Li met recently at a reception, so they don't yet know each other very well.

1. MRS. LI: 谢太太，欢迎，欢迎！请进，请进。
Xiè Tàitai, huānyíng, huānyíng! Qǐng jìn, qǐng jìn.
Mrs. Smith, welcome! Please come in.

2. MRS. SMITH: *(removes her shoes):*
谢谢。
Xièxie.
Thank you.

3. MRS. LI: 请坐，请坐。
Qǐng zuò, qǐng zuò.
Please sit down.

4. MRS. SMITH: 谢谢。李太太，我有一点事，得走了。李太太，谢谢您了。
Xièxie. Lǐ Tàitai, wǒ yǒu yìdiǎn shì, děi zǒule. Lǐ Tàitai, xièxie nín le.
Thank you. (after a while) Mrs. Li, I have something I need to do, I must be going now. Mrs. Li, thank you.

5. MRS. LI: 不客气。慢走啊！
Bú kèqi. Màn zǒu a!
You're welcome. Take care!

6. MRS. SMITH: 再见，再见！
Zàijiàn, zàijiàn!
Goodbye!

New Vocabulary

太太	tàitai	Mrs. (as a title)
欢迎	huānyíng	"welcome"
请	qǐng	"please"
进	jìn	enter
请进	qǐng jìn	"please come in"
坐	zuò	sit
请坐	qǐng zuò	"please sit down"
得	děi	must
谢谢	xièxie	thank
您	nín	you (singular, polite)
不客气	bú kèqi	"you're welcome"
慢走	màn zǒu	"take care"

Supplementary Vocabulary

老师	lǎoshī	teacher
小姐	xiáojie	Miss, Ms. (as a title)
先生	xiānsheng	Mr. (as a title)
我们	wǒmen	we, us
有意思	yǒu yìsi	be interesting
没意思	méi yìsi	not be interesting
你们	nǐmen	you (plural)

Questions on the Conversation

1. 谢太太欢迎李太太，对不对？ Xiè Tàitai huānyíng Lǐ Tàitai, duì bu duì?
2. 谢太太有事吗？ Xiè Tàitai yǒu shì ma?
3. 李太太有事吗？ Lǐ Tàitai yǒu shì ma?
4. 谢太太得走了吗？ Xiè Tàitai děi zǒule ma?

General Questions

1. 你现在有事吗？ Nǐ xiànzài yǒu shì ma?
2. 你现在得走了吗？ Nǐ xiànzài děi zǒule ma?
3. 中文很难吗？ Zhōngwén hěn nán ma?
4. 中文容易不容易？ Zhōngwén róngyi bù róngyi?

5. 中文有意思吗？ **Zhōngwén yǒu yìsi ma?**

6. 你工作吗？你的工作有意思吗？ **Nǐ gōngzuò ma? Nǐde gōngzuò yǒu yìsi ma?**

7. 你爸爸工作吗？他的工作有意思吗？
   Nǐ bàba gōngzuò ma? Tāde gōngzuò yǒu yìsi ma?

8. 你妈妈工作吗？她的工作有意思吗？
   Nǐ māma gōngzuò ma? Tāde gōngzuò yǒu yìsi ma?

9. 你的学习最近怎么样？有意思吗？ **Nǐde xuéxí zuìjìn zěmmeyàng? Yǒu yìsi ma?**

10. 去图书馆学习有意思吗？ **Qù túshūguǎn xuéxí yǒu yìsi ma?**

11. 中文老师的工作有意思吗？ **Zhōngwén lǎoshīde gōngzuò yǒu yìsi ma?**

12. 你的中文老师有意思吗？ **Nǐde Zhōngwén lǎoshī yǒu yìsi ma?**

Notes on the Conversation

Titles

Chinese titles such as **Xiānsheng** "Mr.," **Tàitai** "Mrs.," **Xiáojie** "Miss, Ms.," and **Lǎoshī** come *after* a person's surname, which is the opposite order from English. Here are some examples of Chinese surnames followed by titles: **Xiè Xiānsheng** "Mr. Xie," **Lǐ Tàitai** "Mrs. Li," **Wáng Xiáojie** "Miss Wang, Ms. Wang," **Lín Lǎoshī** "Teacher Lin." Titles are also sometimes used alone, without any surname; for example, **Lǎoshī, qǐng jìn!** "Teacher, please come in!"

Le to indicate a changed situation

In an earlier lesson we learned the phrase **Xiān zǒule** "I'll be leaving now." In this lesson we encounter another sentence with a **le** at the end: **(Wǒ) děi zǒule** "I must be leaving now." The particle **le** attached to the end of a sentence can express a changed situation; either the situation described is new or the speaker has made a new discovery of an existing situation. Here are some more examples of this **le**: **Hǎole** "It's O.K. now," **Tā lèile** "She's become tired," **Nǐ māma hǎole ma?** "Has your mom gotten well?," **Wǒ bú qùle** "I'm no longer going."

Pronouns

As of this lesson, you've learned all the common personal pronouns. Be sure you're thoroughly familiar with them. To recapitulate:

SINGULAR	PLURAL
wǒ "I/me"	**wǒmen** "we/us"
nǐ "you"	**nǐmen** "you" (plural)
nín "you" (polite)	
tā "he/him, she/her"	**tāmen** "they/them"

Reading

New Characters and Words

67.	请	**qǐng**	"please"
68.	坐	**zuò**	sit
	请坐	**qǐng zuò**	"please sit down"
69.	先	**xiān**	first, before someone else
	先生	**xiānsheng**	Mr. (as a title)
70.	走	**zǒu**	leave, depart
71.	了	**le**	(indicates changed status or situation)
	我走了。	**Wǒ zǒule.**	"I'll be leaving now."
	她不去了。	**Tā bú qùle.**	"She's no longer going."
	他好了吗？	**Tā hǎole ma?**	"Is he well now?"
72.	姐	**jiě**	older sister (usually not used alone)
	小姐	**xiáojie**	Miss, Ms. (as a title)

A. SENTENCES

一、王先生、王太太，你们好！请坐，请坐！

二、我好了，他也好了，你也好了吗？

三、我老了，你们也老了，我们都老了！

四、安小姐太忙了，她不去了。

五、李小姐、金小姐她们都去台湾了。

六、文小姐，你不坐吗？

七、我谢谢你，我也谢谢他。

八、何小姐很忙，她先走了。你不太忙，你先请坐。

九、老李，我请你去香港，好不好？

十、我们不去东京了。王大海，你呢？你去不去东京？

B. CONVERSATIONS

一、

谢大文：何大海，你好吗？请坐，请坐。

何大海：谢大文，你好！谢谢！

谢大文：何大海，我们都老了……

何大海：你老，我不老！

二、

王先生：林小姐，你好！

林小姐：王先生，你好！

王先生：林小姐，你忙吗？请坐，请坐。

林小姐：王先生，谢谢你，我不坐了。我很忙，我先走了。

C. NARRATIVES

一、 王太太很忙。她去北京、天津、上海、香港、台北，也去东京。她太忙了！请她坐很难。王先生不太忙。请王先生坐不难。

二、 何先生、林太太、谢小姐，你们好！请坐，请坐！你们去西安吗？太忙了，不去了吗？我也很忙，我也不去西安了。

Notes

A8.   The phrase 你先请坐 here means something like "you first please sit down (for a while, before you do the other things you need to do)."

A9.   In the clause 我请你去香港 "I invite you to go to Hong Kong," the verb 请 is used in its basic sense of "invite."

C1.   As we saw in note A9 above, besides meaning "please," 请 can also be used in its basic sense of "invite." This is how the two 请 in this narrative are used. So 请她坐很难 could be translated as "To invite her to sit down is difficult" and 请王先生坐不难 could be translated as "To invite Mr. Wang to sit down isn't hard."

C2.   Note that in the question 太忙了，不去了吗?, the understood but deleted subject is 你们 "you (all)." So this question could be translated as "Are you all too busy and no longer going?" In Chinese, when a subject or topic is clear from the context (and in this case the subject is clear, since it was mentioned in the first sentence of the paragraph), it is often omitted later in the discourse.

Asking about Name and Nationality

PART ONE

Conversation

Situation: It's registration day at the Mandarin Training Center at National Taiwan Normal University in Taipei. Jerry Parsons is waiting in line to register when a Taiwanese student asks where he's from.

1. TAIWANESE STUDENT: 请问，你是哪国人？
Qǐng wèn, nǐ shi něiguó rén?
Excuse me, what country are you from?

2. PARSONS: 我是美国人。
Wǒ shi Měiguo rén.
I'm an American.

3. TAIWANESE STUDENT: 你叫什么名字？
Nǐ jiào shémme míngzi?
What's your name?

4. PARSONS: 我叫白杰瑞。

Wǒ jiào Bái Jiéruì.

My name is Jerry Parsons.

5. TAIWANESE STUDENT: 你们都是美国人吗？

Nǐmen dōu shi Měiguo rén ma?

Are all of you Americans?

6. PARSONS: 我们不都是美国人。这位同学也是美国人，可是那位同学是加拿大人。

Wǒmen bù dōu shi Měiguo rén. Zhèiwèi tóngxué yě shi Měiguo rén, kěshi nèiwèi tóngxué shi Jiā'nádà rén.

Not all of us are Americans. This classmate is also American, but that classmate is Canadian.

New Vocabulary

问	**wèn**	ask
请问	**qǐng wèn**	"excuse me," "may I ask"
哪	**něi-**	which
哪国	**něiguó**	which country?
人	**rén**	person
美国	**Měiguo**	America
叫	**jiào**	be called or named
什么	**shémme**	what
名字	**míngzi**	name
这	**zhèi-**	this
位	**wèi**	(polite measure for people)
同学	**tóngxue**	classmate
可是	**kěshi**	but
那	**nèi-**	that
加拿大	**Jiā'nádà**	Canada

Supplementary Vocabulary

西班牙	**Xībānyá**	Spain
中国	**Zhōngguo**	China
日本	**Rìběn**	Japan
台湾	**Táiwān**	Taiwan
新加坡	**Xīnjiāpō**	Singapore
马来西亚	**Mǎláixīyà**	Malaysia
华裔	**Huáyì**	person of Chinese descent

Questions on the Conversation

1. 白先生叫什么？ **Bái Xiānsheng jiào shémme?**
2. 他是哪国人？ **Tā shi něiguó rén?**
3. 他的同学都是美国人吗？ **Tāde tóngxué dōu shi Měiguo rén ma?**

General Questions

1. 你叫什么名字？ **Nǐ jiào shémme míngzi?**
2. 你是哪国人？ **Nǐ shi něiguó rén?**
3. 你是美国人吗？ **Nǐ shi Měiguo rén ma?**
4. 你是华裔美国人吗？ **Nǐ shi Huáyì Měiguo rén ma?**
5. 你的同学都是美国人吗？ **Nǐde tóngxué dōu shì Měiguo rén ma?**
6. 你的中文老师叫什么名字？ **Nǐde Zhōngwén lǎoshī jiào shémme míngzi?**
7. 你的中文老师是哪国人？ **Nǐde Zhōngwén lǎoshī shi něiguó rén?**

Notes on the Conversation

The equative verb shì

The verb **shì** "be" is one of the most frequently used verbs in the Chinese language. It indicates that the topic or subject of the sentence is the same as or "equals" the predicate (the part of the sentence after the verb). The verb **shì** is ordinarily pronounced in the neutral tone (**shi**) unless it is stressed. The negative of **shì** is **bú shì**. Here are some examples: **Wǒ shi Měiguo rén** "I am (an) American," **Tā shi wǒ bàba** "He's my dad," **Tāmen bú shi Zhōngguo rén** "They're not Chinese," **Nǐ shi něiguó rén?** "What country are you from?," **Nǐ shi Zhōngguo rén ma?** "Are you Chinese?," **Nǐ shì bu shi Zhōngguo rén?** "Are you Chinese?"

....

Equative Verb Sentences vs. Stative Verb Sentences

Compare the following two sentences, which have the same English structure with the verb "to be" but have different Chinese structures: **Tā shi Zhōngguo rén** "She is Chinese" (Equative Verb Sentence with **shì**) vs. **Tā hěn máng** "She is busy" (Stative Verb Sentence). With stative verbs, remember that "to be" is built into the meaning of the stative verb and that no **shì** is added. In a nutshell, if the predicate *equals* the subject, use **shì**; if the predicate *describes* the subject, use a stative verb.

....

The equative verb jiào

Jiào "be called, be named" is another common equative verb, for example, **Wǒ jiào (Bái) Jiéruì** "My name is (Bai) Jierui." This pattern can indicate either what someone's surname and given name are, or it can indicate given name only. However, it's not possible to give only the surname when using **jiào**. Here are some more examples of **jiào**: **Wǒ māma jiào Guō Zhìlíng** "My mom's name is Guo Zhiling," **Nǐ jiào shémme?** "What's your name?"

....

Nationalities

Nationalities are expressed by saying first the name of the country and then adding **rén** "person." For example, **Měiguo** "America" + **rén** = **Měiguo rén** "American," **Zhōngguo** "China" + **rén** = **Zhōngguo rén** "Chinese."

Question words

Shémme "what" is another example of a question word. You've now had three question words: **zěmmeyàng**, **něiguó**, and **shémme**. Remember that there is no need for a **ma** at the end of questions containing question words like **shémme** because such sentences are already questions. Note that **shémme** can be used either to modify a following noun (as in **Shémme míngzi?** "What name?") or by itself (**Nǐ jiào shémme?** "You are called what?"). Also note that in Chinese questions, the word order is the same as in statements, but in English questions we switch the word order. For "What are you called?" in Chinese you can say only **Nǐ jiào shémme?** (you could never say *Shémme nǐ jiào?).

Bù dōu "not all" vs. dōu bù "all not"

Sentences with **bù dōu** state that the members of a class are not all something, implying that some members of the class are something and other members of the class are not. Sentences with **dōu bù**, on the other hand, state that all members of a class are not something. Contrast the different order of **bù** and **dōu** and the differences in meaning in this pair of sentences: **Wǒmen bù dōu shi Měiguo rén** "We are not all Americans" ("Not all of us are Americans") vs. **Wǒmen dōu bú shi Měiguo rén** "All of us are not Americans" ("None of us is American").

Zhèi- "this" and nèi- "that" as specifiers

Specifiers are adjectival expressions that point to or "specify" a noun or nouns. Specifiers don't occur by themselves but are connected to other words as part of a noun phrase. The basic order is specifier + measure + noun or noun phrase, for example, **zhèiwèi tóngxué** "this classmate" or **nèiwèi lǎoshī** "that teacher." In line 1 of this conversation, you encountered **něi-** "which?" (as in **něiguó rén** "a person from which country"). **Něi-** is both a question word and a specifier. Here is another example with **něi-: Něiwèi lǎoshī?** "Which teacher?"

Measures

Unlike English, where we count or specify most nouns directly ("one classmate," "this classmate"), in Chinese a so-called measure must be used before a noun if it is counted or specified. Chinese specifiers like **zhèi-** "this" and **nèi-** "that" don't ordinarily occur directly before the noun they modify; instead, a measure must occur between the specifier and the noun. Your first example of a measure is **wèi**, which is the polite measure for people. To say "this classmate" in Chinese, you have to say **zhèi** "this" + **wèi** (polite measure for people) + **tóngxué** "classmate" = **zhèiwèi tóngxué** "this classmate." Another example is **nèiwèi lǎoshī** "that teacher."

Reading

New Characters and Words

73.	哪	nǎ-/něi-	which?
74.	国	guó	country
	中国	Zhōngguo	China
	中国人	Zhōngguo rén	Chinese, native of China
	哪国	něiguó/nǎguó	which country?
	哪国人	něiguó/nǎguó rén	a native of which country?
75.	问	wèn	ask
	请问	qǐng wèn	"excuse me," "may I ask"
76.	是	shì	be, is, are, was, were, would be
	不是	bú shi	is not, are not
	是不是	shì bu shi	is it or is it not
77.	美	měi	be beautiful
	美国	Měiguo	America
	美国人	Měiguo rén	American, native of America
78.	叫	jiào	be called or named

A. SENTENCES

一、你是你，我是我。
二、请问，李先生，你是哪国人？
三、李先生、林太太、谢小姐都不是中国人。
四、你叫林国文，是不是？请问，你去哪国？
五、我叫金山，他叫李文。
六、你叫李台生吗？你是台湾人吗？
七、我们都是美国人。你呢？你也是美国人吗？
八、请问，老高、小何他们都是北京人吗？
九、我们不都是美国人。小高是，我不是。
十、王大海是美国人，也是中国人。

B. CONVERSATIONS

一、
李文：你是哪国人？
王台生：我是中国人。
李文：你们都是中国人吗？
王台生：我们不都是中国人。他是美国人。

二、

中国人： 请问，他们都是河北人吗？

美国人： 湖北人？他们都不是湖北人。

中国人： 不是"湖北，"是"河北"！他们都是河北人马？

美国人： 他们不都是河北人。小高、小李是河北人，小林、小王是河南人。

C. NARRATIVES

一、 王先生、王太太都是中国人。王先生叫王大明，他是山西人。王太太叫李小文，她是广东人。王先生、王太太都很忙。何文生先生是美国人，他请王先生、王太太去香港，他们不去。"何先生，我们太忙了。"他请他们去东京，他们也不去。"何先生，谢谢你，我们太忙，太忙了！"

二、 金小姐、谢小姐、林小姐她们不都是美国人，也不都是中国人。金小姐是美国人，谢小姐、林小姐是中国人。你呢？你是哪国人？

Notes

C1.   In this narrative, 请 has the meaning "invite" or "ask" (not "please").

The pinyin for some of the characters is incorrect and reflects Kunming dialect.

PART TWO

Conversation 🎧 LISTEN

Situation: In the women's dormitory at Beijing Normal University, a Chinese student introduces her new roommate, a Chinese-American woman from New Jersey, to a Chinese classmate.

1. FIRST CHINESE: *(hears knock at door):*

请进!

Qǐng jìn!

Come in!

2. SECOND CHINESE: *(enters and greets Chinese classmate, then notices American student):*

诶，小马。噢。

Èi, Xiǎo Mǎ. Ò.

Hi, Little Ma. Oh.

3. FIRST CHINESE: 哦，小陈，我给你介绍一下儿。这是我的新同屋，她叫王爱华。王爱华，这是我的老同学，小陈。

Ò, Xiǎo Chén, wǒ gěi nǐ jièshao yixiar. Zhè shi wǒde xīn tóngwū, tā jiào Wáng Àihuá. Wáng Àihuá, zhè shi wǒde lǎo tóngxué, Xiǎo Chén.

Oh, Little Chen, let me introduce you. This is my new roommate, her name is Ivy Wang. Ivy, this is my old classmate, Little Chen.

4. SECOND CHINESE: 哦，欢迎你到中国来!

Ò, huānyíng nǐ dào Zhōngguo lái!

Oh, welcome to China!

5. AMERICAN: 很高兴认识你，陈小姐!

Hěn gāoxìng rènshi nǐ, Chén Xiáojie!

Happy to meet you, Miss Chen!

6. SECOND CHINESE: 哦，别这么称呼我！还是叫我小陈好了。

Ò, bié zhèmme chēnghu wǒ. Hái shi jiào wǒ Xiǎo Chén hǎole.

Oh, don't address me like this. It's better if you call me Little Chen.

7. AMERICAN: 行。那，你也叫我小王好了。

Xíng. Nà, nǐ yě jiào wǒ Xiǎo Wáng hǎole.

O.K. In that case, why don't you also call me Little Wang.

8. SECOND CHINESE: 好。

Hǎo.

O.K.

New Vocabulary

噢	**ò**	"oh"
给	**gěi**	for
介绍	**jièshao**	introduce
一下儿	**yíxià(r)**	(softens the verb)
这	**zhè**	this
的	**-de**	(indicates possession)
新	**xīn**	be new
同屋	**tóngwū**	roommate
欢迎	**huānyíng**	welcome
来	**lái**	come
高兴	**gāoxìng**	be happy
认识	**rènshi**	be acquainted with, know
别	**bié**	don't
这么	**zhèmme**	like this, in this way, so
称呼	**chēnghu**	address
叫	**jiào**	call (someone a name)
那	**nà**	in that case, so
好	**hǎo**	"all right," "O.K."

Supplementary Vocabulary

那	**nà**	that
谁	**shéi**	who, whom
不要	**búyào**	don't
应该	**yīnggāi**	should
怎么	**zěmme**	how

Questions on the Conversation

1. 王爱华是谁？ **Wáng Àihuá shi shéi?**

2. 王爱华是中国人吗？ **Wáng Àihuá shi Zhōngguo rén ma?**

3. 小陈是谁？ **Xiǎo Chén shi shéi?**

4. 小陈是哪国人？ **Xiǎo Chén shi něiguó rén?**

5. 小马是不是日本人？ **Xiǎo Mǎ shì bu shi Rìběn rén?**

General Questions

1. 欢迎你到中国来！ **Huānyíng nǐ dào Zhōngguo lái!**

2. 我很高兴认识你！ **Wǒ hěn gāoxìng rènshi nǐ!**

3. 我给你介绍一下，这是我的同屋，他叫王京生。
   Wǒ gěi nǐ jièshao yíxià, zhè shi wǒde tóngwū, tā jiào Wáng Jīngshēng.

4. 你认识不认识王爱华？ **Nǐ rènshi bú rènshi Wáng Àihuá?**

5. 我很高兴认识你，你也很高兴认识我吗？
   Wǒ hěn gāoxìng rènshi nǐ, nǐ yě hěn gāoxìng rènshi wǒ ma?

6. 请问，我们应该怎么称呼你？ **Qǐng wèn, wǒmen yīnggāi zěmme chēnghu nǐ?**

Notes on the Conversation

Making verbs less abrupt with yíxià(r)

Yíxià(r), literally "a bit," is often added after certain verbs to soften them and make them sound less abrupt. After a verb, **yíxià(r)** is often in the neutral tone. Here are some examples: **jièshao yixiar** "introduce," **lái yixia** "come," **qù yixia** "go," **tīng yixia** "listen," **wèn yixia** "ask," **zuò yixia** "sit."

Pronoun subjects zhè and nà

Zhè "this" and **nà** "that" are pronouns that can occur as the subjects of sentences. A common formula for making introductions is **Zhè shi A, zhè shi B** "This is A, this is B." Some more examples: **Zhè shi shémme?** "What is this?," **Zhè shi wǒde sùshè.** "This is my dorm.," **Nà shi shéi?** "Who is that?," **Nà shi wǒde tóngwū.** "That is my roommate."

Indicating possession with -de

One important function of **-de** is to indicate possession. In the phrase **wǒde xīn tóngwū** "my new roommate," **wǒde** means "my." Typically, a noun or pronoun will stand before the **-de** and another noun will stand after the **-de**. The meaning is that the second noun is possessed by the first noun or pronoun. Here are some more examples of **-de** indicating possession: **wǒmende túshūguǎn** "our library," **wǒde Zhōngwén lǎoshī** "my Chinese language teacher," **tāmende lǎo tóngxué** "their old classmate," **nèiwèi lǎoshīde sùshè** "that teacher's dormitory." Note that **-de** can be omitted when the possessor is a pronoun and the possessed is a person that the possessor is close to, for example, **wǒ māma** "my mom."

....

Expressing "come to..." with <u>dào...lái</u>

The pattern **dào...lái** expresses where someone is coming. **Dào** literally means "arrive" or "to" and **lái** literally means "come." A place word occurs between the **dào** and the **lái**. Some more examples: **Huānyíng nǐmen dào Měiguo lái!** "Welcome to America!," **Qǐng nǐ dào túshūguǎn lái.** "Please come to the library."

....

<u>Bié</u> and <u>búyào</u> to indicate negative imperative "don't"

The negative imperative (that is, "don't do such-and-such") is formed by using **bié** or **búyào** "don't" plus a verb phrase indicating what it is that you don't want someone to do. The use of a pronoun like **nǐ**, **nín**, or **nǐmen** is common but optional. Adding **qǐng** makes the request more polite. Some examples: **Bié zǒu!** "Don't leave!," **Nǐmen bié jiào wǒ Lǎo Wáng!** "You guys don't call me Old Wang!," **Qǐng nǐ búyào zhèmme jǐnzhāng** "Please don't be so nervous."

....

The pattern SENTENCE + <u>hǎole</u>

A sentence followed by **hǎole** (which consists of **hǎo** plus **le** indicating a changed situation) means "if so-and-so, then it would be good" or "doing such-and-such would be best." The words **hái shi** "still be (better if you consider the alternatives)," are often added before the main verb of the sentence. Some examples: **Nǐ hái shi jiào wǒ Xiǎo Chén hǎole.** "It would be better if you called me Little Chen." **Hái shi qù chīfàn hǎole.** "It would be best to go eat.," **Wǒmen qù Jiā'nádà hǎole.** "Let's go to Canada."

....

Reading

New Characters and Words

79.	的	-de	(indicates possession)
80.	同	tóng	same (can't be said alone)
81.	屋	wū	room (can't be said alone)
	同屋	tóngwū	roommate
82.	别	bié	don't
83.	名	míng	name (can't be said alone)
84.	字	zì	Chinese character
	名字	míngzi	name

A. SENTENCES

一、请问，你同屋的名字是不是林小明？

二、我的同屋是中国人，老谢的同屋是美国人，你的同屋是哪国人？

三、金小姐、谢小姐是同屋，我的同屋是林大一，你的同屋是……？

四、金山街很难去，别去了，我们去南京东路好了。

五、她叫金香川。她的名字很难叫！

六、老林，你别走，你先请坐。

七、请你别叫我王先生，叫我京生好了。

八、你别去台北。谢小姐、李小姐她们都很忙。

九、台湾是不是中国的一省？

十、"王大海"是中国人的名字吗？

B. CONVERSATIONS

一、

小高：你好！我叫高大明。

小文：你好！我叫文中。

小高：你是我的同屋吗？

小文：是，我们是同屋。

二、

李大山：你好！我叫李大山。你的名字是……？

林京生：我叫林京生，你叫我小林好了。

李大山：小林，你是哪国人？

林京生：我是中国人，你呢？

李大山：我是美国人。

C. NARRATIVES

一、 我的名字叫李小明，你们叫我小明好了。我是香港人。我的同屋是美国人，很高，名字叫高大山，我们都叫他"老高"。我请我的同屋去广州，他不去，他太忙了。

二、 我的名字叫何大海。你们别叫我"何先生，"你们叫我"小何"好了。我是中国人，中国四川省成都市人。

Street scene in Kowloon, Hong Kong

Notes

A1.   In the first sentence, look at the phrase 你同屋的名字 "your roommate's name." In general, Chinese people don't like the "sound" of several 的 in a row, so they usually delete all the 的 except the last one. We could say the deeper structure of this phrase was 你的同屋的名字 but, when it became a surface structure, the first 的 was deleted, so that the phrase became 你同屋的名字.

A3.   In 你的同屋是……?, the …… at the end of the sentence indicates an incomplete question. An English translation would be "Your roommate is...?" Incomplete questions like this are often used in Chinese when you doesn't wish to ask too directly.

A5.   The literal meaning of 她的名字很难叫 is "Her name is hard to call out." In more idiomatic English, we would say "Her name is hard to say" or "Her name is hard to pronounce." This is because to a native speaker of Mandarin, the syllables 金香川 **Jīn Xiāngchuān** don't sound pleasant when pronounced one right after another, since they are all in Tone One and all end in nasal finals.

A9.   台湾是不是中国的一省？ means literally "Taiwan is it or is it not China's a province?" In good English, we would translate this as "Is Taiwan a province of China?"

C1.   我请我的同屋去广州，他不去。 "I asked my roommate to go to Guangzhou, but he didn't want to go."

LESSON 6
Introductions

PART ONE

Conversation 🎧

Situation: Suzanne Wood, a foreign service officer at U.S. Embassy Beijing, is attending a reception. Accompanying her is her colleague, Ron Myers. Wood notices a Chinese guest and decides to engage him in conversation.

1. **AMERICAN:** 您贵姓？
   Nín guìxìng?
   What's your last name?

2. **CHINESE:** 我姓高。您贵姓？
   Wǒ xìng Gāo. Nín guìxìng?
   My last name is Gao. What's your last name?

3. **AMERICAN:** 我姓吴，吴素珊。高先生，您在哪个单位工作？
   Wǒ xìng Wú, Wú Sùshān. Gāo Xiānsheng, nín zài něige dānwèi gōngzuò?
   My last name is Wood, Suzanne Wood. Mr. Gao, at which organization do you work?

4. **CHINESE:** 我在外交部工作。您呢？
   Wǒ zài Wàijiāobù gōngzuò. Nín ne?
   I work at the Foreign Ministry. And you?

5. AMERICAN: 我在美国大使馆工作。
Wǒ zài Měiguo Dàshǐguǎn gōngzuò.
I work at the U.S. Embassy.

6. CHINESE: 那位是您的先生吧?
Nèiwèi shi nínde xiānsheng ba?
I suppose that must be your husband?

7. AMERICAN: 不是，不是! 他是我的同事。
Bú shì, bú shì! Tā shi wǒde tóngshì.
No, no! He's my colleague.

8. CHINESE: *(after a while)*

哦，吴女士，对不起。我有一点儿事儿，先走了。再见!
Ò, Wú Nǔshì, duìbuqǐ. Wǒ yǒu yìdiǎnr shìr, xiān zǒule. Zàijiàn!
Oh, Madam Wood, excuse me. I have something I have to do, I have to be going now. Goodbye!

9. AMERICAN: 再见!
Zàijiàn!
Goodbye!

New Vocabulary

贵姓	**guìxìng**	"What's your honorable surname?"
姓	**xìng**	be surnamed
在	**zài**	be located at, at
个	**ge**	(general measure)
单位	**dānwèi**	work unit, organization
工作	**gōngzuò**	work
外交部	**wàijiāobù**	foreign ministry
大使馆	**dàshǐguǎn**	embassy
先生	**xiānsheng**	husband
吧	**ba**	(indicates supposition)
同事	**tóngshì**	colleague
女士	**nǔshì**	madam, lady
对不起	**duìbuqǐ**	"excuse me," "sorry"

Supplementary Vocabulary

太太	**tàitai**	wife
一	**yī**	one, a
家	**jiā**	(for companies, factories)
公司	**gōngsī**	company, firm

学习	**xuéxí**	learn, study
大学	**dàxué**	university, college
香港	**Xiānggǎng**	Hong Kong
香港中文大学	**Xiānggǎng Zhōngwén Dàxué**	Chinese University of Hong Kong
校长	**xiàozhǎng**	head of a school

Questions on the Conversation

1. 吴女士叫什么名字？ **Wú Nǚshì jiào shémme míngzi?**
2. 她在哪个单位工作？ **Tā zài něige dānwèi gōngzuò?**
3. 高先生在哪个单位工作？ **Gāo Xiānsheng zài něige dānwèi gōngzuò?**
4. 那位先生是吴女士的先生吗？ **Nèiwèi xiānsheng shi Wú Nǚshìde xiānsheng ma?**
5. 他是谁？他在哪儿工作？ **Tā shi shéi? Tā zài nǎr gōngzuò?**

General Questions

1. 请问，您贵姓？ **Qǐng wèn, nín guìxìng?**
2. 你的中文老师姓什么？ **Nǐde Zhōngwén lǎoshī xìng shémme?**
3. 你妈妈在一家公司工作吗？ **Nǐ māma zài yìjiā gōngsī gōngzuò ma?**
4. 你爸爸也在一家公司工作吧？ **Nǐ bàba yě zài yìjiā gōngsī gōngzuò ba?**
5. 你是美国人吧？ **Nǐ shi Měiguo rén ba?**
6. 你在哪儿学习中文？ **Nǐ zài nǎr xuéxí Zhōngwén?**
7. 你工作吗？你在哪儿工作？ **Nǐ gōngzuò ma? Nǐ zài nǎr gōngzuò?**
8. 在公司工作有意思吗？ **Zài gōngsī gōngzuò yǒu yìsi ma?**
9. 在大学学习也有意思吧？ **Zài dàxué xuéxí yě yǒu yìsi ba?**

Notes on the Conversation

The honorific prefix guì-

Guì-, which literally means "be expensive, precious, honorable," is an honorific prefix which indicates respect by the person speaking for the person spoken to. By far the most common use of **guì-** is in the question **Nín guìxìng?** "What is your (honorable) last name?" If someone asks you this question, you would answer **Wǒ xìng...** followed by your Chinese surname. You would never answer *Wǒ guìxìng..., because **guì-** is an honorific and can only be used to refer to others, never to oneself.

Equative Verb Sentences with xìng

Xìng is a very common equative verb meaning "be surnamed." Here are some examples: **Wǒ xìng Gāo** "My last name is Gao" (literally, "I am surnamed Gao"), **Tā yě xìng Gāo** "Her last name is also Gao,"

Nǐ xìng shémme? "What's your last name?" If someone asks **Nǐ xìng shémme?** or **Nín guìxìng?**, it is common to answer by first saying **Wǒ xìng...** plus your surname, and then to follow that by saying your whole name. This is what Suzanne Wood does in this conversation when she says **Wǒ xìng Wú, Wú Sùshān** "My last name is Wood, Suzanne Wood."

......

Asking where someone goes to school or works

In line 3 of the conversation, the literal meaning of the question **Nín zài něige dānwèi gōngzuò?** is "You located at which organization work?," in other words, "Which organization do you work in?" We'll take up **zài** "be located in" in more detail in a later lesson. For now, just learn how to ask where someone goes to school or works, and be able to answer when you are asked. Here are some more examples with **zài** plus a main verb: **Nǐ zài nǎr gōngzuò?** "Where do you work?," **Wǒ zài yìjiā gōngsī gōngzuò** "I work at a company," **Nǐ zài nǎr xuéxí?** "Where do you study?," **Wǒ zài Xiānggǎng Zhōngwén Dàxué xuéxí** "I study at the Chinese University of Hong Kong."

......

The final particle ba to indicate supposition

The final particle **ba** can be added to the end of a statement to indicate that the speaker supposes what he or she has said must be so. Take the statement **Tā shi Yīngguo rén** "She's English." By adding **ba** to the end of this statement, we can transform the statement into a supposition: **Tā shi Yīngguo rén ba** "I suppose she's English." Here are some more examples: **Nǐde gōngzuò hěn máng ba?** "Your work must be pretty busy?," **Nǐ lèile ba?** "I suppose you must be tired?," **Tā bú shi nǐde tóngxué ba?** "I guess she's not your classmate, is she?"

......

Tone changes involving yī

By itself the number **yī** "one" or "a" is pronounced in Tone One as **yī**. However, **yī** changes to Tone Four **yì** before syllables in Tones One, Two, and Three; and it changes to Tone Two **yí** before syllables in Tone Four. Examples: **yìjiā gōngsī** "a company," **yìnián** "one year," **yìdiǎnr** "a little," **yíwèi xiáojie** "a young lady."

......

Reading

New Characters and Words

85.	贵	**guì**	be expensive; honorable; (surname)
	贵州	**Guìzhōu**	Guizhou (province)
86.	姓	**xìng**	be surnamed; surname
	贵姓	**guìxìng**	"what's your honorable surname?"
87.	个	**ge**	(general measure)
	哪个	**něige/nǎge**	which one?, which?
88.	您	**nín**	you (polite)
89.	吧	**ba**	(indicates supposition)
90.	兴	**xìng**	interest, excitement (can't be said alone)
	高兴	**gāoxìng**	be happy

A. SENTENCES

一、小姐，请问，您贵姓？

二、我先生是美国人，他姓高，他的名字叫高明。

三、我姓林，您是不是姓王？

四、谢大明是您先生的名字吧？

五、"王小姐"？哪个王小姐？我们都姓王！

六、哪个人好？哪个人不好？他呢？他是不是好人？

七、哪个名字好，哪个名字不好？

八、李小姐不是好人，她走了，我们都很高兴。

九、我去中国，很高兴。你去中国，也很高兴吧？

十、你的老同屋是哪个？是不是他？是不是王大海？

B. CONVERSATIONS

一、

王先生：我很高兴。你也很高兴吧？

李小姐：别问！你是你，我是我。

二、

王先生：请问，您贵姓？

何小姐：我姓何，你叫我小何好了。

王先生：小何，你是中国人吧？

何小姐：我不是中国人，我是美国人。

王先生：中文很难吧？

何小姐：中文不太难。

C. NARRATIVES

一、李文是美国人，她的同屋是中国人，也姓李，名字叫李同。李文
很高兴她的同屋是中国人，李同也很高兴她的同屋是美国人。

二、您好！我的名字叫谢中文，我是美国人。我的先生叫何台生，他
是台湾人。我们都很忙。请问，您贵姓？您是哪国人？您也很忙
吗？哪个是您的先生？是他吧？请问，他叫……请您别走，好不
好？您是不是不高兴了？

Notes

C1.   Notice in this narrative that 高兴 "be happy" sometimes takes an object and then means "be happy that...."

C2.   您是不是不高兴了？ "Is it the case that you've become unhappy?" or "Are you upset?"

PART TWO

Conversation 🎧

Situation: Jan Rogers, an American working for a British firm in Taipei, is attending a reception. She sees a Taiwanese guest whom she doesn't recognize, so she walks over and introduces herself. Standing not far away is Lester Holbrooke, general manager of the trading firm, who is also American.

1. ROGERS: *(taking out her name card):*

你好！我叫罗洁思。请多指教。

Nǐ hǎo! Wǒ jiào Luó Jiésī. Qǐng duō zhǐjiào.

How do you do? My name is Rogers. Please give me much advice.

2. TAIWANESE GUEST: 我姓施。对不起，我没带名片。我在中美贸易公司工作。

Wǒ xìng Shī. Duìbuqǐ, wǒ méi dài míngpiàn. Wǒ zài Zhōng-Měi Màoyì Gōngsī gōngzuò.

My name is Shi. Sorry, I didn't bring name cards. I work at Sino-American Trading Company.

3. ROGERS: *(introduces Shi to Holbrooke):*

总经理，这是中美贸易公司的施小姐。

Zǒngjīnglǐ, zhè shi Zhōng-Měi Màoyì Gōngsīde Shī Xiáojie.

Mr. Holbrooke, this is Ms. Shi from Sino-American Trading Company.

4. HOLBROOKE: *(gives Shi his name card):*

啊，欢迎，欢迎！我姓侯。

À, huānyíng, huānyíng! Wǒ xìng Hóu.

Oh, welcome! My name is Hou.

5. TAIWANESE GUEST: 谢谢。总经理也是英国人吧？

Xièxie. Zǒngjīnglǐ yě shi Yīngguo rén ba?

Thank you. Mr. Holbrooke, I suppose you also must be English?

6. HOLBROOKE: 不，我跟罗小姐都不是英国人。我们是美国人。

Bù, wǒ gēn Luó Xiáojie dōu bú shi Yīngguo rén. Wǒmen shi Měiguo rén.

No, neither Ms. Rogers nor I are English. We're American.

7. TAIWANESE GUEST: 哦，对不起，我搞错了。

Ò, duìbuqǐ, wǒ gǎocuòle.

Oh, sorry, I got it wrong.

8. HOLBROOKE: 没关系。

Méi guānxi.

That's all right.

New Vocabulary

没	méi	(indicates past negative of action verbs)
带	dài	take along, bring
名片	míngpiàn	name card, business card
中美	Zhōng-Měi	Sino-American
贸易	màoyì	trade
贸易公司	màoyì gōngsī	trading company
经理	jīnglǐ	manager
总经理	zǒngjīnglǐ	general manager
的	-de	(indicates what precedes describes what follows)
啊	à	"oh"
英国	Yīngguo	England
跟	gēn	and
搞错	gǎocuò	get or do something wrong
了	-le	(indicates completed action)
没关系	méi guānxi	"never mind," "it doesn't matter"

Supplementary Vocabulary

先生	xiānsheng	gentleman
太太	tàitai	married woman, lady
小姐	xiáojie	young lady

Questions on the Conversation

1. Rogers 小姐的中文名字是什么？ **Rogers Xiáojiede Zhōngwén míngzi shi shémme?**

2. Rogers 小姐带名片了吗？ **Rogers Xiáojie dài míngpiàn le ma?**

3. 谁没带名片？ **Shéi méi dài míngpiàn?**

4. 施小姐是哪国人？ **Shī Xiáojie shì něiguó rén?**

5. 施小姐在哪个单位工作？ **Shī Xiáojie zài něige dānwèi gōngzuò?**

6. 谁在中美贸易公司工作？ **Shéi zài Zhōng-Měi màoyì gōngsī gōngzuò?**

7. 罗洁丝也在中美贸易公司工作吧？
   Luó Jiésī yě zài Zhōng-Měi màoyì gōngsī gōngzuò ba?

8. 罗小姐给谁介绍了谁？ **Luó Xiáojie gěi shéi jièshaole shéi?**

9. 侯先生是谁？ **Hóu Xiānsheng shi shéi?**

10. 侯先生的英文名字是什么？ **Hóu Xiānshengde Yīngwén míngzi shi shémme?**

11. 侯总经理欢迎谁？ **Hóu Zǒngjīnglǐ huānyíng shéi?**

12. 侯总经理是英国人吧？ **Hóu Zǒngjīnglǐ shi Yīngguo rén ba?**

13. 罗小姐是哪国人？ **Luó Xiáojie shi něiguó rén?**

14. 侯总经理、罗小姐都不是英国人吗？
    Hóu Zǒngjīnglǐ, Luó Xiáojie dōu bú shi Yīngguo rén ma?

15. 施小姐说她搞错了，侯总经理说什么？
    Shī Xiáojie shuō tā gǎocuòle, Hóu Zǒngjīnglǐ shuō shémme?

General Questions

1. 对不起！ **Duìbuqǐ!**

2. 你的同学都是美国人吗？ **Nǐde tóngxué dōu shi Měiguo rén ma?**

3. 你的中文老师都是新加坡人吧？ **Nǐde Zhōngwén lǎoshī dōu shi Xīnjiāpō rén ba?**

4. 你的中文老师都是好老师吧？ **Nǐde Zhōngwén lǎoshī dōu shi hǎo lǎoshī ba?**

5. 你在中美贸易公司工作吗？ **Nǐ zài Zhōng-Měi màoyì gōngsī gōngzuò ma?**

6. 你的同学都很困吗？ **Nǐde tóngxué dōu hěn kùn ma?**

7. 你带名片了吗？ **Nǐ dài míngpiàn le ma?**

8. 你的同学都带名片了吗？ **Nǐde tóngxué dōu dài míngpiàn le ma?**

9. 你带功课了吗？ **Nǐ dài gōngkè le ma?**

10. 你爸爸是大学校长吧？ **Nǐ bàba shi dàxué xiàozhǎng ba?**

11. 你妈妈是日本人吧？ **Nǐ māma shi Rìběn rén ba?**

12. 你在香港中文大学学习中文吧？
    Nǐ zài Xiānggǎng Zhōngwén Dàxué xuéxí Zhōngwén ba?

Notes on the Conversation

Past negative of action verbs with méi

The auxiliary verb **méi** in front of an action verb indicates the past negative of the verb, that is, that the action of the verb did not take place. Look at the sentence **Wǒ méi dài míngpiàn** "I didn't bring name cards." In this utterance, **méi dài** means "didn't bring" or "haven't brought." Here are some more examples: **Nǐ méi gǎocuò** "You didn't get it wrong," **Tā méi huí sùshè** "She didn't go back to the dorm," **Tāmen méi lái** "They didn't come."

The particle **-de** to indicate that what precedes describes what follows

In line 3, look at **Zhōng-Měi Màoyì Gōngsīde Shī Xiáojie** "Ms. Shi from Sino-American Trading Company" (literally, "Sino-American Trading Company's Ms. Shi"). The particle **-de** indicates that what precedes it (**Zhōng-Měi Màoyì Gōngsī**) describes what follows it (**Shī Xiáojie**). Here are two more examples: **Zhèiwèi shi Zhōngguo Wàijiāobùde Mǎ Xiānsheng** "This is Mr. Ma from the Chinese Foreign Ministry," **Wǒmen huānyíng Yīngguo Dàshǐguǎnde Xiè Nǚshì!** "Let us welcome Madam Smith from the British Embassy!"

-le to indicate completed action

The verb suffix **-le** attached to an action verb like **gǎocuò** "get something wrong" indicates completed action. **Wǒ gǎocuòle** would mean "I got it wrong" or "I made a mistake." It's possible to add question particle **ma** to a sentence ending in **-le**. For example, **Tāmen láile ma?** "Have they come?" Non-action verbs like **shì** "be" never take **-le** to indicate completed action; with non-action verbs, the context or adverbs of time would make it clear when past time was meant. Here are some more examples of **-le** indicating completed action: **Shìr wǒ dōu bànle** "I took care of all the things," **Lǎo Gāo, Xiǎo Lǐ dōu zǒule** "Old Gao and Little Li have both left," **Xīn tóngxué nǐ dōu jièshaole ma?** "Have you introduced all the new classmates?" The negative form of a sentence containing completed action **-le** is **méi** plus the verb. There is no **-le** in such sentences because the **-le** is cancelled out by the presence of the **méi**.

Mazu Temple in Magong, Penghu Archipelago

Reading

New Characters and Words

91.	片	**piàn**	flat and thin piece of something
	名片	**míngpiàn**	name card
92.	没	**méi**	(indicates past negative of action verbs)
93.	带	**dài**	take along, take, bring
94.	公	**gōng**	public, official (can't be said alone)
95.	司	**sī**	bureau, department; (surname)
	公司	**gōngsī**	company, firm
96.	这	**zhè/zhèi-**	this
	这个	**zhèige**	this, this one

A. SENTENCES

一、你好！我叫林山。这是我们公司的名片。

二、美国人不都带名片，中国人也不都带名片吧？

三、李小姐是哪个公司的？她是不是中美公司的？

四、先生，这是您的名片吧？您是不是叫王国中？

五、这是美国IBM公司的CEO安先生。

六、这是我们公司的谢先生。

七、这是台北中山公司的王小姐。

八、小李没去，小林也没去，他们都没去。

九、我没问，她也没问，我们都没问；你问了吗？

十、大海，请你带我们去你的公司，好吗？

B. CONVERSATIONS

一、

司先生：您好！我姓司。请问，您贵姓？

高先生：我姓高，叫高二明。这是我的名片。

司先生：谢谢！

高先生：司先生，您带名片了吗？

司先生：带了，带了。……我的名片呢？

二、

美国人：李大文，你好！请坐，请坐。

中国人：谢谢，谢谢！我叫林大文，不叫李大文。

美国人：我没叫你李大文。

中国人：这是我们公司的名片。

美国人：谢谢，这是我的名片。你的公司叫"大山公司,"是吗？

中国人：不是。我们公司叫"太山公司"。中文很难吧？

美国人：不难，中文不难！

C. NARRATIVES

一、我姓李，名字叫李文。我是中国人。我的公司的名字叫美山公司。美山公司是一个很大的美国公司。这是我们公司的名片。老王也是美山公司的，小何也是我们公司的。请你去美山公司，好吗？我带你去我们公司，好不好？

二、我是一个北京人。我先生不太好。他不带我去上海，也不带我去香港、台湾。他带我去他的公司，中美公司，我很不高兴。小高是我先生的同屋。这个人很好，他带我去天津，也带我去广州，也带我去美国。小高人太好了！

Entrance to the natatorium at National Taiwan Normal University in Taipei. Notice that the word
游泳馆 yóuyǒngguǎn "natatorium" is here written from right to left.

Notes

A3.   李小姐是哪个公司的？她是不是中美公司的？ Literally, this means "Ms. Li is one from which company? Is she one from Zhongmei Company?" Presumably, in the deep structure of this sentence, there was a noun meaning "person" or "employee," so that the sentence originally may have been something like "Ms. Li is an employee from which company? Is she an employee from Zhongmei Company?" However, that noun was deleted in the surface structure, leaving only 的 to mean "one from." In smoother English, we could translate these two questions as "Ms. Li is with which company? Is she with Zhongmei Company?"

A5.   这是美国IBM公司的CEO "This is the CEO of the American IBM company." Modern Chinese is replete with borrowings from English and other languages that are represented by the letters of the Roman alphabet. Here are some common examples: CD, DIY, DNA, DVD, ID, IQ, IT, KTV, MP3, MTV, OK, PVC.

A6.   这是我们公司的谢先生 "This is Mr. Xie from our company."

A10.   请你带我们去你的公司 "Please take us to your company." Note that the verb 带 can be used to mean "take" or "bring" things or, as here, people.

B1.   您带名片了吗？ "Did you bring a name card?"

B2.   In the last line by the Chinese speaker, 我们公司 means "our company." Though it would not be incorrect to say 我们的公司, very often in Chinese a 的 is dropped when there is an especially close connection between a pronoun and a noun. This holds true for body parts ("my hand"), for relatives ("my mother"), and—as we see here—for institutions to which there is a strong sense of belonging. Also, note that the speaker says not "my company" but "*our* company." This is related to the strong sense of group affiliation in Chinese society as compared to the more individual outlook in Western society.

C2.   Look at the word 人 in 小高人太好了！ This 人 means not just "person" but "as a person" or "the manner in which a person conducts herself or himself." We could translate the whole sentence as "As a person, Little Gao is wonderful!"

LESSON 7
"How Many Students in Your Class?"

PART ONE

Conversation

Situation: Zhang Xiaohui, an English major at Beijing Foreign Studies University, asks her friend Jerry Freeman about the Chinese class he's taking at the university's Chinese language training center.

1. **ZHANG:** 你们班上有几位同学？
   Nǐmen bānshang yǒu jǐwèi tóngxué?
   How many students are there in your class?

2. **FREEMAN:** 有十位。
   Yǒu shíwèi.
   There are ten.

3. **ZHANG:** 都是美国人吗？
   Dōu shi Měiguo rén ma?
   Are they all Americans?

4. FREEMAN: 不都是美国人。有七个美国人，两个德国人跟一个法国人。

Bù dōu shi Měiguo rén. Yǒu qíge Měiguo rén, liǎngge Déguo rén gēn yíge Fǎguo rén.

They're not all Americans. There are seven Americans, two Germans and one Frenchman.

5. ZHANG: 几个男生，几个女生？

Jǐge nánshēng, jǐge nǚshēng?

How many male students and how many female students?

6. FREEMAN: 一半儿一半儿。五个男的，五个女的。

Yíbànr yíbànr. Wǔge nánde, wǔge nǚde.

Half and half. Five men and five women.

7. ZHANG: 那，你们有几位老师呢？

Nà, nǐmen yǒu jǐwèi lǎoshī ne?

So, how many teachers do you have?

8. FREEMAN: 一共有三位。两位是女老师，一位是男老师。

Yígòng yǒu sānwèi. Liǎngwèi shi nǚlǎoshī, yíwèi shi nánlǎoshī.

There are three in all. Two are female teachers, and one is a male teacher.

New Vocabulary

班	**bān**	class
班上	**bānshang**	in a class
有	**yǒu**	there is, there are
几	**jǐ-**	how many
十	**shí**	ten
七	**qī**	seven
两	**liǎng-**	two
德国	**Déguo**	Germany
法国	**Fǎguo**	France
几个	**jǐge**	how many?
男生	**nánshēng**	male student
女生	**nǚshēng**	female student
半	**bàn**	half
一半(儿)	**yíbàn(r)**	one-half
五	**wǔ**	five
男的	**nánde**	man, male
女的	**nǚde**	woman, female
一共	**yígòng**	in all

三	**sān**	three
女老师	**nǔlǎoshī**	female teacher
男老师	**nánlǎoshī**	male teacher

Supplementary Vocabulary

一	**yī**	one
二	**èr**	two
三	**sān**	three
四	**sì**	four
五	**wǔ**	five
六	**liù**	six
七	**qī**	seven
八	**bā**	eight
九	**jiǔ**	nine
十	**shí**	ten

Notes on the Conversation

Yǒu to indicate existence

Besides indicating possession, the verb **yǒu** can also indicate existence, that is, "there is" or "there are." Examples: **Bānshang yǒu qíge tóngxué** "In the class there are seven classmates," **Túshūguǎn yǒu jǐge rén?** "How many people are there in the library?," **Míngtiān yǒu gōngkè ma?** "Is there homework (for) tomorrow?"

Jǐ- plus a measure

Jǐ- attached to a measure means "how many?" It's used when the number is expected to be ten or fewer. **Jǐge** "how many?" can be used alone or before a noun. **Jǐwèi** is a polite expression meaning "how many (people)?" Some examples of **jǐ-** attached to the measures **wèi** and **ge**: **Yǒu jǐge?** "How many are there?," **Nǐ yǒu jǐge tóngxué?** "How many classmates do you have?" **Jǐwèi lǎoshī?** "How many teachers?"

Numbers from one to ten

Be sure to memorize the numbers from 1–10 thoroughly. The basic forms of the numbers are used for counting and citing telephone numbers, addresses, and years. To count nouns with numbers, in other words, to indicate how many of something, a measure such as **ge** or **wèi** has to be added. The number **èr** "two" changes to **liǎng-** when a measure follows (for example, **liǎngge** or **liǎngwèi**; you could NEVER say *èrge). Also, note that **yī**, **qī**, and **bā** usually change to Tone Two before Tone Four syllables (for example, **yíge**, **qíge**, **báge**); and **yī** changes to **yì** before syllables in Tone One, Tone Two, and Tone Three.

Reading

New Characters and Words

97.	几	jǐ-	how many?
	几个	jǐge	how many? (people or things)
98.	位	wèi	(polite measure for people)
	哪位	něiwèi/nǎwèi	which one? (polite)
	几位	jǐwèi	how many? (people; polite)
99.	两	liǎng-	two
	两个	liǎngge	two (people or things)
	两位	liǎngwèi	two (persons; polite)
100.	男	nán-	man, male
	男的	nánde	man, male
	男生	nánshēng	male student
101.	女	nǚ-	woman, female
	女的	nǚde	woman, female
	女生	nǚshēng	female student
102.	师	shī	teacher
	老师	lǎoshī	teacher
	男老师	nánlǎoshī	male teacher
	女老师	nǚlǎoshī	female teacher

A. SENTENCES

一、这位女生的名字是金小山吗？

二、他们不都是男生。八个是男生，两个是女生。

三、请问，小安是男的吧？小金呢？小金是女的吧？

四、请问，几位去成都，几位去广州？

五、这个男生是美国人。请问，哪个女生是台湾人？

六、这是高老师先生的公司吗？不是吗？哪个是？

七、她的先生姓李，是一位很好的老师。

八、两位男老师去天津街了，三位女老师去上海路了。

九、我的中文老师是男老师，你的中文老师也是男的吗？

十、王大海是男生，他的同屋也是男的吧？

B. CONVERSATIONS

一、

中国人：先生，您好！请问，几位？

美国人：两位。

二、
老师：几个男生，几个女生？
男生：一个男生，两个女生。

三、
师先生：他们都是中国人吧？
李小姐：不，他们不都是中国人。六位是中国人，两位是美国人。
师先生：几个男的，几个女的？
李小姐：三个男的，五个女的。

C. NARRATIVE

这位老师是我们的中文老师。他姓高，叫高国公，我们都叫他高老师。高老师是北京人。他的太太也是我们的老师，她的名字叫何文香。何老师不是北京人，她是四川人。高老师、何老师他们两位都很忙。这是高老师的名片，何老师的名片我没带。他们两位老师都很好，我们很高兴他们都是我们的老师。

Notes

A6. Look at the phrase 高老师先生的公司 "Teacher Gao's husband's company." At a deeper level, the grammatical structure of this phrase was originally 高老师的先生的公司, with two 的 in it, but because Chinese people don't like the "sound" of several 的 in a row and usually delete all 的 except the last one, this phrase became 高老师先生的公司, with only one 的 in it.

A7. Look at the sentence 她的先生姓李，是一位很好的老师 "Her husband's last name is Li; he's a very good teacher." First, note that the Chinese comma is sometimes equivalent to an English semicolon (translating as "Her husband's last name is Li, he's a very good teacher" would create an English run-on sentence). Second, note that in the Chinese there is no subject for the second clause (literally, it says "is a very good teacher"). Be aware that if the subject or topic has already been made clear, it's perfectly normal not to repeat it later. In fact, excessive repetition of the subject is considered poor, Western-influenced style.

A8. Depending on the context, 两位男老师……三位女老师…… could mean either "Two male teachers...three female teachers..." or "The two male teachers...the three female teachers... ."

B1. This dialog takes place in a restaurant.

C. As we saw in the previous unit, 高兴 sometimes functions as a verb taking a following clause as object and means "be happy that..." So the sentence 我们很高兴他们都是我们的老师 could be translated as "We are very happy that they're both our teachers."

PART TWO

Conversation 🎧

Situation: Sylvia Thompson, a foreign student who is enrolled in a study abroad program in Beijing, is showing photographs of her family to one of her teachers.

1. **TEACHER:** *(looking at a photograph):*

   这是你父亲吗？他多大了？

   Zhè shi nǐ fùqin ma? Tā duō dà le?

   This is your father? How old is he?

2. **THOMPSON:** 我想想看。他今年五十三岁了——不，五十四岁了。

   Wǒ xiángxiang kàn. Tā jīnnián wǔshisānsuì le – bù, wǔshisìsuì le.

   Let me try to think. He's 53 this year – no, 54.

3. **TEACHER:** 哦。那，这位是你母亲吧？

   Ò. Nà, zhèiwèi shi nǐ mǔqin ba?

   Oh. So I suppose this must be your mother?

4. **THOMPSON:** 对，她今年四十八岁了。

   Duì, tā jīnnián sìshibāsuì le.

   Right, she's 48 this year.

5. **TEACHER:** 这是你妹妹，对不对？她很可爱！她几岁了？

   Zhè shi nǐ mèimei, duì bu dui? Tā hěn kě'ài! Tā jǐsuì le?

   This is your younger sister, right? She's very cute! How old is she?

6. **THOMPSON:** 她八岁。下个月就九岁了。

   Tā bāsuì. Xiàge yuè jiù jiǔsuì le.

   She's 8 years old. Next month she'll be 9.

New Vocabulary

父亲	**fùqin**	father
多大	**duō dà**	how big?, how old? (of people)
想想看	**xiángxiang kàn**	try to think
今年	**jīnnián**	this year
岁	**suì**	year of age
母亲	**mǔqin**	mother
对	**duì**	be correct
对不对?	**duì bu duì?**	right?
妹妹	**mèimei**	younger sister
可爱	**kě'ài**	be loveable, cute
下个月	**xiàge yuè**	next month
就	**jiù**	then

Supplementary Vocabulary

哥哥	**gēge**	older brother
姐姐	**jiějie**	older sister
弟弟	**dìdi**	younger brother
没有	**méiyou**	not have; there is not, there are not
上个	**shàngge yuè**	last month

Notes on the Conversation

Asking someone's age

The most common way to ask someone's age is **Nǐ duō dà le?** "How old are you?" (literally, "You are how big of age?"). The reason there is no question particle **ma** at the end of this question is that **duō** "how" is itself a question word; remember that if there is already a question word in a sentence, **ma** isn't added at the end.

....

Giving your age

The pattern for saying how old you are is: SUBJECT + TIME WORD + NUMBER + **suì**. Since age is always changing, there is often a **le** at the end of the sentence. For example, **Wǒ jīnnián shíbāsuì le** "This year I'm 18 years old."

....

The numbers from 11 to 19

To create the numbers between 11 and 19, say **shí** "ten" followed immediately by the additional number. Examples: **shíyī** "11," **shí'èr** "12," **shísān** "13, **shísì** "14," **shíwǔ** "15," **shíliù** "16," **shíqī** "17," **shíbā** "18," **shíjiǔ** "19."

Multiples of 10

To create multiples of ten, say the number of times you want to multiply, followed immediately by **shí**. Examples: **èrshí** "20," **sānshí** "30," **sìshí** "40," **wǔshí** "50," **liùshí** "60," **qīshí** "70," **bāshí** "80, **jiǔshí** "90."

Forming numbers from 21 to 99

To create the numbers between one multiple of ten and the next, say the multiple of ten, then say **shí**, and then say the additional number. Examples: **èrshiyī** "21," **liùshisān** "63," **jiǔshijiǔ** "99." When **shi** is the middle syllable in a three-syllable number, it usually loses its tone.

Tag questions

Look at the first sentence in line 5: **Zhè shi nǐ mèimei, duì bu dui?** "This is your younger sister, right?" You could also ask **Zhè shi nǐ mèimei, shì bu shì?** or **Zhè shi nǐ mèimei, shì ma?** "This is your younger sister, isn't it?" Questions such as this, where an affirmative-negative question or a **ma** question has been "tagged on" at the end of a statement to transform the statement into a question, are common in Chinese and are called tag questions.

Le to indicate a changed situation in the future

In the sentence **Xiàge yuè jiù jiǔsuì le** "Next month (my little sister) will be 9 years old," the **le** at the end of the sentence indicates a changed situation, even though that change (the little sister's becoming 9 years old) has not yet occurred and is anticipated in the future.

Using méiyou to indicate "not have, there isn't, there aren't"

Méiyou "not have, there isn't, there aren't" is the negative form of **yǒu** "to have, there is, there are." The question **Yǒu méiyou** "Have or don't have?" or "Is there or isn't there?" is very common, for example: **Nǐ yǒu méiyou gēge?** "Do you have older brothers?"

Reading

New Characters and Words

103.	多	**duō**	how; be many
	多大	**duō dà**	how old?
104.	年	**nián**	year
105.	纪	**jì**	to record
	年纪	**niánji**	age
	多大年纪	**duō dà niánji**	how many years old?

106.	今	**jīn**	now (can't be used alone)
	今年	**jīnnián**	this year
107.	岁	**suì**	year of age
	几岁	**jǐsuì**	how many years old? (of a child)
108.	对	**duì**	be correct

A. SENTENCES

一、这是你的姐姐吗？她今年多大年纪了？

二、我姐姐的先生是美国人，他的中文很好，他是中文老师。

三、我的名字叫司小文，今年十九岁，我姐姐叫司文香。

四、你几岁了？五岁了，对不对？

五、你的同屋是中国人吧？他今年多大了？二十岁，对不对？

六、李老师的两个姐姐也都是老师，对不对？她们的年纪都不小了吧？

七、我们今年的中文老师是上海人，不是吗？

八、这个公司的人都是男的吗？这是不对的！

九、小何的两位老师都是美国人，年纪都不大。

十、王大海的两位中文老师年纪都很大，一位八十岁，一位七十五岁。

B. CONVERSATIONS

一、

老先生：老太太，您多大年纪了？

老太太：我年纪不小了，今年八十三岁了。老先生，您呢？

老先生：我今年八十四岁了！

二、

大海：你多大年纪了？

文山：我二十一岁了。你呢？你多大了？

大海：请你别问，好不好？

C. NARRATIVES

一、我的名字叫李小明，今年二十九岁了。我的姐姐叫李中明，今年三十六岁了。我们两个都是湖北人。我的姐姐是一位中文老师，她的先生也是中文老师。我姐姐的先生叫王中山，他是河南人，今年四十岁了。这是他们两位的名片。

二、我的名字叫安东山，今年六岁，他们都叫我"东东"。我是男生，北京人。我姐姐叫安东文，今年九岁，他们都叫她"文文"。

Notes

A6.   她们的年纪都不小了吧？ literally means "Their age is, for all of them, not small, I suppose?" In good English, we could translate as "I guess they're all not so young, huh?" or "I guess they must all be rather old?"

A7.   In the question 我们今年的中文老师是上海人，不是吗?, the tag question 不是吗 literally means "is it not so?" In smoother English, we could translate the whole question as "Our Chinese teacher this year is from Shanghai, right?"

A8.   In this sentence, 这是不对的！ means "This isn't right!" (in the sense of "This isn't as it should be!").

A9.   In this sentence, 年纪都不大 literally means "age both not big." In better English, we could translate "neither of them is very old" or "both of them are rather young."

B1.   In Chinese, addressing an elderly woman as 老太太, literally "old lady," is considered quite polite and respectful, not at all rude as it would be in English.

C1.   In the sentence 这是他们两位的名片, the pronoun 这 means "these" rather than "this." We know this from the context, because it wouldn't make sense to interpret the sentence as "This is the name card of the two of them," since two people would not normally share one name card.

Stand in southern Taiwan selling coconuts

LESSON 8
Buying Things

PART ONE

Conversation 🎧

Situation: Jonathan Little, who is spending six months as an intern in a law firm in Beijing, passes a store selling clothing and kitchenware. He first asks the salesman how much one of the coats on display costs, then asks how much a tea cup costs.

1. LITTLE: *(looking at a coat)*

请问，这个多少钱？

Qǐng wèn, zhèige duōshǎo qián?

Excuse me, how much is this?

2. SALESMAN: 一百九十八块。

Yìbǎi jiǔshibākuài.

One hundred and ninety-eight dollars.

3. LITTLE: 哟，太贵了！这个杯子多少钱？

Yò, tài guìle! *(pointing at a cup)* **Zhèige bēizi duōshǎo qián?**

Gosh, that's too expensive! How much is this cup?

4. SALESMAN: 那个只要三块五。

Nèige zhǐ yào sānkuài wǔ.

That only costs three dollars and fifty cents.

5. LITTLE: 我看看，行不行？
Wǒ kànkan, xíng bu xíng?
Would it be all right if I took a look at it?

6. SALESMAN: 行，您看吧。
Xíng, nín kàn ba.
Sure, take a look.

7. LITTLE: *(looking at the cup)*

好，我买两个。
Hǎo, wǒ mǎi liǎngge.
O.K., I'll buy two.

New Vocabulary

多少	**duōshǎo**	how much?, how many?
钱	**qián**	money
百	**-bǎi**	hundred
块	**kuài**	dollar (monetary unit)
哟	**yò**	"gosh," "wow"
贵	**guì**	be expensive
杯子	**bēizi**	cup
只	**zhǐ**	only
要	**yào**	want, need, cost, take
吧	**ba**	(indicates suggestions)
买	**mǎi**	buy

Supplementary Vocabulary

毛	**máo**	ten cents, dime
分	**fēn**	fen, cent
零	**líng**	zero
公事包	**gōngshìbāo**	briefcase, attache case
千	**-qiān**	thousand
卖	**mài**	sell
背包	**bēibāo**	knapsack, backpack
袋子	**dàizi**	bag
便宜	**piányi**	be cheap
加	**jiā**	add; plus
减	**jiǎn**	subtract; minus

Notes on the Conversation

Zhèige and nèige

The very common words **zhèige** "this, this one" and **nèige** "that, that one" are both composed of a specifier (**zhèi-** or **nèi-**) plus the general measure **ge**. **Zhèige** and **nèige** can function either as adjectives that describe a following noun (**Wǒ mǎi zhèige bēizi** "I'll buy this cup") or as pronouns (**Wǒ mǎi zhèige** "I'll buy this one"). Some more examples: **zhèige bān** "this class," **nèige nánde** "that guy," **Zhèige, bú shi nèige!** "This one, not that one!" Be sure to contrast carefully the corresponding question word **něige** "which one?" and note that some speakers say **zhège**, **nàge**, and **nǎge** instead of **zhèige**, **nèige**, and **něige**.

....

Duōshǎo vs. jǐ-

The question word **duōshǎo** "how much?, how many?" is used where the number is known or expected to be 10 or more. The question word **jǐ-**, followed by an appropriate measure, is used when the number is under 10. Study carefully the following examples: **Nǐ yǒu duōshǎo qián?** "How much money do you have?" vs. **Nǐ yǒu jǐkuài qián?** "How many dollars do you have?" (the assumption is that it's under 10 dollars); and **Yígòng yǒu duōshǎo rén?** "How many people are there in all?" vs. **Yígòng yǒu jǐge rén?** "How many people are there in all?" (again, the assumption is that it's under 10 people).

....

Numbers from 100 to 999 with -bǎi

The pattern for forming the words for hundreds is multiplier times **-bǎi** "hundred." The multiples of a hundred are: **yībǎi** "100," **liǎngbǎi** "200," **sānbǎi** "300," **sìbǎi** "400," **wǔbǎi** "500," **liùbǎi** "600," **qībǎi** "700," **bābǎi** "800," **jiǔbǎi** "900." To create numbers that fall between two multiples of a hundred (such as "358"), simply say the multiple of a hundred ("300" or **sānbǎi** in this case) followed directly by the word for the number under one hundred ("58" or **wǔshibā**), resulting in **sānbǎi wǔshibā** "358."

....

Le after tài in affirmative sentences

Notice that in the sentence **Yò, tài guìle** "Gosh, that's too expensive," there is a **le** after the stative verb **guì** "be expensive." When stative verbs (and, less commonly, some auxiliary verbs) are preceded by a **tài** "too" in affirmative sentences, they are often followed by a **le**.

....

Yào to indicate price

The pattern in Chinese for indicating the price of something is: item + **yào** + price. Examples: **Zhèige bēizi yào sānkuài wǔ** "This cup costs three fifty," **Nèige yào duōshǎo qián?** "How much does that one cost?"

....

Reduplication of verbs

Some verbs are reduplicated, that is, repeated so as to give a relaxed, casual sense to the verb and make the sentence they occur in sound smoother and less abrupt. The basic meaning is the same as when they are not reduplicated. For example, the verb **kàn** "look" is often reduplicated into the form **kànkan** "take a look." The second iteration of the verb is often in the neutral tone. Some other verbs you've had that can be reduplicated in this manner: **tīng** "listen" → **tīngting**, **wèn** "ask" → **wènwen**, **xiǎng** "think" → **xiángxiang**.

....

Ba to indicate suggestions

The particle **ba** can be added to the end of a statement to indicate a suggestion, as in **Nín kàn ba** "Why don't you take a look?" Common English translations of this **ba** include "why don't you," "how about," and "let's." More examples: **Zuò ba!** "Why don't you sit down?," **Nǐ yě mǎi yíge ba** "Why don't you buy one, too?," **Wǒmen zǒu ba** "Let's leave."

Numbers from 1,000 to 9,999 with -qiān

The pattern for forming the words for thousands is multiplier times **-qiān** "thousand." The multiples of a thousand are: **yìqiān** "1,000," **liǎngqiān** "2,000," **sānqiān** "3,000," **sìqiān** "4,000," **wǔqiān** "5,000," **liùqiān** "6,000," **qīqiān** "7,000," **bāqiān** "8,000," **jiǔqiān** "9,000." Note that **-qiān**, like **-bǎi**, can't be said alone.

Reading

New Characters and Words

109.	那	**nà/nèi-**	that; in that case, so
	那个	**nèige**	that one, that
	那位	**nèiwèi**	that (person; polite)
110.	少	**shǎo**	be few
	多少	**duōshǎo**	how much?, how many?
111.	钱	**qián**	money
112.	块	**kuài**	dollar (monetary unit)
113.	百	**-bǎi**	hundred (can't be used alone)
114.	千	**-qiān**	thousand (can't be used alone)

A. SENTENCES

一、这位男老师姓高，那位女老师姓钱。

二、五十块钱？太贵了！那，这个多少钱？

三、中国多少人姓王？美国多少人姓Smith？

四、先生，两个人去中国，两千块钱，太贵了！

五、我们的公司很大，七百人。你的公司多少人？

六、九十九岁的那位中国老太太姓安，对不对？

七、她不是香港人？那，她是台湾人吧？

八、他叫李南，今年四岁了，你们叫他"南南"吧。

九、谢太太，今年去不好，您今年别去了！

十、小王，这个太贵了，那个多少钱？

B. CONVERSATIONS

一、

美国人：那个多少钱？
中国人：哪个？
美国人：那个。
中国人：是这个吗？
美国人：不是这个，是那个！

二、

美国人：小姐，请问，这个多少钱？
香港人：这个……一百九十九块。
美国人：太贵了。那个呢？那个多少钱？
香港人：那个二十三块五。

C. NARRATIVE

你问我去北京一个人多少钱？好，去北京一个人一百二十块。去香山多少钱？去香山两百八十块。去天津呢？去天津四百五十块。去上海呢？去上海一个人一千四百块。去美国一个人多少钱？这个你别问我；请你问那个人吧！

Notes

A4.　两个人去中国，两千块钱，太贵了！ "$2,000 for two people to go to China is too expensive!"

A5.　七百人 means the same as 七百个人. In writing and sometimes in speaking, measures can be omitted between 百 or 千 and 人.

C.　你问我去北京一个人多少钱？ "You're asking me how much it costs for one person to go to Beijing?" This sentence involves the Question Word Question 去北京一个人多少钱？ being embedded within the Intonation Question 你问我？

Chinese currency

PART TWO

Conversation 🎧

Situation: Paige Haynes, who is in China on a two-year assignment teaching English at a language institute, walks up to a ticket window at Beijing West Railway Station to purchase a ticket to Tianjin.

1. HAYNES:　请问，下一趟到天津的火车几点开？
　　　　　　Qǐng wèn, xiàyítàng dào Tiānjīnde huǒchē jǐdiǎn kāi?
　　　　　　Excuse me, when does the next train to Tianjin depart?

2. TICKET AGENT:　九点二十。可是现在已经九点一刻了，恐怕您来不及了。
　　　　　　Jiǔdiǎn èrshí. Kěshi xiànzài yǐjīng jiǔdiǎn yíkè le, kǒngpà nín láibujíle.
　　　　　　Nine twenty. But it's now already a quarter past nine, I'm afraid you're not going to make it.

3. HAYNES:　那么，再下一趟呢？
　　　　　　Nèmme, zài xiàyítàng ne?
　　　　　　Well, what about the one after that?

4. TICKET AGENT:　我看看。再下一趟是十点半。
　　　　　　Wǒ kànkan. Zài xiàyítàng shi shídiǎn bàn.
　　　　　　Let me see. The one after that is at 10:30.

5. HAYNES:　好。那，我就坐十点半的。多少钱？
　　　　　　Hǎo. Nà, wǒ jiù zuò shídiǎn bànde. Duōshǎo qián?
　　　　　　O.K. In that case, I'll take the ten thirty one. How much is it?

6. TICKET AGENT:　十一块五。
　　　　　　Shíyīkuài wǔ.
　　　　　　Eleven dollars and fifty cents.

7. HAYNES: 到天津要多长时间？
Dào Tiānjīn yào duō cháng shíjiān?
How long does it take to get to Tianjin?

8. TICKET AGENT   差不多要两个半钟头。
Chàbuduō yào liǎngge bàn zhōngtóu.
It takes about two and a half hours.

9. HAYNES: 好，谢谢您！
Hǎo, xièxie nín.
O.K., thanks.

New Vocabulary

趟	**tàng**	(for runs by trains, buses)
到	**dào**	arrive, reach
天津	**Tiānjīn**	Tianjin
火	**huǒ**	fire
车	**chē**	vehicle (car, cab, bus, bicycle)
火车	**huǒchē**	train
点	**diǎn**	o'clock, hour
开	**kāi**	depart (of a train, bus, ship)
现在	**xiànzài**	now
已经	**yǐjīng**	already
刻	**kè**	quarter of an hour
恐怕	**kǒngpà**	"I'm afraid that"; probably
及	**-jí**	reach a goal in time
来不及	**láibují**	not have enough time
那么	**nèmme**	then, in that case, well
再	**zài**	again
坐	**zuò**	travel by, take
长	**cháng**	be long
时间	**shíjiān**	time
差不多	**chàbuduō**	almost, about
钟头	**zhōngtóu**	hour

Supplementary Vocabulary

钟	**zhōng**	clock, o'clock; bell
分	**fēn**	minute
差	**chà**	lack

Notes on the Conversation

-de following long phrases to indicate modification

The particle **-de** can indicate that what precedes it describes what follows it. This holds true whether the descriptive phrase with **-de** consists of one word or a phrase containing many words. In **xiàyítàng dào Tiānjīnde huǒchē**, the **-de** indicates that the part before it (**xiàyítàng dào Tiānjīn** "the next trip of it goes to Tianjin") describes the part after it (**huǒchē** "train"), resulting in the meaning "the next train which goes to Tianjin." More examples: **wǒ yào mǎide bēizi** "the cup that I want to buy," **zài Měiguo gōngzuòde nèige Zhōngguo nánshēng** "that male Chinese student who works in America," **sāndiǎn zhōng zuò huǒchē dào Běijīng qùde nèiwèi Yīngguo xiáojie** "that young English woman who took the train at three o'clock to go to Beijing."

-de to create nominal phrases

Compare the following two phrases: **shídiǎn bànde huǒchē** "the 10:30 train" vs. **shídiǎn bànde** "the 10:30 one." If the noun following a **-de** is dropped, the phrase that remains can substitute for the missing noun and has a meaning such as "the...one" or "the one that..." More examples: **wǒ mǎide** "the ones I bought," **tā yàode** "what she wanted," **xìng Gāode** "the one who is surnamed Gao," **mài bēizide** "the one who sells cups, the cup seller."

Time when before the verb

Time expressions indicating the point in time when something happens, happened, or will happen are placed immediately after the subject and before the verb. Note that this order is different from English, since in English time when is indicated after the verb. The same rule applies to question words like **jǐdiǎn** "at what o'clock?, when?" Examples: **Wǒ bādiǎn zhōng qù.** "I go at eight o'clock," **Huǒchē jǐdiǎn lái?** "When is the train coming?," **Wǒ míngtiān hěn máng.** "I'm busy tomorrow."

Clock times

The pattern for creating clock times is: number of the hour + **diǎn** + **zhōng** "o'clock," for example, **sāndiǎn zhōng** "three o'clock." In the same way that in English the "o'clock" can be omitted, in Chinese the **zhōng** may be omitted, so you could say just **sāndiǎn** "three." The number of minutes is indicated by adding after **diǎn** the number of minutes + **fēn** "minute," for example, **sāndiǎn'èrshisānfēn** "3:23." **Yíkè** "quarter after" and **bàn** "thirty" are used with times involving 15 and 30 minutes after the hour. Examples: **liùdiǎn yíkè** "6:15," **qīdiǎn bàn** "7:30." **Chà**, literally "lack," can be used to indicate a point of time between the 31st minute and the 59th minute before the next hour, for example, either **yīdiǎn chà wǔfēn** or **chà wǔfēn yīdiǎn** "12:55." The question for "What time is it (now)?" is **Xiànzài jǐdiǎn zhōng le?** or just **Xiànzài jǐdiǎn?**

Number of hours

To express the number of hours, say the number followed by the general measure **ge** followed by the noun **zhōngtóu** "hour." Examples: **yíge zhōngtóu** "one hour," **liǎngge zhōngtóu** "two hours," **èrshisìge zhōngtóu** "twenty-four hours," **Jǐge zhōngtóu?** "How many hours?." Carefully contrast and memorize the following pair of expressions with **zhōngtóu** that are easily confused: **bàn'ge zhōngtóu** "half an hour" vs. **yíge bàn zhōngtóu** "an hour and a half." Also, be careful to distinguish both **bàn'ge zhōngtóu** and **yíge bàn zhōngtóu** from **yīdiǎn bàn**, which means "1:30."

Reading

New Characters and Words

115.	点	**diǎn**	o'clock (can't be used alone)
116.	刻	**kè**	quarter of an hour (can't be used alone)
117.	半	**bàn**	half (can't be used alone)
	一半	**yíbàn**	one-half
	一半一半	**yíbàn yíbàn**	half and half
118.	差	**chà**	lack
	差不多	**chàbuduō**	almost, about
119.	钟	**zhōng**	bell; clock
	几点钟?	**Jǐdiǎn zhōng?**	What time (of the clock) is it?
120.	头	**tóu**	head; (common noun suffix)
	钟头	**zhōngtóu**	hour

A. SENTENCES

一、这位先生，请问，几点钟了？

二、九点一刻了，我不坐了，我先走了。

三、差一刻六点了，我们走吧！

四、别太高兴，这个钟很贵，一千六百块钱！

五、我的四位老师，一半是男的，一半是女的。

六、三个是男生，三个是女生，一半一半。

七、你也去成都吗？我坐三点的，你坐几点的？

八、五点钟去台北的那位老先生姓文，不姓王。

九、名字叫李京生的那个女的是小李的姐姐，不是我的姐姐。

十、没带钱的那个男生是王大海，不是我！

B. CONVERSATIONS

一、

老李：几点了？

老谢：十一点三刻了。

老李：十一点三刻了吗？

老谢：不对，不对。十点三刻。

二、

美国人：天津，十点半的。多少钱？

中国人：十一块五。

美国人：好，这是钱，十一块五。去天津几个钟头？

中国人：差不多两个半钟头。

美国人：好，谢谢您！

C. NARRATIVE

老高是我的同屋，小何是小李的同屋。我们四个人三点半去北京的"中美公司"。去北京不太难，差不多一个半钟头，一个人差不多十五块钱。老高很高兴，他带了她的名片，也带了一点钱，差不多两百块吧。小李也很高兴，他也带了一点钱，差不多一百块，没带名片。我太忙了，没带名片，也没带钱。没带钱不太好吧？

Notes

A1.   In this sentence, 这位先生, literally "This gentleman," is used as a vocative expression to address the person that this question is addressed to. It's probably best translated as "Sir."

A4.   别太高兴 "Don't be too happy" or "Don't get too happy."

A7.   我坐三点的，你坐几点的？ "I'm taking the 3:00 one, which one are you taking?" In this question, it's understood from the context that some means of transportation—most likely a train, possibly an airplane—is being talked about.

C.   没带钱不太好吧？ literally means "Didn't bring money, not too good, I suppose?" We could translate this into more colloquial English as "Not to have brought money wasn't such a cool thing to do, huh?"

These characters can be read in any direction to mean "(National Taiwan) Normal University" or "great teacher"

Numbers, Dates, and Time (I)

PART ONE

Conversation 🎧

Situation: Jessica Osbourne walks up to the language lab attendant at the Mandarin Training Center of National Taiwan Normal University to ask about the schedule.

1. OSBOURNE:

请问，语言实验室每天几点钟开门，几点钟关门？

Qǐng wèn, yǔyán shíyànshì měitiān jǐdiǎn zhōng kāimén, jǐdiǎn zhōng guānmén?

Excuse me, what time every day does the language lab open and what time does it close?

2. LANGUAGE LAB ATTENDANT:

早上八点开门，晚上九点半关门。

Zǎoshang bādiǎn kāimén, wǎnshang jiǔdiǎn bàn guānmén.

It opens at 8:00 in the morning and closes at 9:30 at night.

3. OSBOURNE:

星期六开不开？

Xīngqīliù kāi bu kāi?

Is it open on Saturdays?

4. LANGUAGE LAB ATTENDANT:

星期六开半天。上午开，下午不开。

Xīngqīliù kāi bàntiān. Shàngwǔ kāi, xiàwǔ bù kāi.

Saturdays it's open half-days. It's open in the morning but not in the afternoon.

5. OSBOURNE: 星期天呢?
                                          Xīngqītiān ne?
                                          And on Sundays?

6. LANGUAGE LAB ATTENDANT: 星期天休息。
                                          Xīngqītiān xiūxi.
                                          It's closed on Sundays.

7. OSBOURNE: 谢谢你。
                                          Xièxie nǐ.
                                          Thank you.

8. LANGUAGE LAB ATTENDANT   哪里。
                                          Náli.
                                          Sure.

New Vocabulary

语言	**yǔyán**	language
实验	**shíyàn**	experiment
实验室	**shíyànshì**	laboratory
语言实验室	**yǔyán shíyànshì**	language lab
每	**měi-**	each, every
天	**tiān**	day
开	**kāi**	open
门	**mén**	door, gate
开门	**kāimén**	open a door, open
关	**guān**	close
关门	**guānmén**	close a door, close
早上	**zǎoshang**	in the morning
晚上	**wǎnshang**	in the evening
星期六	**xīngqīliù**	Saturday
上午	**shàngwǔ**	morning, A.M.
下午	**xiàwǔ**	afternoon, P.M.
星期天	**xīngqītiān**	Sunday
休息	**xiūxi**	rest, take time off
哪里	**náli**	"not at all"

Supplementary Vocabulary 🎧

平常	**píngcháng**	usually, ordinarily
起床	**qǐchuáng**	get up from bed, rise
睡觉	**shuìjiào**	sleep, go to bed
睡	**shuì**	sleep
星期	**xīngqī**	week
礼拜	**lǐbài**	week
星期一	**xīngqīyī**	Monday
星期二	**xīngqī'èr**	Tuesday
星期三	**xīngqīsān**	Wednesday
星期四	**xīngqīsì**	Thursday
星期五	**xīngqīwǔ**	Friday
星期六	**xīngqīliù**	Saturday
星期天	**xīngqītiān**	Sunday
星期日	**xīngqīrì**	Sunday
星期几	**xīngqījǐ**	which day of the week?
礼拜一	**lǐbàiyī**	Monday
礼拜二	**lǐbài'èr**	Tuesday
礼拜三	**lǐbàisān**	Wednesday
礼拜四	**lǐbàisì**	Thursday
礼拜五	**lǐbàiwǔ**	Friday
礼拜六	**lǐbàiliù**	Saturday
礼拜天	**lǐbàitiān**	Sunday
礼拜日	**lǐbàirì**	Sunday
礼拜几	**lǐbàijǐ**	which day of the week?

Notes on the Conversation

Tiān as a measure meaning "day"

Even though in English the word "day" is a noun, in Chinese **tiān** functions grammatically as a measure, not as a noun. Therefore, to say "every day," you place the specifier **měi-** directly before **tiān** and say **měitiān**. Because **tiān** is itself a measure, nothing is inserted between **měi-** and **tiān**. Similarly, to say "one day," you place the number **yī** directly before **tiān** and say **yìtiān** (it would be a big mistake to say *yíge tiān). This is very different from the situation with nouns, where a measure must be inserted between the number or specifier and the noun, for example, **yíge xīngqī** "one week" or **měige yuè** "every month."

Verb-object compounds

The expression **kāimén** "open" ("open the door") is your first example of a verb-object compound. These are verbal compounds composed of a one-syllable verb plus a one-syllable object which are often best translated into English as a verb without an object. There are several other verb-object compounds in this lesson: **guānmén** "close" ("close a door"), **qǐchuáng** "get up" ("rise from bed"), and **shuìjiào** "sleep" ("sleep a sleep").

Time spent after the verb

In line 4 of this lesson, you'll notice that the time expression **bàntiān** "for half the day" follows the verb **kāi** "open," but that the time words **xīngqīliù** "Saturday," **shàngwǔ** "in the morning," and **xiàwǔ** "in the afternoon" all precede **kāi**. The reason for this is that there is a very important rule in Chinese grammar that time expressions indicating when something happens ("time when") precede the verb; but that time expressions indicating for how long something happens ("time spent") follow the verb. Example: **Yǔyán shíyànshì xīngqīliù kāi bàntiān** "The language lab is open for half the day on Saturday."

Days of the week

Xīngqī, literally "star period," is a common word for "week." In Taiwan and occasionally in mainland China, **xīngqī** is pronounced **xīngqí**, with Tone Two on the second syllable. The words for the days of the week are formed by suffixing to **xīngqī-** the number for the particular day of the week, from **yī** "one" to **liù** "six," with "Monday" being considered the first day and counting in this manner up to "Saturday," the sixth day. "Sunday" is different, with two possible forms: **xīngqītiān** and **xīngqīrì**. Be careful to contrast the pronunciations and meanings of **xīngqī'èr** "Tuesday" and **xīngqīrì** "Sunday." The question word for "which day of the week?" is **xīngqījǐ**. A more colloquial word for "week" is **lǐbài**. As with **xīngqī**, the number for the day of the week is suffixed to **lǐbài-**, there being two forms for "Sunday," **lǐbàitiān** and **lǐbàirì**, as well as a question form **lǐbàijǐ** "which day of the week?."

Reading

New Characters and Words

121.	谁	**shéi**	who, whom
122.	开	**kāi**	open; depart (of a train, bus, ship)
123.	门	**mén**	door, gate
	开门	**kāimén**	open a door, open
	金门	**Jīnmén**	Quemoy (island off the coast of Fujian Province)
124.	关	**guān**	close
	关门	**guānmén**	close a door
125.	星	**xīng**	star
126.	期	**qī**	period of time (can't be used alone)
	星期	**xīngqī**	week
	星期几	**xīngqījǐ**	which day of the week?

星期一	**xīngqīyī**	Monday
星期二	**xīngqī'èr**	Tuesday
星期三	**xīngqīsān**	Wednesday
星期四	**xīngqīsì**	Thursday
星期五	**xīngqīwǔ**	Friday
星期六	**xīngqīliù**	Saturday
星期天	**xīngqītiān**	Sunday
上个星期	**shàngge xīngqī**	last week
这个星期	**zhèige xīngqī**	this week

A. SENTENCES

一、请问，星期一去北京的那位小姐是谁？

二、这个星期请你们别开这个门，请你们开那个门，好吗？

三、请问，台北的公司几点钟开门，几点钟关门？

四、金门多大？多少人？金门人都是中国人，对不对？

五、钱老师去湖南，去了两天半了。

六、这个门很难开，请老王开吧。

七、台湾的公司星期六开半天，星期天关门。

八、今天星期几？你姐姐去北京几天了？

九、请问，那个女的是谁？是小王的姐姐吗？

十、王大海上个星期天去中国了，很高兴。

B. CONVERSATIONS

一、

老师：是谁开了门？你别开门，好不好？

女生：我没开门，也没关门。

老师：我问你，那个女生是谁？

女生：她是我的同屋，她叫关小星。

二、

何小山：您星期六去公司吗？

王大中：去。香港的公司星期六开半天。

何小山：那，星期天您不去公司吧？

王大中：对，星期天我不去。星期天公司不开门。

C. NARRATIVES

一、 小谢的公司是中国公司，叫"大安公司"。星期一、二、三、四、五八点钟开门，五点钟关门。星期六开半天，八点开门，十二点半关门。星期天不开。小谢星期一八点钟去了公司，公司没开门。他不太高兴，走了。

二、 上个星期我们的两位中文老师带我们去了台湾。去台湾不太贵，差不多一千多块钱，差不多十八个钟头。我们去台湾去了五天：星期一去了台中、星期二去了台南、星期三去了台东、星期四去了台北、星期五去了金门。那五天，我们都很高兴！

Notes

A1. 星期一去北京的那位小姐是谁? could be translated as either "Who is that young lady that went to Beijing on Monday?" or "Who is that young lady that is going to Beijing on Monday?" The real world context and prior knowledge that the speaker and listener bring to the task would make the meaning clear.

A5. 钱老师去湖南，去了两天半了 means "Teacher Qian has gone to Hunan for two and a half days now" or "Teacher Qian has been in Hunan for two and a half days now." The implication is that this situation is continuing up to the present and that Teacher Qian is still in Hunan. In sentences indicating duration of time, a sentence-final particle 了 at the end of the sentence indicates that the action of the verb has been continuing for a period of time up to and including the present.

A8a. The question 今天星期几? means "What day of the week is it today?" No verb 是 is needed after 今天, though it would not be wrong to add one.

A8b. 你姐姐去北京几天了? "For how many days now has your older sister been in Beijing?" (literally, "Your older sister went to Beijing for how many days now?").

Kowloon Station in Hong Kong

PART TWO

Conversation

Situation: Vernice Johns, an Australian student in Taipei, goes to a neighborhood clinic to see a doctor. A nurse helps her fill out the registration form.

1. **NURSE:** 你叫什么名字?
   Nǐ jiào shémme míngzi?
   What's your name?

2. **JOHNS:** 我叫张文英。张是"弓""长"张，文是"文化"的文，英是
   "英国"的英。
   Wǒ jiào Zhāng Wényīng. Zhāng shi "gōng" "cháng" Zhāng, wén shi "wénhuà" de wén, yīng shi "Yīngguo" de yīng.
   My name is **Zhāng Wényīng**. The **Zhāng** is the **Zhāng** made up of "bow" and "long," the **wén** is the **wén** in the word for "culture," and the **yīng** is the **yīng** in the word for "England."

3. **NURSE:** 你是哪年出生的?
   Nǐ shi něinián chūshēngde?
   Which year were you born?

4. **JOHNS:** 一九八零年，就是民国六十九年。
   Yī-jiǔ-bā-líng-nián, jiù shi Mínguó liùshijiǔnián.
   In 1980, the sixty-ninth year of the Republic.

5. **NURSE:** 几月几号?
   Jǐyuè jǐhào?
   Which month and which day?

6. JOHNS: 四月十三号。
Sìyuè shísānhào.
April 13th.

7. NURSE: 你的地址是……
Nǐde dìzhǐ shi...
Your address is...

8. JOHNS: 和平东路一段，二十七巷，三弄，一百五十四号，八楼。
Hépíng Dōng Lù yīduàn, èrshiqīxiàng, sānlòng, yībǎi wǔshisìhào, bālóu.
Heping East Road Section One, Lane 27, Alley 3, Number 154, Eighth Floor.

9. NURSE: 好，请等一下。
Hǎo, qǐng děng yíxià.
All right, please wait a moment.

New Vocabulary

弓	**gōng**	bow (the weapon)
文化	**wénhuà**	culture
年	**nián**	year
出生	**chūshēng**	be born
就	**jiù**	precisely, exactly
民国	**Mínguó**	the Republic (of China)
几月	**jǐyuè**	which month of the year?
号	**hào**	day of the month
几号	**jǐhào**	which day of the month?
四月	**sìyuè**	April
地址	**dìzhǐ**	address
和平	**hépíng**	peace
东	**dōng**	east
路	**lù**	road
和平东路	**Hépíng Dōng Lù**	Heping East Road
段	**duàn**	section
巷	**-xiàng**	lane
弄	**-lòng**	alley
号	**hào**	number (in addresses, sizes)
楼	**lóu**	floor (of a building)
等	**děng**	wait, wait for

Supplementary Vocabulary 🎧

今天	**jīntiān**	today
明天	**míngtiān**	tomorrow
昨天	**zuótiān**	yesterday
今年	**jīnnián**	this year
明年	**míngnián**	next year
去年	**qùnián**	last year
一月	**yīyuè**	January
二月	**èryuè**	February
三月	**sānyuè**	March
四月	**sìyuè**	April
五月	**wǔyuè**	May
六月	**liùyuè**	June
七月	**qīyuè**	July
八月	**bāyuè**	August
九月	**jiǔyuè**	September
十月	**shíyuè**	October
十一月	**shíyīyuè**	November
十二月	**shí'èryuè**	December
生日	**shēngrì**	birthday

Notes on the Conversation

Shi...-de to express time or place of known past actions

The **shi...-de** pattern is frequently used to indicate the time or place of known past actions. When using **shi...-de**, you and your interlocutor are already aware of the fact that something has happened in the past; what you don't know is when or where the known past action took place. The **shi** is placed before the time or place, while the **-de** is usually placed at the end of the sentence. Examples: **Wǒ shi yī-jiǔ-bā-wǔ-nián chūshēngde** "I was born in 1985," **Wǒ shi zài Měiguo chūshēngde** "I was born in America." Memorize the following two questions along with the appropriate responses for yourself: **Nǐ shi něinián chūshēngde?** "Which year were you born?" and **Nǐ shi zài nǎr chūshēngde?** "Where were you born?"

Nián as measure meaning "year"

As in the case of **tiān** "day," the Chinese word **nián** "year" is a measure, not a noun. This means that, when specified or counted, **nián** is preceded directly by a number and not first by a measure like **ge**. Also, unlike most measures, **nián** and **tiān** are not normally followed by nouns. Examples: **yìnián** "one year," **liǎngnián** "two years," **jǐnián** "how many years?," **měinián** "every year."

Time before place

If you want to ask or state not only when but also where someone was born, the time expression must come before the place. For example, you would ask: **Qǐng wèn, nǐ shi něinián zài nǎr chūshēngde?** "Excuse me, when and where were you born?" The other person might then reply: **Wǒ shi yī-jiǔ-jiǔ-sān-nián zài Měiguo chūshēngde** "I was born in 1993 in America."

Years of the calendar with <u>nián</u>

To create the words for the years of the calendar, the numbers representing the year are usually read off one digit at a time followed by **nián** "year." Examples: **yī-jiǔ-jiǔ-bā-nián** "the year 1998," **èr-líng-líng-líng-nián** "the year 2000," **èr-líng-yī-bā-nián** "the year 2018." In English the word "year" is often omitted, but in Chinese **nián** is usually included.

Days of the month with <u>hào</u>

The days of the month are indicated by the number of the day plus the measure **hào**, which literally means "number." Examples: **yīhào** "1st day of month," **shíyīhào** "11th day of month," **èrshiyīhào** "21st day of month," **sānshiyīhào** "31st day of month." The expression for "Which day of the month?" is **Jǐhào?**

Dates

When discussing categories of things in Chinese, there is a general habit of first mentioning the more general category and then moving to the more specific category, which is the opposite of the English habit of moving from the specific to the general. You've already seen this in Chinese names, where the surname precedes the given name (since in Chinese the category of people sharing the same surname is larger than the category of people with the same given name). The order of dates in Chinese is also the opposite of English. In Chinese, you begin with the largest category—the year, and then, in succession, mention the month, day of the month, and day of the week. Example: **èr-líng-líng-wǔ nián shíyīyuè èrhào xīngqīyī** "Monday, November 2, 2005."

Addresses

As with dates, the order of the elements in a Chinese address is the opposite of English. Again, in Chinese you move from the largest category to the smallest one. What in English is "2nd Floor, 40 Whitman Street, Williamstown, Massachusetts, U.S.A.," would in Chinese be (translated back into English literally) "U.S.A., Massachusetts, Williamstown, Whitman Street, Number 40, 2nd Floor." Example: **Zhōngguo Guǎngdōng Guǎngzhōu Zhōngshān Lù wǔhào sānlóu** "3rd Floor, No. 5, Zhongshan Road, Guangzhou, Guangdong, China."

Floors of buildings with <u>lóu</u>

The floors of buildings are indicated by the number of the floor followed by the measure **lóu** "floor." Examples: **yīlóu** "first floor," **èrlóu** "second floor," **sānlóu** "third floor." The expression for "Which floor?" is **Jǐlóu?**

Months of the year with <u>yuè</u>

The months of the year are indicated by the number of the month plus the word **yuè** "month," which, literally, means "moon." The names of the months are: **yīyuè** "January," **èryuè** "February," **sānyuè** "March," **sìyuè** "April," **wǔyuè** "May," **liùyuè** "June," **qīyuè** "July," **bāyuè** "August," **jiǔyuè** "September,"

shíyuè "October," **shíyīyuè** "November," and **shí'èryuè** "December." Be sure to distinguish carefully between the names of the months, on the one hand, and the expressions for numbers of months, on the other. That is, **yīyuè** means "January," but **yíge yuè** means "one month"; similarly, **sānyuè** is "March" but **sān'ge yuè** means "three months." To say "this month" say **zhèige yuè**; to say "last month" say **shàngge yuè**; and to say "next month" say **xiàge yuè**. The expression for "Which month?" is **Jǐyuè?**.

Reading

New Characters and Words

127.	什	shén	(first syllable of word for "what")
128.	么	me	(second syllable of several common words)
	什么	shénme	what (pronounced **shémme**)
	这么	zhème	like this, in this way, so (pronounced **zhèmme**)
	那么	nàme	then, in that case, so (pronounced **nèmme**)
129.	就	jiù	then; precisely, exactly; only
	就是	jiù shi	be precisely, be exactly, be none other than
130.	月	yuè	month
	几月	jǐyuè	which month?
	一月	yīyuè	January
	二月	èryuè	February
	三月	sānyuè	March
	四月	sìyuè	April
	五月	wǔyuè	May
	六月	liùyuè	June
	七月	qīyuè	July
	八月	bāyuè	August
	九月	jiǔyuè	September
	十月	shíyuè	October
	十一月	shíyīyuè	November
	十二月	shí'èryuè	December
	上个月	shàngge yuè	last month
131.	号	hào	number; day of the month (in speech)
	几号	jǐhào	which day of the month?
132.	日	rì	day; day of the month (in writing); Japan
	星期日	xīngqīrì	Sunday
	生日	shēngrì	birthday
	日文	Rìwén	Japanese (especially written Japanese)

A. SENTENCES

一、对，那就是你问的我们公司的名片。

二、你高兴，我就高兴；你不高兴，我就不高兴。

三、钱老师，请问，"五月八日"就是"五月八号，"对不对？

四、明天，也就是五月五号，是我的生日；我明天就不去公司了，好吗？

五、请你们别这么叫她，好不好？她很不高兴。

六、去年是一九九九年，今年是两千年，明年是二○○一年，是不是？

七、你们是哪年几月几号去中国的？

八、你去年的日文老师是谁？是不是中川先生？

九、今天是六月十三号星期五。十三号星期五不好吗？

十、王大海上个月去了河南，这个月去湖北，明年二月去四川。

B. CONVERSATIONS

一、

安先生：何小姐，你好！

何小姐：安先生，你好！你这个星期不去台南吗？

安先生：六号是我的生日，我就不去了。

何小姐：六号？明天就是六号。那，明天你多大了？

安先生：我明天三十岁了，老了！

二、

美国女生：这是谁？

李先生：这是小明。

美国女生：小明，你好！你今年几岁了？

小明：我四岁。明天是我的生日。明天我就五岁了！

C. NARRATIVE

我的先生年纪很大，他明年就八十岁了。我的姐姐年纪也不小，她今年七十六岁了。我今年七十四岁了。我先生的生日是一九三○年六月十号，我姐姐的生日是一九三三年六月十号。我的生日是一九三五年六月十号。我、我先生、我姐姐，我们三个人的生日都是六月十号！

Notes

A2.   你高兴，我就高兴；你不高兴，我就不高兴 "If you're happy, then I'm happy; if you're unhappy, then I'm unhappy." Notice the implied conditional "if." In Chinese, when there are two clauses in succession, the first one often expresses the condition under which the second clause applies. This is especially likely when the second clause contains a 就 "then."

A6a.   去年是一九九九年，今年是两千年，明年是二〇〇一年 "Last year was 1999, this year is 2000, next year will be 2001." The equative verb 是 here has three different English equivalents! As a translation strategy, always check dates and timewords in a sentence before deciding on the tense of any verbs in the translation.

A6b.   For "the year 2000," some Chinese say 二〇〇〇年 and others say 两千年.

B1.   Since this is a conversation between two people that consists of direct quotations, 六号 is used rather than written-style 六日.

Numbers, Dates, and Time (II)

PART ONE

Conversation 🎧

Situation: Ben Ross, an American businessman, is staying at a Beijing hotel. While waiting for the elevator, he encounters the bellhop.

1. ROSS: 你好！
Nǐ hǎo!
How are you?

2. BELLHOP: 你好！你是美国人吗？
Nǐ hǎo! Nǐ shi Měiguo rén ma?
How are you? Are you American?

3. ROSS: 对，我是美国人。
Duì, wǒ shi Měiguo rén.
Yes, I'm American.

4. BELLHOP: 这是你第一次到中国来吗？
Zhè shi nǐ dìyīcì dào Zhōngguo lái ma?
Is this your first time in China?

5. ROSS: 不，这是第二次。我去年来过一次。
Bù, zhè shi dì'èrcì. Wǒ qùnián láiguo yícì.
No, this is the second time. I came once before last year.

6. BELLHOP: 嗨，你这次要住多久？
M, nǐ zhèicì yào zhù duō jiǔ?
Uh, how long are you going to stay this time?

7. ROSS: 大约半个月。我十二号回国。
Dàyuē bàn'ge yuè. Wǒ shí'èrhào huíguó.
About half a month. I return home on the 12th.

8. BELLHOP: 你住哪个房间？
Nǐ zhù něige fángjiān?
Which room are you staying in?

9. ROSS: 我住三零六。
Wǒ zhù sān líng liù.
I'm staying in 306.

10. BELLHOP: *(Sees another guest approaching)*

哦，对不起，我得走了。再见！
Ò, duìbuqǐ, wǒ děi zǒule. Zàijiàn!
Oh, sorry, I have to go now. Goodbye!

11. ROSS: 再见！
Zàijiàn!
Goodbye!

New Vocabulary

第	**dì-**	(forms ordinal numbers)
次	**cì**	time
过	**-guo**	(indicates experience)
嗨	**m**	(hesitation sound; pause filler)
要	**yào**	be going to, will
住	**zhù**	live (in), stay (in)
久	**jiǔ**	be long (of time)
大约	**dàyuē**	approximately, about
回国	**huíguó**	return to one's home country
房间	**fángjiān**	room

Supplementary Vocabulary

说	**shuō**	say, speak
然后	**ránhòu**	afterward, then
家	**jiā**	family, home
回家	**huíjiā**	return to one's home
中午	**zhōngwǔ**	noon

白天	**báitiān**	in the daytime
夜里	**yèli**	at night
前天	**qiántiān**	day before yesterday
后天	**hòutiān**	day after tomorrow
前年	**qiánnián**	year before last
后年	**hòunián**	year after next

Notes on the Conversation

dì- to create ordinal numbers

To create ordinal numbers where you designate the place occupied by an item in an ordered sequence, place the specifier **dì-** before the number, for example, **dìyī** "first," **dì'èr** "second," **dìsān** "third." The number is often, but not always, followed by a measure, for example, **dìyīcì** "the first time," **dìshítiān** "the 10th day," **dì'èrnián** "the second year," **dìyíge rén** "the first person," **dì'èrwèi xiānshēng** "the second gentleman." The question form is **dìjǐ**, for example, **Dìjǐge?** "The number which one?" or **Dìjǐcì** "The number which time?" In narrating past events, where in English we would say "the next day" or "the next year," in Chinese you would say **dì'èrtiān** "the second day" and **dì'èrnián** "the second year." However, to express which floor of a building, you simply say number + **lóu**, as in **qīlóu** "seventh floor."

....

-guo to express experience

The verb suffix **-guo**, which has the basic meaning "go through, pass," stresses that the subject of the sentence has in the past gone through the experience of performing the action of the verb. The **-guo** is usually suffixed to a verb, though it can occasionally be suffixed to a whole sentence. Examples: **Wǒ qùguo** "I've gone there" or "I've been there," **Tā zuòguo huǒchē** "She's taken a train before," **Wǒ yě shíqī, shíbāsuìguo** "I also was once 17 or 18." Since past time is involved, the negative of **-guo** is always with **méi**, never with **bù**. The **méi** stands right before the verb, with the **-guo** coming right after the verb. Example: **Wǒ méi zuòguo huǒchē** "I've never taken a train before." To make questions with verbs that have a **-guo** attached, you can either add **ma** at the end or use the affirmative-negative question pattern. Examples: **Nǐ zuòguo huǒchē ma?** or **Nǐ zuòguo méi zuòguo huǒchē?** "Have you ever taken a train?."

....

Reading

New Characters and Words

133.	第	**dì-**		(forms ordinal numbers)
	第一	**dìyī**		first
	第一个	**dìyíge**		the first one
	第一位	**dìyíwèi**		the first one (of people; polite)
134.	次	**cì**		time

几次	jǐcì	how many times?
一次	yícì	one time
第几次	dìjǐcì	the number what time?
第一次	dìyícì	the first time
上次	shàngcì	last time

135.	来	lái	come
136.	过	-guo	pass; (indicates past experience)
	来过	láiguo	have come to some place before
	去过	qùguo	have gone to some place before
137.	要	yào	want, need, cost, take; will, be going to
	不要	búyào	don't
138.	住	zhù	live (in), stay (in)

A. SENTENCES

一、那次我太忙，没去北京，这次我要去。

二、请问，这是你第几次来中国？你要住几天？

三、她的第一个先生是台湾人，第二个先生是香港人。

四、来，来，来，公司开门了，八点就开了。今天第一天开，不要走！

五、我问你，他姓什么，叫什么名字？他要来台北住几天？

六、林先生要来我们的公司问什么？你要带他来吗？

七、我要坐三点的，去南京。您呢？您要坐几点的？

八、钱先生住广东大街，钱太太住四川路。

九、我们住二〇六，他们住三〇八，是谁来了？我去开门。

十、王大海去过北京、香港、台北，没去过东京。

B. CONVERSATIONS

一、

中国男生：这是你第一次来中国吗？

美国女生：不，这是第二次。我去年来过一次。

中国男生：你这次要住几天？

美国女生：差不多半个月吧。

二、

台湾人：你来过台湾几次？

美国人：我来过两次。第一次是去年三月。

台湾人：你去过北京吗？

美国人：去过。北京，我去过五、六次。
台湾人：北京好？台北好？
美国人：北京、台北都很好！

C. NARRATIVE

我去过中国，去过两次。第一次是二〇〇八年，第二次是二〇一〇年。二〇一〇年那次我十九岁，中文也不太好。我们先去上海住了两、三天，也去了北京、西安、成都、广州、香港。我们是四个男生、十个女生，我们的中文老师王老师也去了。我们很高兴，明年一月王老师要带我们去台湾。我们都没去过台湾。我们要住台北，要住差不多两个星期。

Notes

B2a.   五、六次 means "five or six times."

B2b.   北京好？台北好？ means "Is Beijing better or is Taipei better?" One of the most common ways to indicate alternatives is simply by listing them, one directly after another.

Beijing Railway Station

PART TWO

Conversation 🎧

Situation: Derek Miller, a student in a study abroad program in Beijing, asks his teacher about the population of China and several Chinese cities.

1. **MILLER:** 孙老师，请问，中国有多少人？
   Sūn Lǎoshī, qǐng wèn, Zhōngguo yǒu duōshǎo rén?
   Excuse me, Mr. Sun, how many people are there in China?

2. **SUN:** 中国差不多有十三亿人。
   Zhōngguo chàbuduō yǒu shísānyì rén.
   China has about one billion three hundred million people.

3. **MILLER:** 北京有多少人？
   Běijīng yǒu duōshǎo rén?
   How many people are there in Beijing?

4. **SUN:** 北京有一千多万人。
   Běijīng yǒu yìqiānduōwàn rén.
   Beijing has more than ten million people.

5. **MILLER:** 那么，南京呢？
   Nèmme, Nánjīng ne?
   And what about Nanjing?

6. **SUN:** 南京的人口比较少。好像只有五百万。
   Nánjīngde rénkǒu bǐjiào shǎo. Hǎoxiàng zhǐ yǒu wǔbǎiwàn.
   The population of Nanjing is smaller. It seems it has only five million.

New Vocabulary

父亲	**fùqin**	father
亿	**-yì**	hundred million
万	**-wàn**	ten thousand
千万	**-qiānwàn**	ten million
多	**duō**	be many, much, more
人口	**rénkǒu**	population
比较	**bǐjiào**	comparatively, relatively
少	**shǎo**	be few, less
好像	**hǎoxiàng**	apparently, it seems to me
百万	**-bǎiwàn**	million

Supplementary Vocabulary

十万	**shíwàn**	one hundred thousand
课	**kè**	class
上课	**shàngkè**	have class
迟到	**chídào**	arrive late, be late
常常	**chángcháng**	often
逃课	**táokè**	skip class

Notes on the Conversation

Large numbers

The basic units for the Chinese higher numbers are **-wàn** "ten thousand" and **-yì** "one hundred million"; like **-bǎi** "hundred" and **-qiān** "thousand," these are never said alone. The secondary units are formed as follows: **yíwàn** "ten thousand," **shíwàn** "one hundred thousand" (literally, "ten ten thousands"), **yìbǎiwàn** "one million" (literally, "one hundred ten thousands"), **yìqiānwàn** "ten million" (literally, "one thousand ten thousands"), **yíyì** "one hundred million," and **shíyì** "one billion" (literally, "ten one hundred millions"). While it helps to understand the underlying logic, it is best to memorize these as set expressions rather than trying to construct them on the spot. Examples of some larger numbers: **liǎngwàn** "20,000," **wǔshiwàn** "500,000," **sānbǎiwàn** "3,000,000," **liǎngqiānwàn** "20,000,000," **sānyì** "300,000,000," **sānshiyì** "three billion."

....

Duō and shǎo

The stative verb **duō** "be many, be much, be more" is very common. Examples: **Hǎo rén bù duō** "There are not many good people," **Lǎo Lǐ rènshi hěn duō rén** "Old Li knows lots of people," **Chídàode tóngxué duō ma?** "Were there many classmates who arrived late?" **Duō** must be preceded by an adverb like **hěn** when used to modify a noun. Examples: **hěn duō rén** "lots of people," **hěn duō qián** "much money," **hěn duō shíjiān** "much time." When it occurs after a numerical expression, **duō** indicates "more than" the amount stated. Examples: **yìbǎiduō rén** "more than a hundred people," **yìqiānduōkuài** "more than a thousand dollars," **yíge duō zhōngtóu** "more than an hour," **yíwèi yìbǎiduōsuìde lǎo tàitai** "an old woman more than a hundred years old." The stative verb **shǎo** "be few, be less" is also common and important. Examples: **Rén hěn shǎo** "There weren't many people," **Qùde rén bù shǎo** "Quite a few people went," **Bù duō yě bù shǎo** "Neither many nor few."

Hǎoxiàng

The adverb **hǎoxiàng** "apparently, it seems to me" is very common and useful when you wish, as is common in Chinese, not to be overly direct and emphatic, or when you want to avoid committing yourself too strongly to a certain viewpoint so as to save your own or someone else's face. Chinese speakers will sometimes use **hǎoxiàng** even when they are completely sure of the facts. **Hǎoxiàng** may occur directly before the verb but it may also occur at the beginning of the sentence. Some examples with **hǎoxiàng**: **Tāmen hǎoxiàng hái méi lái** "It seems they haven't come yet," **Hǎoxiàng tā xìng Zhào** "Apparently her surname is Zhao," **Nǐ hǎoxiàng bú tài gāoxìng** "It seems as though you're not very happy," **Tā hǎoxiàng méi qùguo Zhōngguo** "I think she's never been to China before."

Reading

New Characters and Words

139.	有	**yǒu**	have; there is, there are
	没有	**méiyou**	not have; there isn't, there aren't
	有没有	**yǒu méiyou**	have or not have? is there or isn't there?
140.	口	**kǒu**	mouth (can't be used alone)
	人口	**rénkǒu**	population (literally, "human mouths")
	海口	**Hǎikǒu**	Haikou (capital of Hainan Province)
141.	像	**xiàng**	resemble
	好像	**hǎoxiàng**	apparently, it seems to me
142.	万	**-wàn**	ten thousand (can't be used alone)
	一万	**yíwàn**	ten thousand
	十万	**shíwàn**	hundred thousand
	百万	**-bǎiwàn**	million (can't be used alone)
	一百万	**yìbǎiwàn**	one million
	千万	**-qiānwàn**	ten million (can't be used alone)
	一千万	**yìqiānwàn**	ten million
143.	比	**bǐ**	compare
144.	较	**jiào**	compare (can't be used alone)
	比较	**bǐjiào**	comparatively, relatively

A. SENTENCES

一、一年有十二个月，一个月有四个多星期，一个星期有七天。

二、您好像是第一次来中国吧？中文难不难？

三、那个大街我好像去过，是不是叫南京大街？

四、好像九月去北京比较好；七月去不太好，别七月去。

五、谁比较高？是你？是他？好像是他。

六、这个月公司好像比较忙，星期日也不关门。

七、去香港差不多要八百块。去北京比较贵，对不对？

八、小李有个同屋，姓万，海南人，海口来的。我没有同屋。你有没有？

九、河北省山很少，山西省也很少，广西省比较多。

十、王大海有一个姐姐，二十六岁，她明年要去广州住。

B. CONVERSATIONS

一、

美国男生：高老师，请问，天津有多少人？

高老师　：天津有一千多万人。

美国男生：那么，南京呢？

高老师　：南京的人口比较少，好像有五百万吧。

二、

美国同屋：小王，你有没有五块钱？

中国同屋：我没有。我今天没带钱。

美国同屋：那，我去问老谢吧。

中国同屋：你别问他，好像他也没带钱。你去问老王比较好，好像他
　　　　　带了很多钱。

C. NARRATIVES

一、上海人太多。香港人口比较少，七百万。香港有香港人、广东
　　人、上海人，也有不少美国人。香港有很多公司。有香港人开的
　　公司，有中国人开的公司，也有美国人开的公司。住香港很贵，
　　一个月差不多要两万块钱。香港的人好像都很忙。有很多人去了
　　香港，就不走了。

二、中国有二十多个省，人口差不多有1,300,000,000。广东、河南、山
　　东、四川都是中国的大省。2005年广东有九千五百多万人，河南
　　有九千四百多万人，山东也有差不多九千四百万人，四川有八千
　　一百多万人。

Notes

A8.   This sentence is in informal, conversational style. A literal translation would be "Little Li has a roommate, (he/she) is surnamed Wan, (he/she is) from Hainan, (he/she) has come from Haikou." In informal, conversational style, measures, subjects or topics, and the verb 是 are sometimes omitted. 有个同屋 is short for 有一个同屋, 海南人 is short for 他/她是海南人, and 海口来的 is short for 他/她是海口来的.

A fruit store in Beijing

Locating Persons, Places, and Things (I)

PART ONE

Conversation 🎧

Situation: Sarah Eng, who is teaching English at a college in Beijing, recently met a young Chinese woman whom she knows only as "Mary Wang." She goes to the address the woman gave her to visit her.

1. **CHINESE:** 请进！
   Qǐng jìn!
   Come in, please!

2. **ENG:** 对不起，我想找一下儿王小姐。请问，她在不在？
   Duìbuqǐ, wǒ xiǎng zhǎo yixiar Wáng Xiáojie. Qǐng wèn, tā zài bu zai?
   Excuse me, I'd like to find Ms. Wang. May I ask, is she in?

3. **CHINESE:** 哪位王小姐？
   Něiwèi Wáng Xiáojie?
   Which Ms. Wang?

4. **ENG:**   实在抱歉。我是美国华侨，中文不太好。我不知道她的中文名字。不过，她的英文名字叫"Mary 王"。

Shízài bàoqiàn. Wǒ shi Měiguo Huáqiáo, Zhōngwén bú tài hǎo. Wǒ bù zhīdào tāde Zhōngwén míngzi. Búguò, tāde Yīngwén míngzi jiào "Mary Wang."

I'm really sorry. I'm an overseas Chinese from America and my Chinese isn't too good. I don't know her Chinese name. But her English name is "Mary Wang."

5. **CHINESE:**   哦，我知道了。是王国丽。不过，她现在不在这儿。

Ò, wǒ zhīdaole. Shi Wáng Guólì. Búguò, tā xiànzài bú zài zhèr.

Oh, now I know. It's Wang Guoli. But she's not here right now.

6. **ENG:**   请问，你知道她在哪儿吗？

Qǐng wèn, nǐ zhīdao tā zài nǎr ma?

Excuse me, would you know where she is?

7. **CHINESE:**   她在老板的办公室。

Tā zài lǎobǎnde bàngōngshì.

She's in the boss's office.

8. **ENG:**   那，我可不可以给她留一个条子？

Nà, wǒ kě bu kéyi gěi tā liú yíge tiáozi?

In that case, may I leave her a note?

9. **CHINESE:**   当然可以。

Dāngrán kéyi.

Of course you may.

10. **ENG:**   谢谢。

Xièxie.

Thanks.

New Vocabulary

想	**xiǎng**	want to, would like to
找	**zhǎo**	look for
在	**zài**	be present; be located at
实在	**shízài**	really, truly
抱歉	**bàoqiàn**	feel sorry, regret
华侨	**Huáqiáo**	overseas Chinese
知道	**zhīdao**	know
不过	**búguò**	however
英文	**Yīngwén**	English (language)
这儿	**zhèr**	here
老板	**lǎobǎn**	boss, owner
办公室	**bàngōngshì**	office

可以	**kéyi**	may, can
留	**líu**	leave (someone something)
条子	**tiáozi**	note
当然	**dāngrán**	of course

Supplementary Vocabulary

哥哥	**gēge**	older brother
要是	**yàoshi**	if
怎么办	**zěmme bàn**	"what should be done?"
桌子	**zhuōzi**	table
椅子	**yǐzi**	chair
那儿	**nàr**	there
张	**zhāng**	(measure for tables, name cards)
把	**bǎ**	(measure for chairs, umbrellas)

Notes on the Conversation

Zài as main verb

Zài is one of the most common verbs in Chinese. It has a number of different functions and usages. You've seen it before used as a coverb in sentences like **Nín zài něige dānwèi gōngzuò?** "In which organization do you work?" In line 2 of this conversation, **Tā zài bu zài?** "Is she present?," **zài** is used as a main verb, without any object, to mean "be present" or "be there." The answers to this question would be **Tā zài** "He/she is present" or **Tā bú zài** "He/she isn't present." As another example, when roll is called in Chinese schools or places of work, as the person in charge reads off each person's name, that person answers with a loud **Zài!** meaning "Present!" In lines 5, 6, and 7 of this conversation, **zài** is also used as a main verb but with a place word as object. When **zài** has an object, it's usually best translated as "be located at" or "be at," so we could translate **Tā xiànzài bú zài zhèr** as "She's not here now," **Tā zài nǎr?** as "Where is she?," and **Tā zài lǎobǎnde bàngōngshì** as "She's in the boss's office." Even though **zài** often translates into English with a form of the verb "to be," be careful to use **zài** and not **shì** for sentences expressing location. For example, English "Where are my name cards?" would be **Wǒde míngpiàn zài nǎr?** and could never be said as *Wǒde míngpiàn shi nǎr?

....

Embedded questions

Examine the question **Qǐng wèn, nǐ zhīdao tā zài nǎr ma?** "Excuse me, do you know where she is?" This sentence is an example of an embedded question, or question within a question; that is, the question **Tā zài nǎr?** "Where is she?" has here been embedded within the question **Nǐ zhīdao ma?** "Do you know?" Because this is an embedded question, both a question word (**nǎr**) and the question particle (**ma**) are present in the same sentence. In normal, unembedded questions, you could never have both a question word and **ma**. More examples: **Nǐ zhīdao tā shi shéi ma?** "Do you know who she is?," **Nǐ zhīdao jīntiān jǐhào ma?** "Do you know what the date is today?," **Nǐ zhīdao zhèige duōshǎo qián ma?** "Do you know how much this is?"

....

Deletion of second syllable of two-syllable verbs in affirmative-negative questions

In line 8, look at the question **Wǒ kě bu kéyi gěi tā liú yíge tiáozi?** "May I leave her a note?" The **kě bu kéyi** here is an abbreviation of the full form **kéyi bu kéyi**. It would not be incorrect to use the full form, but when forming affirmative-negative questions involving two-syllable verbs, Chinese speakers frequently drop the second syllable of the affirmative part of the question. More examples: **zhīdao bu zhīdào → zhī bu zhīdào** "know or don't know?," **yīnggāi bu yīnggāi → yīng bu yīnggāi** "should or should not?," **gāoxìng bu gāoxìng → gāo bu gāoxìng** "happy or unhappy?"

Gěi as a coverb

The literal meaning of **gěi** is "give," but when it co-occurs with other verbs, **gěi** often translates as English "for." In this conversation we see **Wǒ gěi tā liú yíge tiáozi** "I'm going to leave a note for her." The negative of this sentence would be formed by placing **bù** or **méi** right before the **gěi**: **Wǒ bù gěi tā liú yíge tiáozi** "I'm not going to leave a note for her." We actually have encountered **gěi** as a coverb meaning "for" previously in the phrase **wǒ gěi nǐ jièshao yixiar** "let me introduce you." More examples: **Wǒ gěi nǐ mǎile yíge xīnde gōngshìbāo** "I bought a new briefcase for you," **Xiǎo Lǐ gěi Xiǎo Bái kāimén le** "Little Li opened the door for Little Bai."

Reading

New Characters and Words

145.	可	**kě**	may, can; but
	可是	**kěshi**	but
146.	以	**yǐ**	take; use; with (can't be used alone)
	可以	**kéyi**	may, can; be O.K.
147.	知	**zhī**	know (can't be used alone)
148.	道	**dào**	road, way; Taoism (can't be used alone)
	知道	**zhīdao**	know
149.	在	**zài**	be located in, at, on; be present
150.	找	**zhǎo**	look for

A. SENTENCES

一、高先生，请问，您知道今天几月几号吗？

二、我们可不可以去上海住两、三个星期？

三、你知道不知道王太太今天在不在台北？

四、要是她们去湖南省，那我们也要去湖南省。

五、请问，您找谁？是不是找小李的同屋？他今天不在！

六、钱小姐，你知道谢先生在哪个公司吗？

七、我可不可以问您，您今年多大年纪了？

八、您知道广州的人口是多少吗？我不知道。

九、我知道老李的日文不好，可是小关的日文好像也不太好。

十、王大海去找他姐姐，可是他姐姐不在。

B. CONVERSATIONS

一、

美国人：先生贵姓？

中国人：我姓何，我叫何大一。何是"人"、"可"何，大是"大小"的大，一是"一二三"的一。

二、

女：先生，您好！我找王小姐。请问，她在不在？

男：王小姐？哪位王小姐？

女：我是美国人，中文不太好。我不知道她的中文名字。

男：我知道了。是王国金小姐。不过，她不在。她今天没来公司。

C. NARRATIVES

一、今天差不多三点半老万来找我，可是我不在。我去南京的一个公司了，不过我的同屋小王不知道我去了哪个公司。他请老万明天九点来找我。可是，老万明天很忙，他就不来了。

二、我不知道在南京东路的那个公司明天几点开门、几点关门。不过我可以去找我的同屋小金。要是我问她，她也不知道，我就不去了。

"(We) welcome male, female, old, young (to) beautify (their) hair"

Notes

A2. 我们可不可以去 "Can we go...?" is an abbreviated form of 我们可以不可以去, with the same meaning.

A3. It just happens that in this sentence, the full form of the affirmative-negative question is used: 你知道不知道 "Do you know...?" However, the speaker might just as well have asked 你知不知道, with exactly the same meaning.

B1. 先生贵姓? "Sir, what is your honorable surname?" Be aware that this question is being addressed to the person whose last name the speaker wishes to find out; this isn't about a third person. In very polite style, pronouns like 你 and 您 tend to be avoided, people's titles or roles being mentioned instead. In Chinese it would be normal to ask questions that would translate literally into English as "Is this the school president's first trip to America?" or "Does the general manager have any areas where he needs me to help?"

B2a. In the written record of this conversation, 女 and 男 have been used to indicate who is speaking. These are examples of written-style Chinese. In speech, 男 and 女 would not be said alone; instead, you would say 男的 or 男人 for "man," and 女的 or 女人 for "woman."

B2b. 我知道了 "Now I know." Initially, the man didn't know which "Ms. Wang" the woman was looking for, but now he knows.

C1. 可是，老万明天很忙，他就不来了 "But Old Wan is busy tomorrow, so he's not coming."

C2. 要是我问她，她也不知道，我就不去了 "If I ask her, and if she doesn't know either, then I won't go."

PART TWO

Conversation 🎧

Situation: Cindy Han, who is studying Chinese in Beijing, has ordered noodles at a stand in Beijing. She sits down at a table with a young Chinese woman whom she has never met before.

1. HAN:

请问，这个位子有人吗？

Qǐng wèn, zhèige wèizi yǒu rén ma?

Excuse me, is there anyone in this seat?

2. CHINESE WOMAN:

没有，没有。您坐吧。

Méiyou, méiyou. Nín zùo ba.

No. Go ahead and sit down.

3. HAN:

您常来这儿吃午饭吗？

Nín cháng lái zhèr chī wǔfàn ma?

Do you often come here to eat lunch?

4. CHINESE WOMAN:

我常来。您呢？

Wǒ cháng lái. Nín ne?

I come often. And you?

5. HAN:

我也常在这儿吃。您是学生吗？

Wǒ yě cháng zài zhèr chī. Nín shi xuésheng ma?

I eat here often, too. Are you a student?

6. CHINESE WOMAN:

不，我是工人，在北京第一皮鞋厂工作。您呢？

Bù, wǒ shi gōngrén, zài Běijīng Dìyī Píxié Chǎng gōngzuò. Nín ne?

No, I'm a laborer. I work at Beijing Number One Shoe Factory. How about you?

7. HAN: 我在美国是大学生，现在在这儿学中文。
Wǒ zài Měiguo shi dàxuéshēng, xiànzài zài zhèr xué Zhōngwén.
I'm a college student in America, now I'm learning Chinese here.

8. CHINESE WOMAN: 您在哪儿学习？
Nín zài nǎr xuéxí?
Where are you studying?

9. HAN: 在北大的汉语培训中心。
Zài Běidàde Hànyǔ péixùn zhōngxīn.
At the Chinese language training center at Peking University.

10. CHINESE WOMAN: *(looking at her watch)*

哟！快一点了。我得走了。再见！
Yò! Kuài yīdiǎn le. Wǒ děi zǒule. Zàijiàn!
Gosh! It'll soon be one o'clock. I have to be going now. So long!

11. HAN: 再见！
Zàijiàn!
So long!

New Vocabulary

位子	**wèizi**	seat, place
常	**cháng**	often
吃	**chī**	eat
午饭	**wǔfàn**	lunch
学生	**xuésheng**	student
工人	**gōngrén**	worker, laborer
皮	**pí**	leather, skin
鞋	**xié**	shoe
皮鞋	**píxié**	leather shoe
厂	**chǎng**	factory
大学生	**dàxuéshēng**	college student
学	**xué**	learn, study
北大	**Běidà**	Peking University
汉语	**Hànyǔ**	Chinese (language)
培训	**péixùn**	train
中心	**zhōngxīn**	center
快	**kuài**	soon, quickly

Supplementary Vocabulary

早饭	**zǎofàn**	breakfast
中饭	**zhōngfàn**	lunch
晚饭	**wǎnfàn**	dinner, evening meal
饭	**fàn**	rice (cooked); food
吃饭	**chīfàn**	eat food, eat
菜	**cài**	food

Notes on the Conversation

Lái + verb to indicate purpose

The verb **lái** "come" followed by another verb can indicate purpose, for example, **Nín cháng lái zhèr chī wǔfàn ma?** "Do you often come here in order to eat lunch?" A place word, such as **zhèr**, is frequently inserted after the **lái** and before the second verb. Examples: **Yǎwén lái Běijīng zhǎo tāde tóngxué** "Yawen came to Beijing to look for her classmates," **Lín Tàitai měige xīngqīliù lái Táiběi mǎi cài** "Mrs. Lin comes to Taipei every Saturday to buy food." **Nèige Měiguo dàxuéshēng lái wǒmen jiā zuò shémme?** "What is that American college student coming to our house for?"

....

Zài as coverb

Examine the following sentence: **Wǒ zài yìjiā gōngsī gōngzuò** "I work at a company." There are two verbs in this sentence, **zài** "be located at" and **gōngzuò** "work." When **zài** occurs first in a sentence followed by another verb, it is said to be a coverb. Though from the Chinese point of view **zài** is a verb, from the English point of view it often corresponds to prepositions like "in," "at," or "on." One important thing to remember concerning **zài** as a coverb is that in English, the phrase with the "in," "at," or "on" usually occurs after the verb; but in Chinese, the phrase with **zài** always occurs before the main verb. More examples: **Nǐmen zài nǎr shàngkè?** "Where do you have class?," **Tā zài Zhōngguo xuéxí Hànyǔ** "She's studying Chinese in China," **Wǒ bú zài shítáng chīfàn** "I don't eat in the cafeteria."

....

College and university abbreviations

Most Chinese college and university names consist of four syllables—a two-syllable word indicating a place or person after which the university was named, followed by the two-syllable word **dàxué** "college, university." The usual way to abbreviate college and university names is to retain the first and third syllables but drop the second and fourth syllables. Examples: **Běijīng Dàxué → Běidà** "Peking University," **Táiwān Dàxué → Táidà** "Taiwan University," **Zhōngshān Dàxué → Zhōngdà** "Sun Yat-sen University."

....

Kuài (yào)...le to indicate an imminent action or situation

In the conversation, look at the sentence **Kuài yīdiǎn le** "Soon it will be one o'clock." The adverb **kuài** here means "soon," with the **le** at the end of the sentence indicating anticipated change in a situation. The whole sentence means something like "Soon it will be one o'clock and, once it is, the situation will be different than it is now." The auxiliary verb **yào** "will" is commonly added after **kuài** to emphasize the imminent future situation. Examples: **Tā kuài yào zǒu** le "She'll be leaving soon," **Nǐ kuài yào chídào le!** "You'll soon be late!," **Tā kuài sānsuì le** "Soon he'll be three years old."

....

Reading

New Characters and Words

151.	吃	**chī**	eat
152.	饭	**fàn**	cooked rice, food
	吃饭	**chīfàn**	eat food, eat
	中饭	**zhōngfàn**	lunch
	中国饭	**Zhōngguo fàn**	Chinese food
153.	学	**xué**	learn, study
	同学	**tóngxué**	classmate
	学生	**xuésheng**	student
	男学生	**nánxuésheng**	male student
	女学生	**nǔxuésheng**	female student
	大学	**dàxué**	university, college
	大学生	**dàxuéshēng**	college student
154.	工	**gōng**	work
	工人	**gōngrén**	worker, laborer
155.	子	**zi**	(common noun suffix)
	位子	**wèizi**	seat, place
156.	儿	**ér**	(common word suffix)
	这儿	**zhèr**	here
	那儿	**nàr**	there
	哪儿	**nǎr**	where?
	一点儿	**yìdiǎnr**	a little, some
	门儿	**ménr**	door, gate
	同屋儿	**tóngwūr**	roommate
	一半儿	**yíbànr**	half

A. SENTENCES

一、美国人吃美国饭，中国人吃中国饭。你是哪国人？你吃什么饭？

二、这儿很好，也不贵。老师、学生、工人都可以在这儿吃中饭。

三、南京大学也叫南大，在南京市，有32,000个学生，有500多位老师。

四、我们要吃饭了。请男学生坐这儿，请女学生坐那儿。

五、这个位子不太好，那个位子比较好，请您坐那儿吧！

六、我找北京大学。您知道北大在哪儿吗？是不是在这儿？

七、我找高子文，他是我在台大的同学。您知道他在哪儿吗？

八、那个女的好像不是一个大学生，她是一个工人吧。

九、今年在很多美国大学，学中文的女学生多，男学生少。

十、大海，你不要走，先吃一点儿饭吧。

B. CONVERSATIONS

一、

万小姐：李老师，你今年有多少男学生，多少女学生？

李老师：一半儿一半儿吧。

万小姐：你有多少中国学生，多少美国学生？

李老师：也是一半儿一半儿吧。

万小姐：李老师，这儿的学生去哪儿吃饭呢？

李老师：这个……我就不知道了。

二、

学　生：请问，这个位子有人吗？

工　人：没有，没有。你坐吧。

学　生：谢谢！

工　人：你第一次来这儿吃饭吗？

学　生：不，我来过很多次。你是学生吗？

工　人：不，我是工人。你呢？

学　生：我是美国来的大学生，今年在北大学中文。

工　人：一点钟了，我走了。

学　生：我也走了。

C. NARRATIVES

一、我们大学在台湾是很好的大学，叫台湾大学，也叫"台大"。台大在台北市。这个大学很大，有差不多三万个学生，有三千多位老师。台大的学生都很好，在那儿要找好的老师也不太难。我是台大的学生，这是我在那儿的第一年。我姐姐也是台大的学生，这是她的第三年。

二、那个美国大学生问我，在哪儿学中文比较好？我知道在北大学中文很好。那儿有很多很好的中国学生，美国学生也不少。那儿的老师也都比较好。美国学生可以在北大住，也可以在那儿吃饭，都不贵。吃、住一个月好像一千多块钱。中文很难，可是你要是要学，在北大学比较好。这是北京大学王国安老师的名片。你明天可以去北大找王老师问问。

Notes

A7.　他是我在台大的同学 "He's a classmate of mine at Taiwan University."

A9.　学中文的女学生多，男学生少 "There are many female students studying Chinese, but few male students." In the case of contrasting clauses like this, in Chinese it's often not necessary to have a 可是 or 不过. However, a "but" can sometimes be added to the English to make the translation smoother.

B2.　我是美国来的大学生 "I'm a college student from America."

C2.　你明天可以去北大找王老师问问 "Tomorrow you can go to Peking University and look for Teacher Wang and ask." Regarding the verb duplication of 问问, some one-syllable verbs are frequently reduplicated (that is, repeated) so as to give a relaxed, casual sense to the verb and make the sentence they occur in sound smoother and less abrupt. The meaning is the same as when they are not reduplicated. Note that 问问 is pronounced with a neutral tone on the second syllable as **wènwen**.

Locating Persons, Places, and Things (II)

PART ONE

Conversation 🎧

Situation: Adam Norris, a businessman on a brief trip to Beijing, has a lunch appointment with his Chinese friend, Li Zongxian. Late due to a traffic jam, he finally arrives at the restaurant and asks the cashier where the restroom is.

1. **NORRIS:** 请问，厕所在哪儿?

   Qǐng wèn, cèsuǒ zài nǎr?

   Excuse me, where's the bathroom?

2. **CASHIER:** 在那边儿。

   Zài nèibianr.

   It's over there.

3. **NORRIS:** *(emerges from restroom and walks over to Li's table):*

   小李，对不起，让你久等了。

   Xiǎo Lǐ, duìbuqǐ, ràng nǐ jiǔ děngle.

   Little Li, sorry, I made you wait a long time.

4. LI: 没事儿，没事儿。小罗，好久不见了！你可瘦了一点儿。
            你这回来北京住在哪儿？

            Méi shìr, méi shìr. Xiǎo Luó, hǎo jiǔ bú jiànle! Nǐ kě shòule yidianr. Nǐ zhèihuí lái Běijīng zhùzai nǎr?

            That's O.K. Adam, haven't seen you for a long time! You sure have gotten thinner. Where are you staying on this trip to Beijing?

5. NORRIS: 住在长城饭店，七一五号房间。你还是住在老地方吗？

            Zhùzai Cháng Chéng Fàndiàn, qī-yāo-wǔ-hào fángjiān. Nǐ hái shi zhùzai lǎo dìfang ma?

            I'm staying at the Great Wall Hotel, room 715. Are you still living where you were before?

6. LI: 不，我们去年就搬到香山了。

            Bù, wǒmen qùnián jiù bāndao Xiāng Shān le.

            No, last year we moved to Fragrant Hills.

7. NORRIS: 香山在哪儿？

            Xiāng Shān zài nǎr?

            Where is Fragrant Hills?

8. LI: 在北京城的北边儿。

            Zài Běijīng chéngde běibiānr.

            To the north of Beijing city.

New Vocabulary

厕所	cèsuǒ	toilet
那边(儿)	nèibian(r)	that side, there
让	ràng	let, cause, make
让你久等了	ràng nǐ jiǔ děngle	"made you wait a long time"
没事(儿)	méi shì(r)	"it's nothing," "never mind"
可	kě	indeed, certainly
瘦	shòu	be thin, lean, skinny
回	huí	time
在	-zài	at, in, on
长城	Cháng Chéng	Great Wall
饭店	fàndiàn	hotel
长城饭店	Cháng Chéng Fàndiàn	Great Wall Hotel
一	yāo	one
地方	dìfang	place
搬	bān	move (a thing or one's home)
到	-dào	arrive at, to

香山	xiāng	be fragrant, smell good
山	shān	mountain, hill
香山	Xiāng Shān	Fragrant Hills
城	chéng	city
北边(儿)	běibiān(r)	north

Supplementary Vocabulary 🎧

哪边	něibiān	which side, where
南边	nánbiān	south
东边	dōngbiān	east
西边	xībiān	west
这边	zhèibian	this side, here
胖	pàng	be fat (of people or animals)

Notes on the Conversation

Stative verb + yìdiǎn(r) to express "a little more…"

The pattern stative verb + **yìdiǎn(r)** means "a little more…," for example, **Nèige guì yìdiǎnr** "That one is a little more expensive." The **yìdiǎn(r)** often loses its tones to become neutral tone **yidian(r)** and the syllable **yi** is often dropped in rapid speech; the final **r**-suffix is optional. More examples: **Zhèige piányi dianr** "This one is a little cheaper," **Yǒu hǎo yìdiǎnde ma?** "Are there better ones?," **Nǐ pàngle yidianr!** "You've gotten a little fatter!"

....

-zài as postverb

You've previously learned **zài** as a main verb and coverb. In this lesson you learn **zài** as a postverb, which is a type of verb that is suffixed onto the main verb of a sentence to link the action of the main verb to a following object. For example, in the sentence **Wǒ zhùzai Cháng Chéng Fàndiàn** "I'm staying at the Great Wall Hotel," **zhù** "live, stay" is the main verb and **-zài** "at, in, on" is the postverb. The number of postverbs in Chinese is limited, **-zài** and **-dào** being the most common ones. In rapid conversation, postverbs frequently lose their tone. Examples with **-zài**: **Lǐ Tàitai zhùzai nǎr?** "Where does Mrs. Li live?," **Wǒ zhùzai Nánjīng** "I live in Nanjing," **Nín zuòzai zhèr, hǎo ma?** "Why don't you sit here, all right?" It would be possible to transform all of these sentences into coverb sentences with **zài**, for example, **Lǐ Tàitai zhùzai nǎr?** → **Lǐ Tàitai zài nǎr zhù?** "Where does Mrs. Li live?" In rapid, colloquial speech, the postverb **-zài** is sometimes omitted.

....

-dào as postverb

In the sentence **Wǒmen qùnián jiù bāndao Xiāng Shān le** "Last year we moved to Xiang Shan," we encounter our second postverb, **-dào**. In this sentence, **bān** is the main verb, **-dào** is a postverb meaning "to," and **Xiāng Shān** is the object of **-dào**. As in the case of the postverb **-zài**, in rapid conversation **-dào** often becomes neutral tone, being pronounced as **-dao**. Examples: **Tāmen bāndao nǎr le?** "Where did they move to?," **Wǒ yào zuòdao Tiānānmén** "I'm going to take it (a bus or trolley) to Tiananmen,"

Wǒ xiǎng zhùdao xià xīngqī'èr "I'd like to stay until next Tuesday," **Yǔyán shíyànshì xiàwǔ kāidao wǔdiǎn zhōng** "The language lab is open in the afternoon until five o'clock."

....

Points of the compass

The words for the four basic points of the compass, in the order they are usually said in Chinese, are: **dōng** "east," **nán** "south," **xī** "west," **běi** "north." Grammatically speaking, these terms are localizers and, with few exceptions, can't be said alone. They are usually combined with **-biān(r)** "side" to create the place words **dōngbiān(r)** "east, east side," **nánbiān(r)** "south, south side," **xībiān(r)** "west, west side," **běibiān(r)** "north, north side."

....

Reading

New Characters and Words

157.	地	**dì**	the ground; place
158.	方	**fāng**	square, open space (can't be used alone)
	地方	**dìfang**	place
159.	边	**biān**	side
	这边	**zhèbian**	this side, here
	那边	**nàbiān**	that side, there
	哪边	**nǎbiān**	what side?, where?
	东边	**dōngbiān**	in the east
	南边	**nánbiān**	in the south
	西边	**xībiān**	in the west
	北边	**běibiān**	in the north
160.	事	**shì**	matter, thing (abstract)
	一点事	**yìdiǎn shì**	a little something to do
	没事儿	**méi shìr**	"it's nothing," "never mind"
	同事	**tóngshì**	colleague
161.	回	**huí**	go back to; time
	回国	**huíguó**	return to one's native country
	第一回	**dìyīhuí**	the first time
162.	店	**diàn**	shop, store
	饭店	**fàndiàn**	hotel

A. SENTENCES

一、香山那个地方不难找，我有两位老同事住在那儿。

二、你的那位同事住在什么地方？他是不是住在南京路？

三、这个地方大学很多，北边有一个大学，南边也有一个大学。

四、你们要是没事儿，五点半回饭店吃饭比较好。

五、你去年是不是回过国？回了几天呢？

六、这回我们回中国，好像饭店都贵了一点儿，人也都老了一点儿。

七、广西省在广东省的西边，海南省在广东省的南边。

八、山东省在河南省的东边，山西省在河南省的北边。

九、这个地方的人口比较多，那个地方的人口比较少。

十、王大海知道，有很多事，第一回很难，第二回、第三回就不难了。

B. CONVERSATIONS

一、

小王：小李，问你一下儿，我星期日带同学来，可以吗？

小李：可以。这个地方星期日不关门。

小王：谢谢你！

小李：没事儿。

二、

高先生：小李，你这回来北京住在哪儿？

李先生：我住在北京饭店，七一五号。

高先生：北京饭店在哪儿呢？

李先生：在北京市的东边儿。你住在老地方？

高先生：对，我们住在香山，你去年去过。

李先生：老高，我这回来北京，有很多事儿谢谢你！

高先生：没事儿，没事儿。

"Beijing Hotel"

C. NARRATIVES

一、我住的地方在我们公司的东边。公司的南边有一个大学，叫南山大学。有一个美国人在那个大学学中文。他没事儿就来我的公司找我，差不多一个星期来一、两次。要是我不在，他就来找我的同事老王。

二、北京在河北省，在中国的北边。北京市北边、西边都是山，西边那儿的山叫"西山"。北京是一个很老的地方，有三千多年了。2010年北京人口有差不多22,000,000。

Notes

A1a. 香山那个地方 literally means "Fragrant Hills, that place." In better English, we might translate this as "That place called Fragrant Hills" or just "The place called Fragrant Hills." It's common in Chinese to add an appositive phrase after a noun that further describes the noun.

A1b. The 老 of 老同事 "old colleagues" refers to colleagues whom you've worked with for a long time, not "aged" colleagues.

A5. 你去年是不是回过国？回了几天呢？ "Did you return to your native country last year? For how many days did you return?" Since 回国 is a Verb-Object Compound, it can be split by grammatical suffixes like 过 in this way.

A7. 广西省在广东省的西边. Grammatically, this could mean either "Guangxi Province is to the west of Guangdong Province" or "Guangxi Province is in the west of Guangdong Province." Of course, common sense tells us that the second interpretation isn't possible.

B2. 你住在老地方？ "You're living in the same place as before?" This is an Intonation Question.

C1a. 他没事儿就来我的公司找我 "When he has nothing to do, he comes to my company looking for me." Here 没事儿 retains its literal meaning of "not have matters (that one has to do)" rather than being an idiomatic expression used after someone thanks you that means "never mind" or "don't mention it."

C1b. 差不多一个星期来一、两次 "He comes about once or twice a week."

C2. Though Beijing municipality is surrounded on all sides by Hebei Province, administratively it isn't considered part of it.

PART TWO

Conversation 🎧

Situation: Guo Zhiwen, a Taipei businessman, has invited Peter Walters, who works part-time at Guo's office, to visit him. The two men are chatting in the living room of Guo's condominium when Guo suggests they go to his study to look at the new computer he has just bought.

1. **GUO:**   Peter, 我买了一台新电脑，在书房里。你要不要看看？
    Peter, wǒ mǎile yìtái xīn diànnǎo, zài shūfángli. Nǐ yào bu yao kànkan?
    Peter, I bought a new computer, it's in the study. Do you want to see it?

2. **WALTERS:**   好啊！呃，是一台五八六吗？里面有多少RAM？
    Hǎo a! E, shi yìtái wǔ-bā-liù ma? Lǐmiàn yǒu duōshǎo RAM?
    Sure! Uh, is it a Pentium? How much RAM is there in it?

3. **GUO:**   三十二个。
    Sānshi'èrge.
    32.

4. **WALTERS:**   *Walters (sits down at computer and tries to turn it on):*

    开关应该在旁边吧？
    Kāiguān yīnggāi zài pángbiān ba?
    The switch ought to be on the side, I suppose?

5. **GUO:**   不对，在前面。
    Bú duì, zài qiánmian.
    No, it's in front.

6. WALTERS: 哦。呃，我可不可以看看使用手册？

              Ò. E, wǒ kě bu kéyi kànkan shǐyòng shǒucè?

              Oh. Uh, could I see the operating manual?

7. GUO: 当然可以。就在你左边的那个书架上——哦，不对，不对，是在你后面的那把椅子上。

              Dāngrán kéyi. Jiù zài nǐ zuǒbiānde nèige shūjiàshang—ò, bú duì, bú duì, shi zài nǐ hòumiande nèibǎ yǐzishang.

              Of course you can. It's right on that bookcase to your left—oh, no, it's on that chair in back of you.

8. WALTERS: 哎哟，桌子底下是什么东西啊？

              Āiyò, zhuōzi dǐxia shi shémme dōngxi a?

              Hey, what is that under the table?

9. GUO: 哦，是来福，我们家的狗。你不要管它！

              Ò, shi Láifú, wǒmen jiāde gǒu. Nǐ búyào guǎn ta.

              Oh, it's Laifu, our family's dog. Don't worry about him.

New Vocabulary 🎧

台	**tái**	(measure for computers, TV sets)
电脑	**diànnǎo**	computer
书房	**shūfáng**	study
里	**lǐ**	in, inside
要	**yào**	want to
五八六	**wǔ-bā-liù**	Pentium® (brand of computer)
里面	**lǐmiàn**	in, inside
开关	**kāiguān**	switch
旁边	**pángbiān**	at or on the side, next to
前面	**qiánmian**	in front, front
使用	**shǐyòng**	use, employ
手册	**shǒucè**	handbook, manual
使用手册	**shǐyòng shǒucè**	operating manual
左边	**zuǒbian**	left side, left
书架	**shūjià**	bookshelf, bookcase
上	**shàng**	on top, on
后面	**hòumian**	in back, back
哎哟	**āiyò**	(indicates surprise)
底下	**dǐxia**	underneath
东西	**dōngxi**	thing

狗	gǒu	dog
管	guǎn	concern oneself with
它	tā	it (animal or thing)

Supplementary Vocabulary 🎧

哥哥	gēge	older brother
前	qián	in front, front
前头	qiántou	in front, front
前边	qiánbian	in front, front
前面	qiánmian	in front, front
后	hòu	in back, back
后头	hòutou	in back, back
后边	hòubian	in back, back
后面	hòumian	in back, back
里	lǐ	in, inside
里头	lǐtou	in, inside
里边	lǐbian	in, inside
里面	lǐmiàn	in, inside
外	wài	outside
外头	wàitou	outside
外边	wàibian	outside
外面	wàimian	outside
上	shàng	on top, on
上头	shàngtou	on top, on
上边	shàngbian	on top, on
上面	shàngmian	on top, on
下	xià	on the bottom, under, below
下头	xiàtou	on the bottom, under, below
下边	xiàbian	on the bottom, under, below
下面	xiàmian	on the bottom, under, below
左	zuǒ	left
左边	zuǒbian	left side, left
右	yòu	right
右边	yòubian	right side, right

Notes on the Conversation

-le in sentences with quantified objects to indicate completed action

In a sentence with a verb and a quantified object (such as "a table" or "two chairs"), we must attach a **-le** to the verb if we want to indicate completed action; there is no **le** at the end of the sentence. Look at the first sentence of this conversation: **Wǒ mǎile yìtái xīn diànnǎo** "I bought a new computer." Because there is a verb with a quantified object ("a new computer") and the speaker intends to indicate completed action, a **-le** is attached to **mǎi**, forming **mǎile** and there is no **le** at the end of the sentence. Here are some more examples of **-le** in sentences with quantified objects to indicate completed action: **Lǎo Bái liúle yíge tiáozi** "Old Bái left a note," **Lǎobǎn jīntiān màile wǔtái diànnǎo** "Today the boss sold five computers," **Xiǎo Chén chīle hěn duō dōngxi** "Little Chen ate a lot of things."

Localizers and place words

Localizers are noun-like forms that are used in combination with other words to indicate location. In the sentence **Xīn diànnǎo zài shūfánglǐ** "The new computer is in the study," **lǐ** "in" is a localizer which is attached to the noun **shūfáng** "study" to create the place word **shūfánglǐ** "in the study." The two most common localizers are **lǐ** "in" and **shàng** "on"; they often lose their tones to become **li** and **shang**. Examples: **shūfángli** "in the study," **fángjiānli** "in the room," **shítángli** "in the cafeteria"; **zhuōzishang** "on the table," **diànnǎoshang** "on the computer," **yǐzishang** "on the chair." **Lǐ** and **shàng** frequently combine with the suffixes **-miàn** "side," **-tou** (noun suffix), and **-biān(r)** "side" to create place words. Examples:

Group One (three forms for each):

-miàn	-tou	-biān(r)	English
lǐmiàn	lǐtou	lǐbian(r)	"inside"
wàimian	wàitou	wàibian(r)	"outside"
qiánmian	qiántou	qiánbian(r)	"in front"
hòumian	hòutou	hòubian(r)	"in back"
shàngmian	shàngtou	shàngbian(r)	"on top"
xiàmian	xiàtou	xiàbian(r)	"on the bottom"

Group Two (only one form for each):

		zuǒbian(r)	"left side"
		yòubian(r)	"right side"
		pángbiān(r)	"on the side, next to"
		dǐxia	"underneath"

For the place words in Group One, the forms ending in **-miàn** are considered more "written-style" while the ones ending in **-tou** or **-biānr** are considered more conversational. Place words are always placed directly after the noun they refer to. Examples: **zhuōzi dǐxia** "underneath the table," **túshūguǎn wàimian** "outside the library." This is the opposite order from English. Notice that most of the localizers and place words introduced in this lesson divide into four pairs of opposites based on the following eight word roots, which you should memorize: **qián** "front," **hòu** "back," **lǐ** "inside," **wài** "outside," **shàng** "above," **xià** "below," **zuǒ** "left," **yòu** "right."

Reading

New Characters and Words

163. 里	**lǐ**	in, inside
里边	**lǐbian**	in, inside
里头	**lǐtou**	in, inside
哪里	**náli**	not at all
164. 外	**wài**	outside
外边	**wàibian**	outside
外头	**wàitou**	outside
165. 左	**zuǒ**	left
左边	**zuǒbian**	left side, left
166. 右	**yòu**	right
右边	**yòubian**	right side, right
167. 下	**xià**	on the bottom, under, below; next
下边	**xiàbian**	on the bottom, under, below
下头	**xiàtou**	on the bottom, under, below
下次	**xiàcì**	next time
下个月	**xiàge yuè**	next month
一下	**yíxià**	(softens the verb)
168. 面	**miàn**	side, surface; face
里面	**lǐmiàn**	in, inside
外面	**wàimian**	outside
上面	**shàngmian**	on top, on, above
下面	**xiàmian**	on the bottom, under, below

Sign at the Great Wall in Badaling

A. SENTENCES

一、那个东西我先去找一下儿，要是没有，我们可以在里面问一下儿。

二、坐在高先生左边的那个小姐是谁？高太太在哪儿呢？

三、你要是找我们，我们不是在上面，就是在下面。

四、我上个星期去西安了，这个星期要去成都，下个星期要回天津。

五、我不知道这个公司里头有多少人，可是我知道不少。

六、你的名片就在你左边的那个位子上。

七、这个饭店里有多少工人？好像今天有很多没来，是不是？

八、那个大钟下头是什么东西？

九、那三个人里头一个是我的老师，一个是我的同学，一个是我的学生。

十、王大海在里边找，在外边找，在上边找，在下边找，在左边找，在右边找，可是都没有。

B. CONVERSATIONS

一、

边外山：这边儿的位子上有东西，我们去右边儿坐吧。

金文明：右边儿的位子上也有东西。我们去哪儿呢？

边外山：里边儿的位子上好像没有东西，我们去里边儿坐吧。

二、

方大年：你去哪儿？

左明生：我去里头找开关。

方大年：开关不是在外头吗？

左明生：我不知道。谢谢你！

方大年：哪里，哪里。

C. NARRATIVE

上个月我的同事老金第一次去广州。在广州他先去了中大，就是中山大学。那边的学生很多，差不多八万四千人，也有不少美国学生。老师有八千一百多位。中大里边、外边都有很多饭店可以住，不过外边的饭店比较贵。吃饭也不难，可以在大学里面吃，也可以在外面吃，可是在中大里面吃比较好。老金很高兴他去了广州，也很高兴他住在中山大学的饭店里。下个月十五号他要第二次去广州，这次他的太太也去。

"Cold drinks, food, fruit"

Notes

A2.   坐在高先生左边的那个小姐 "that young lady sitting to the left of Mr. Gao."

A3.   The pattern 不是……就是…… means "if not...then... ."

A6.   你的名片就在你左边的那个位子上 "Your name cards are located at the seat to your left." The 就 here means "exactly, precisely," but in English we would probably not say this.

A9.   那三个人里头 "Of those three people" or "Among those three people." 里头 usually means "in" or "inside," but sometimes it can be translated as "of" or "among."

A10.   可是都没有 "but it was nowhere" (literally, "but in all cases it was not present").

B2a.   开关不是在外头吗？ "Isn't the switch outside?" This is a rhetorical question that indicates the speaker believes the switch is outside.

B2b.   Given the context, 我不知道 here doesn't mean "I don't know" but rather means "I didn't know (the fact that the switch is outside)." In Chinese you could not say *我没知道, since 没 can only be used with action verbs.

Review of Lessons 1–12

Part One: Oral Translation

Instructions: To review the major grammar patterns introduced in the preceding lessons, try interpreting the following English phrases and sentences into spoken Chinese.

LǍO and XIǍO before Monosyllabic Surnames

1. Old Gao
2. Little Wang
3. Old Li
4. Little Zhao
5. Old He
6. Little Lin

TITLES

1. Mr. Wang
2. Ms. Gao
3. Mrs. He
4. Miss Ke
5. Teacher Li
6. Mr. Xie
7. Teacher He
8. Ms. Wang
9. Teacher Lin
10. Mrs. Zhao

QÙ + PLACE WORD to indicate "go to a certain place"

1. She's going to the dining hall.
2. I'm going back to my dorm.
3. Wang Jingsheng is going to the library.
4. We're all going to the cafeteria.
5. He's going to the library to take care of some stuff.
6. I'm going back to my dorm to take care of something.
7. They're all going to the dining hall to work.
8. We're all going to the library to study Chinese.

DÀO...QÙ "go to..."

1. Where is Ke Lei'en going?
2. Where are you going?
3. I'm going to the library.
4. She's also going to the library.
5. Where is Teacher Li going?

QUESTION WORD QUESTIONS

1. Where is he going?
2. Where are they going?
3. Where are your children going?
4. Where are your mom and dad going?
5. Where is Teacher Wang going?

USE of **YĚ** "also, too"

1. Wang Jingsheng is going; Ke Lei'en is also going.
2. The children are going to the library; the teacher is also going.
3. You're going to the dining hall; I'm going, too.
4. She is busy; I'm busy, too.
5. He's returning to his dorm; I'm returning to the dorm, too.

STATIVE VERB SENTENCES

1. I'm sleepy.
2. He is good.
3. My mom is busy.
4. Her husband is tired.
5. They're all fine.

6. Chinese is hard.
7. Their studies are intense.
8. He's very old.
9. We are nervous.
10. They're tall; I'm short.

MA to transform Statements into Questions

1. Are you going to the library?
2. Are you tired?
3. Is she going to the dining hall?
4. Is your dad well?
5. Are you going to take care of some things?
6. Are they all busy?
7. Are you returning to the dorm?
8. Are your spouse and children all well?

IMPERATIVES with **QǏNG**

1. Please go to the library.
2. Please go to the cafeteria.
3. Please go back to your dorm.
4. Please sit down.

5. Please thank her.
6. Please leave.
7. Please come in.

AFFIRMATIVE-NEGATIVE QUESTIONS

1. Is Chinese easy?
2. Are you sleepy?
3. Is your father busy?
4. Is she nervous?
5. Is your mother all right?

6. Are you exhausted?
7. Are they all going?
8. Is your work busy?
9. Are your studies intense?
10. Does she study Chinese?

BÙ/BÚ to negate Verbs

1. I won't go.
2. He's not happy.
3. She doesn't work.
4. We're not busy.
5. Mr. Wang isn't nervous.
6. They don't study Chinese.
7. I'm not going back to the dormitory.

NE as Final Particle to abbreviate Questions

1. I work. And you?
2. I'm fine. How about you?
3. They're all going. And you all?
4. I study Chinese. And you?
5. I'm not busy. How about you?
6. We're not going. How about you all?
7. I'm going to the dining hall. And what about you?
8. She's returning to her dorm. And you?
9. I'm going to the library. How about you?
10. Ke Lei'en is going to do some things. How about Wang Jingsheng?

STATIVE VERBS before Nouns as Adjectives

1. a good mother
2. a good father
3. a good teacher
4. small matters
5. good jobs
6. the (same) old way (as before)

TĬNG...-DE

1. quite intense
2. quite easy
3. very nervous
4. very good
5. very old
6. very busy
7. very sleepy
8. very exhausted
9. very difficult

LE to indicate a Changed Situation

1. I'm O.K. now.
2. I have to be leaving now.
3. Have they gotten well?
4. We're not going anymore.
5. Is your father all right now?
6. He's gone to the library.
7. Where've you gone?
8. He's not nervous anymore.
9. I'm not working any longer.
10. They're not learning Chinese any more.
11. She's no longer small.
12. I won't sit any longer.

SHÌ in EQUATIVE VERB SENTENCES

1. I'm American.
2. She's Japanese.
3. He's Chinese.
4. What nationality are you?
5. Little Gao is English.
6. She's a teacher.
7. I'm a teacher, too.
9. Are you Spanish?
10. You're not Taiwanese?

Attention! The next few sentences mix up stative verbs and equative verbs. Which is which?

11. They're all from Hong Kong.
12. They're all busy.
13. Is she Malaysian?
14. Is she happy?
15. He's Chinese.
16. He's happy.
17. They're teachers.
18. They're tired.
19. He's Singaporean.
20. Chinese is interesting.

QUESTION WORD SENTENCES

1. Where do you work?
2. Where is he going?
3. What's your name?
4. How are you? (said to a classmate)
5. What are you bringing?
6. How are your mom and dad? (said to a classmate)
7. What country are you from?
8. Which one? (of several things)
9. Who is she? What's her name?
10. Where are you going?

MÉI to indicate Past Negative of Action Verbs

1. I didn't go.
2. He didn't work.
3. She didn't leave.
4. They didn't come.
5. I didn't call him Little Li.
6. We didn't welcome him.
7. I didn't sit.
8. I didn't bring name cards.
9. I didn't get it wrong.
10. They didn't ask.
11. They didn't welcome me.

JIÀO in EQUATIVE VERB SENTENCES

1. My name is **Bái Jiéruì**.
2. My name is **Zhào Guócái**.
3. My name is **Zhāng Lìxiàn**.
4. My name is **Zāng Tīngshēng**.
5. His name is **Dīng Kǎi**.
6. Her name is **Wáng Yíng**.
7. What is your name?
8. What is her name?
9. What are their names?

XÌNG in EQUATIVE VERB SENTENCES

1. My last name is Chen.
2. Her family name is Bai.
3. That manager's surname is Hou.
4. That teacher's name is Wu.
5. This gentleman's last name is Luo.
6. That lady's family name is Zhao.
7. That Chinese-American's name is Wang.
8. What's your last name?
9. Is your last name Zhao, too?
10. That school president's name is Wang.

Now be careful! Some of the following require **jiào** *while others require* **xìng**.

11. His name is Li.
12. That teacher's name is **Zhào Guócái**.
13. What's your last name?
14. My name is Wang.
15. What's your whole name?
16. My name is **Wáng Táishēng**.
17. My name is **Hé, Hé Zhìwén**.
18. His name is **Hé Zhìwén**, too!
19. My name isn't He, my name is Li

BÙ DŌU "not all" vs. DŌU BÙ "all not"

1. We're not all Americans.
2. None of us is American.
3. None of them is Chinese.
4. Not all of them are Chinese.
5. Not all of us are teachers.
6. None of us are teachers.
7. We're all unhappy.
8. Not all of us are happy.
9. None of us work at the embassy.
10. Not all of us work at the embassy.
11. None of us is a colleague of hers.
12. Not all of us are colleagues of hers.

*The following sentences involve **méi dōu** "didn't all" vs. **dōu méi** "all didn't," which operate similarly to **bù dōu** vs. **dōu bù**.*

1. We didn't all go.
2. None of us went.
3. They didn't all leave.
4. None of them left.

5. Not all of them came.
6. None of them came.
7. Not all of them asked.
8. None of them asked.

ZHÈ and NÀ as Pronoun Subjects

1. This is **Wáng Àihuá**.
2. That is **Chén Lì**.
3. Who's that?
4. This is my name card.
5. This is my teacher.
6. That's my dad.
7. That's my mom.
8. This is Malaysia. (for example, on a map)
9. That is Hong Kong. (for example, on a map)
10. Is that Singapore? (for example, pointing down from an airplane)

ZHÈI- and NÈI- as Specifiers with the Polite Measure WÈI

1. this teacher
2. that school president
3. this fellow student
4. that (unmarried) young lady
5. this teacher
6. that (married) lady
7. which gentleman?
8. which teacher?

9. that Mr. Zhao
10. this Miss Li
11. that colleague
12. which Mr. Shi?
13. which manager?
14. this Chinese-American
15. that general manager

-DE to indicate Possession

1. my roommate
2. your new classmate
3. her college
4. his company
5. Mr. Wang's new colleague
6. our school president
7. our teacher

8. my name card
9. Mrs. Chen's name card
10. your child
11. your name
12. their company
13. our embassy
14. their unit/organization

-DE to indicate that what precedes describes what follows

1. Mr. Zhang from our library (= "our library's Mr. Zhang")
2. Ms. Gao from our dining hall (= "our dining hall's Ms. Gao")
3. a person from the U.S. Embassy (= "U.S. Embassy's person")
4. Mr. Wang from the Canadian Embassy
5. Miss Li from Sino-American Trading Company
6. Mrs. Xie from the English Embassy
7. the general manager of our firm
8. the Chinese University of Hong Kong's president

BIÉ OR BÚYÀO to indicate Negative Imperative

1. Don't go!
2. Don't leave!
3. Don't be nervous.
4. Don't say it like that.
5. Don't bring name cards.
6. Don't call me Mr. Gao.
7. Don't call her Miss Shi.
8. Don't come to America.
9. Don't go to China.
10. Don't address me like that.

BA to indicate Supposition

1. I guess you're American, too?
2. I suppose you're busy, too?
3. Your work also must be pretty intense?
4. I suppose you also are a classmate of hers?
5. I guess you don't know him either?
6. I guess this is your name card?
7. She must be your wife?
8. I guess you also work at that company?
9. I guess they're Japanese, too?
10. I guess your husband isn't Taiwanese?
11. I suppose she's English.
12. I suppose you must be tired?

DÀO...LÁI

1. Welcome to America!
2. Welcome to Britain!
3. Welcome (you, singular) to China!
4. Welcome (you, plural) to America!
5. Please come to the library.
6. Please come to the dining hall.
7. Please come to the embassy.
8. Please come to the work unit.
9. Please (you, plural) come to the company.
10. Please (you, plural) come to the Foreign Ministry.

-LE to indicate Completed Action

1. He went.
2. They came.
3. I asked.
4. You got it wrong.
5. Have they gone?
6. She brought them. (for example, name cards)
7. The matters, we took care of all of them.
8. Dad, Mom, and the children all left.
9. Have the new classmates all come?
10. The new teachers, he introduced them all.

YÍXIÀ(R) after Verbs to make them less abrupt

1. go
2. come
3. ask
4. say
5. listen
6. ask
7. sit
8. introduce

TIĀN as Measure meaning "day"

1. one day
2. two days
3. how many days?
4. that day
5. which day?
6. every day

DAYS of the WEEK

1. Sunday
2. Friday
3. Which day of the week?
4. Thursday
5. Monday, Wednesday, Friday
6. Tuesday, Thursday, Saturday
7. What day of the week is today?
8. Today is Tuesday.
9. Yesterday was Monday.
10. Tomorrow is Wednesday.

DAYS of the MONTH

1. the first
2. the thirty-first
3. the tenth
4. July 4th
5. December 25th
6. October 2nd
7. May 3rd
8. January 1st
9. February 28th
10. September 6th
11. Which day of the month?
12. Which day in August?

MONTHS of the YEAR

1. November
2. March
3. September
4. June
5. October
6. April (careful!)
7. four months (careful!)
8. December
9. August
10. May
11. July
12. January
13. Which month?
14. February
15. two months (careful!)

YEARS of the CALENDAR

1. 1999
2. 1985
3. 2002
4. 1987
5. 1793
6. Which year?
7. This year is 2012.
8. Last year was 2011.
9. Next year is 2013.
10. The year before last was 2010.
11. The year after next will be 2014.
12. Which year?

Large Numbers from 10,000 to One Billion

1. 10,000; 20,000; 30,000
2. 100,000; 200,000; 300,000
3. 1,000,000; 2,000,000; 3,000,000
4. 10 million, 20 million, 30 million
5. 100 million, 200 million, 300 million
6. 800 million, 900 million, one billion
7. 1,001
8. 10,001
9. 100,001

DUŌ to express "more than"

1. more than $100
2. more than $1,000
3. more than $2,000
4. more than $5,000
5. more than 100 people
6. more than 1,000 people
7. more than 10,000 people

TIME "when" before PLACE

1. I was born in 1985 in America.
2. She was born in 1989 in England.
3. He was born in 1992 in Spain.

4. My roommate was born in 1994 in Malaysia.
5. My teacher was born in 1949 in China.

TIME SPENT after the verb

1. I'll come tomorrow for two hours.
2. In 2001 I went for three months.
3. She came for six weeks last year.
4. The language lab is open half the day on Saturday.
5. The library is open for eight hours on Sunday.

Floors of Buildings with **LÓU**

1. first floor
2. second floor
3. third floor
4. fourth floor

5. 8th floor
6. 15th floor
7. 23rd floor
8. Which floor?

DÌ- to create Ordinal Numbers

1. the second person
2. the fourth time
3. The number what time?
4. the first teacher
5. the first day
6. the second day
7. the tenth day

8. the first year
9. the second year
10. the third person
11. the first one
12. the second one
13. the third one

-GUO to express Experience

1. Have you ever been to China?
2. I've been to China.
3. I've been four times.
4. She's never been to Beijing.
5. Have you ever been to Taibei?
6. I've been to Taibei twice.
7. They haven't ever been to Taibei.
8. Have you ever taken a train?
9. I've taken a train before.
10. My little sister has also taken a train before.
11. My little brother has never taken a train before.

NUMBER + MEASURE + NOUN

1. one person
2. two teachers (ordinary speech)
3. two teachers (polite speech)
4. three roommates
5. four months

6. five days (careful!)
7. six years (careful!)
8. seven cups
9. fifty backpacks
10. 200 bags

SPECIFIER + MEASURE + NOUN

1. this person
2. that person
3. this dining hall
4. that library
5. that address
6. that day (careful!)
7. Which day? (careful!)
8. How many days? (careful!)
9. this week
10. that month
11. How many teachers? (ordinary speech)
12. How many teachers? (polite speech)
13. that Canadian
14. this organization
15. Which year?
16. How many years?

SHI...-DE to express TIME or PLACE of Known Past Actions

1. What year did they come?
2. They came in 2005.
3. Where were you born?
4. I was born in America.
5. He was born in China.
6. She was born in Taiwan.
7. When were you (plural) born?
8. I was born in 1993.
9. She was born in 1999.
10. He was born in 2003.
11. Mr. Duval was born in 1986 in France.
12. When was your father born?
13. He was born in 1966.
14. When was your mother born?
15. She was born in 1964.
16. What day and what month were you born?
17. I was born on November 24, 2005.
18. What day did he leave?
19. He left last Thursday.
20. They came by train.

HǍOXIÀNG ("it seems," "it looks like...")

1. It seems it's not her.
2. It seems Little Li has already come.
3. It seems Old Xie has not yet come.
4. Apparently her last name is Bai.
5. It seems like you're not very happy.
6. I think they've never been to Malaysia before.
7. It seems like he's come here before.

Part Two: Written Translation

Instructions: Translate the following 50 sentences into Pinyin and/or characters and hand them in to your instructor for correction. These sentences were designed to review the most important grammar patterns and vocabulary in the preceding lessons.

1. Mr. Zhao is a good teacher; he is very interesting.
2. Chinese isn't too hard and it also isn't too easy.
3. Miss Ke, welcome! Please come in, please sit down.
4. Mrs. Li, has your work been busy recently? (be polite)
5. I'm going to take care of some things. How about you?
6. She is very tall; her mom and dad are also both very tall.
7. I'll go to the library; you please go back to the dormitory.
8. We've all gotten tired. Have you (plural) also gotten tired?
9. I have a little something to do; I must be going now. Goodbye!
10. Little Lin, how are you? Long time no see! Where are you going?

11. I know Ms. Ma from the U.S. Embassy.

12. I suppose your studies must be very intense.

13. General Manager He, welcome to America! (be polite)

14. A: Sorry, I got it wrong, I didn't bring name cards. B: Never mind.

15. Excuse me, who is that? What's her name? What unit does she work in?

16. Don't address me like that. It would be better if you called me Little Wu.

17. My mother and I work at a trading company, my dad doesn't work anymore.

18. I'll introduce you: this gentleman is my new colleague; his last name is Bai.

19. Old Wang, don't go back to the dining hall. It would be better if you went to the library.

20. They're my classmates; they're not all Americans. Little Lin is Chinese; she's very busy.

21. How much is nine plus eight minus six?

22. This bag is cheap. Why don't you buy one too?

23. I don't have an older brother, I also don't have an older sister.

24. In our Chinese class, in all there are twelve classmates, right?

25. This one costs $4,000, that one costs $5,000. Too expensive!

26. Would it be all right if I took a look at your name card? Thanks!

27. I'm afraid the classmate who works in the library is no longer coming.

28. Let me try to think... My mom will be forty-seven years old next month.

29. My mom and dad are coming at 11:45; it will still take an hour and a half.

30. A: How much does that cup cost? B: This cup only costs two dollars and ninety-eight cents.

31. She was born in Taipei on July 23, 1995.

32. This is the third time that he's going to China.

33. It seems that Hong Kong has more than seven million people.

34. It seems yesterday was October 17, a Wednesday. Is that right?

35. This is my second time coming here; this time I'm going to stay for three months.

36. That trading company is open half-days on Saturdays; it's closed on Sundays.

37. The library opens daily at 8:45 in the morning and closes at 7:30 in the evening.

38. I've been to Shanghai, but I've never been to Guangzhou. Have you been there?

39. The first person wants to go for one day; the second person wants to go for one year.

40. Her address is 6th Floor, No. 108, Alley 22, Lane 345, Nanjing East Road Section Three.

41. If you're tired, you may sleep here.

42. Little Sun, do you know where the boss is?

43. Miss Zhang was not in. I left her a message.

44. Is she also studying Chinese at Peking University?

45. Last year they moved to Tianjin; it's east of Beijing.

46. Next month Mrs. Chen is coming here to study English.

47. The dog was on the bookshelf; the child was under the table.

48. This computer is a little cheaper, that computer is a little more expensive.

49. It will soon be 12:00. The shoe factory workers will soon be eating lunch.

50. A: Where does Mr. Bai live? B: He lives in Nanjing, to the west of Shanghai.

LESSON 14
Conversation with a Six-year-old

PART ONE

Conversation 🎧

Situation: Harvey Rosenthal, who is studying Chinese in Beijing, has been invited to visit his teacher's home. While he's sitting in the living room of his teacher's apartment, the teacher's six-year-old son enters the room.

1. CHILD: 叔叔，你好！
Shūshu, nǐ hǎo!
Hello, uncle!

2. ROSENTHAL: 你好！你叫什么名字？
Nǐ hǎo! Nǐ jiào shémme míngzi?
How are you? What's your name?

3. CHILD: 我叫冬冬。
Wǒ jiào Dōngdong.
My name is Dongdong.

4. ROSENTHAL: 冬冬，你几岁了？
Dōngdong, nǐ jǐsuì le?
Dongdong, how old are you?

5. CHILD:　　六岁了。
　　　　　　　Liùsuì le.
　　　　　　　Six.

6. ROSENTHAL:　你上小学了吧?
　　　　　　　Nǐ shàng xiǎoxué le ba?
　　　　　　　I guess you already go to elementary school?

7. CHILD:　　对，已经上一年级了。
　　　　　　　Duì, yǐjīng shàng yīniánjí le.
　　　　　　　Yes, I'm already in first grade.

8. ROSENTHAL:　*(takes a package from his backpack):*

　　　　　　　冬冬，这是我送给你的小礼物。
　　　　　　　Dōngdong, zhè shi wǒ sònggěi nǐde xiǎo lǐwù.
　　　　　　　Dongdong, this is a little present for you.

9. CHILD:　　谢谢叔叔。
　　　　　　　Xièxie shūshu.
　　　　　　　Thank you, uncle.

10. ROSENTHAL:　不客气。
　　　　　　　Bú kèqi.
　　　　　　　You're welcome.

11. CHILD:　　嗯，真好吃!
　　　　　　　M, zhēn hǎochī!
　　　　　　　Mm, it's really delicious!

New Vocabulary

叔叔	shūshu	uncle (father's younger brother)
上	shàng	go to, attend
小学	xiǎoxué	elementary school
年级	niánjí	grade, level (in school)
一年级	yīniánjí	first grade
送	sòng	give (as a present)
给	-gěi	give; for, to
送给	sònggěi	give (someone as a present)
礼物	lǐwù	gift, present
真	zhēn	really
好吃	hǎochī	be good to eat, delicious

Supplementary Vocabulary

朋友	péngyou	friend
男朋友	nánpéngyou	boyfriend, male friend
女朋友	nǔpéngyou	girlfriend, female friend
好看	hǎokàn	be good-looking
阿姨	āyí	aunt (mother's sister)
喜欢	xǐhuan	like
糖	táng	candy; sugar
初中	chūzhōng	junior high school
高中	gāozhōng	senior high school
中学	zhōngxué	middle school
初一	chūyī	first year in junior high school
初二	chū'èr	second year in junior high school
初三	chūsān	third year in junior high school
高一	gāoyī	sophomore year in high school
高二	gāo'èr	junior year in high school
高三	gāosān	senior year in high school
大一	dàyī	first year in college
大二	dà'èr	sophomore year in college
大三	dàsān	junior year in college
大四	dàsì	senior year in college

Junior high school in Taiwan

Notes on the Conversation

School system and grade in school

The Chinese educational system is divided into **xiǎoxué** "elementary school," **zhōngxué** "middle school," and **dàxué** "university." **Zhōngxué** is in turn divided into **chūzhōng** "junior high school" and **gāozhōng** "senior high school." The verb **shàng** can be used with all of these to mean "go to, attend." Year or grade in a school is expressed by the appropriate number followed by **niánjí** "grade in school." Examples: **èrniánjí** "second grade," **wǔniánjí** "fifth grade." The question word is **jǐniánjí** "which grade?" If you wish to indicate the grade in a certain level of school, then first give the name of the school followed by the grade. Examples: **xiǎoxué sānniánjí** "third grade in elementary school," **chūzhōng èrniánjí** "second year in junior high school," **dàxué sìniánjí** "fourth year at the university." For junior high school and above, it is very common to abbreviate the full expressions for grade in a certain type of school by means of this formula: first syllable of the type of school + the number of the year in school. Examples: **chūyī** "seventh grade," **gāosān** "twelfth grade," **dàyī** "first year in college."

Reading

New Characters and Words

169.	喜	**xǐ**	like, happy, joy (can't be used alone)
170.	欢	**huān**	happy (can't be used alone)
	喜欢	**xǐhuan**	like
171.	朋	**péng**	friend (can't be used alone)
172.	友	**yǒu**	friend (can't be used alone)
	朋友	**péngyou**	friend
	男朋友	**nánpéngyou**	boyfriend
	女朋友	**nǔpéngyou**	girlfriend
173.	真	**zhēn**	real, really
174.	级	**jí**	rank, grade
	年级	**niánjí**	grade (in school)
	几年级	**jǐniánjí**	which grade?
	一年级	**yīniánjí**	first grade

A. SENTENCES

一、我喜欢北京，可是我的朋友都比较喜欢上海。

二、我们要是没事儿，喜欢去北京饭店吃饭，那儿的饭真好吃。

三、我有两个高中同学，一个叫王安，一个叫万安，他们都是我很好
　　的朋友。

四、朋友，你喜欢吃中国饭吗？里边的东西可好吃了，来吧！

五、要是好吃你就多吃一点儿，要是不好吃你就少吃一点儿。

六、金山大一那年，没有朋友。他今年大四，朋友可真多！

七、明年我要上大二，我的女朋友要上大三。

八、这位同学，你多大了？你上几年级？

九、我的同屋是大一的学生，她的男朋友是大四的学生。

十、大海上大学四年级，文文上高中三年级。

B. CONVERSATIONS

一、

美国太太　　：小朋友，你叫什么名字？

中国小朋友：我叫小明。

美国太太　　：小明，你几岁了？

中国小朋友：六岁了。

美国太太　　：你上小学了吧？

中国小朋友：对，上一年级了。
美国太太　：来，这是你的。你喜欢不喜欢？
中国小朋友：我很喜欢，谢谢！真好吃！

"Double happiness"

二、
男：你有没有男朋友？
女：我有男的朋友，可是没有男朋友。
男：你喜欢我吗？
女：你别问我这个！

C. NARRATIVES

一、什么叫"好朋友"？你有事儿可以去找他，他有事儿也可以来找你，这个叫好朋友。坐在那边的那个人就是我的好朋友小王。他的名字叫王大川，他是天津人，今年三十岁。我们小学、中学都是同学。上了大学，大一、大二、大四我们是同屋。我很喜欢小王，小王也很喜欢我。我们两个是好朋友！

二、我去老李的公司找老李，可是老李不在。我问老钱老李在哪儿，可是老钱也不知道老李去什么地方了。老钱要我先在他们公司里吃饭。他们公司的饭真好吃！

"Buffet and lunch boxes" (written from right to left)

Notes

A4a. 朋友 is here used as a vocative. That is, it is addressed to someone and said to attract their attention, much as in English we might say "Hey, friend, could you do me a favor?"

A4b. 里边 "inside" here probably refers to "inside" a restaurant.

A4c. 东西 "things" can be used to refer to food; in fact, 吃的东西 is a common way to say "things to eat" or "food."

A5a. 要是……就…… means "if...then... ."

A5b. 多吃一点儿 means "eat a little more." Similarly, 少吃一点儿, which occurs later in this same sentence, means "eat a little less."

A6a. 金山大一那年 should be parsed as follows: 金山 + 大一 + 那年. Hints: 金山 is a person's name, and 大一 is an abbreviation of 大学一年级.

A6b. 他今年大四，朋友可真多！ "He's a senior this year, and he has really many friends!" (literally, "He this year university fourth grade, friends indeed really many!")

A8. 这位同学, literally "This classmate," is here said to address the student concerned and attract her or his attention. The best English equivalent might be "Excuse me, young lady" or "Excuse me, young man." 这位同学 could be said by anybody (for example, a visitor to the school), not only by a fellow classmate.

B1. 小朋友, literally "Little friend," is often used to address children whose name you don't know, much like English "Little boy" or "Little girl."

B2. For many Chinese speakers, there is a distinction between 男朋友 "boyfriend" and 男的朋友 "male friend," or between 女朋友 "girlfriend" and 女的朋友 "female friend."

C1a. 你有事儿可以去找他 "When you have something (you need help with, you) can go seek him out."

C1b. 坐在那边的那个人 "That person (who is) sitting over there."

C2. 老钱要我先在他们公司里吃饭 "Old Qian wants me to eat in their company first." Regarding 他们公司里, note that there is often no 的 between a personal pronoun and the word 公司, because the connection between a person and her or his company is considered so close. Also, in China many larger companies have dining rooms or canteens for their employees, so it's sometimes possible to invite a person from the outside to join you for a meal in your company.

PART TWO

Conversation 🎧

Situation: Wayne Hammond, a consular officer at the American Institute in Taiwan, is sitting on a bench at the Chiang Kai-shek Memorial in Taipei reading a newspaper, when a Taiwanese man sits down and begins conversing with him.

1. **TAIWANESE MAN:** Hello! 你好！你是美国人吗？
Hello! Nǐ hǎo! Nǐ shi Měiguo rén ma?
Hello! How are you? Are you American?

2. **HAMMOND:** 对，我是美国人。
Duì, wǒ shi Měiguo rén.
Yes, I'm an American.

3. **TAIWANESE MAN:** 美国什么地方？
Měiguo shémme dìfang?
What place in America?

4. **HAMMOND:** 我在纽约出生，然后在旧金山长大的。你是哪里人？
Wǒ zài Niǔyuē chūshēng, ránhòu zài Jiùjīnshān zhǎngdàde. Nǐ shi náli rén?
I was born in New York and then grew up in San Francisco. Where are you from?

5. **TAIWANESE MAN:** 我是台北人。你看起来很年轻诶！还不到三十吧？
Wǒ shi Táiběi rén. Nǐ kànqilai hěn niánqīng ei! Hái bú dào sānshí ba?
I'm a native of Taipei. You sure look young! I suppose you must be under 30?

6. **HAMMOND:** 我今年二十九。
Wǒ jīnnián èrshijiǔ.
I'm twenty-nine.

7. **TAIWANESE MAN:** 结婚了吗？
   Jiéhūnle ma?
   Are you married?

8. **HAMMOND:** 已经结婚了。
   Yǐjīng jiéhūnle.
   Yes, I'm married.

9. **TAIWANESE MAN:** 有没有小孩？
   Yǒu méiyǒu xiǎohái?
   Do you have kids?

10. **HAMMOND:** 有，我们有两个孩子。一个儿子，一个女儿。
    Yǒu, wǒmen yǒu liǎngge háizi. Yíge érzi, yíge nǚ'ér.
    Yes, we have two children. One son and one daughter.

New Vocabulary

纽约	**Niǔyuē**	New York
旧金山	**Jiùjīnshān**	San Francisco
长	**zhǎng**	grow
大	**-dà**	big
长大	**zhǎngdà**	grow up
哪里	**náli**	where
起来	**-qǐlai**	in the VERBing
看起来	**kànqilai**	in the looking
年轻	**niánqīng**	be young
诶	**ei**	(indicates liveliness)
结婚	**jiéhūn**	marry, get married
小孩(儿)	**xiǎohái(r)**	small child, kid
儿子	**érzi**	son
女儿	**nǚ'ér**	daughter

Supplementary Vocabulary

这里	**zhèli**	here
那里	**nàli**	there
做	**zuò**	do, make
搬家	**bānjiā**	move one's home
离婚	**líhūn**	divorce, get divorced
意思	**yìsi**	meaning

Notes on the Conversation

The resultative verb ending -qilai to indicate "in the (verb) -ing"

The resultative verb ending **-qilai** means "in the (performing of the action of some verb)." Examples: **Tā kànqilai hěn lǎo** "She looks very old" ("She in the looking is very old"), **Zhōngwén xuéqilai hěn yǒu yìsi** "Chinese is interesting to learn" ("Chinese in the learning of it is interesting"), **Shuōqilai róngyi, zuòqilai nán** "Easier said than done" ("Talking about it is easy, doing it is hard"), **Zhèige càide míngzi tīngqilai bú tài hǎotīng, kěshi chīqilai zhēn hǎochī!** "The name of this food doesn't sound very nice, but it really tastes great!"

....

How to express "get married to" and "get divorced from"

Jiéhūn is a verb-object compound which means "get married." Example: **Nǐ jiéhūnle ma?** "Are you married?" ("Have you gotten married?") The typical answers to this question would be either **Wǒ yǐjīng jiéhūnle** "I already have married" or **Wǒ hái méi jiéhūn** "I haven't yet gotten married." To say "marry someone," add the coverb **gēn** "with" and say **gēn...jiéhūn**, for example, **Wǒ yào gēn tā jiéhūn, kěshi tā bú yào gēn wǒ jiéhūn** "I want to marry him, but he doesn't want to marry me." **Jiéhūn** is a verb-object compound, so it can be split up as in **Tā yǐjīng jiéguo sāncì hūn le** "He's already been married three times." Notice that the usual way to say "I'm not married" is **Wǒ hái méi jiéhūn** "I haven't gotten married yet." The reason for the **hái méi** "not yet" is that in Chinese society, everyone is expected to marry. If you say **Wǒ bù jiéhūn**, that would mean "I'm not going to get married." To say "get divorced from," you say in Chinese **gēn...líhūn**, for example, **Tā gēn tā xiānsheng líhūnle** "She's gotten divorced from her husband."

....

Communication strategies

Engaging in conversation with a Chinese native speaker can at first be daunting, but you should realize that when conversing with someone, you do have some control over the conversation. For example, you can ask for repetition of key points, you can confirm meanings, you can to some extent choose the subjects you want to talk about, and you can bring the conversation to an end. It can be helpful for you to have at your disposal phrases and strategies that will help you control a conversation. For example, in the Classroom Expressions section of this textbook, you learned the expression **Qǐng nǐ zài shuō yíbiàn** "Please say it again." If someone has said something you don't understand, use this phrase to ask them to repeat, perhaps expanded a bit into the less abrupt: **Duìbuqǐ, wǒde Zhōngwén hái bú tài hǎo, kě bu kéyi qǐng nín zài shuō yíbiàn?** Even more natural than asking someone to repeat something word for word would be to confirm your understanding of what the other person has said by using a pattern such as **"X" de yìsi shi "Y,"** for example, **Ò, suóyi nínde yìsi shì...** "Oh, so what you mean is...." Similarly, it's important to learn phrases for facilitating and managing your own language learning. Some of these you learned in Lesson 2, such as **Duì bu duì?** "Is it correct?," **Qǐng nǐ dà shēng yidianr** "A little louder, please," **Qǐng nǐ kuài yidianr** "A little faster, please," and **Qǐng nǐ màn yidianr** "A little slower, please." It can also be useful to know how to ask the meaning of something. A common formula for doing this is: **Qǐng wèn, X shi shémme yìsi?** "Excuse me, what does X mean?" The answer to this question would be: **"X" shi "Y"de yìsi** "The meaning of X is Y." Circumlocution, that is, using simpler words to "talk around" the more difficult word you don't know or have forgotten, can similarly be a useful communication strategy. You could say: **Wǒde yìsi shi shuō...** "What I mean is...." We hope that most of the time you'll manage to cope without resorting to English. However, if you need to know the Chinese equivalent of an English term and you have access to a Chinese native speaker who knows English, you could ask: **Qǐng wèn, X Zhōngwén zěmme shuō?** "Excuse me, how do you say X in Chinese?"

....

Reading

New Characters and Words

175. 长	**cháng; zhǎng**	be long; grow
长大	**zhǎngdà**	grow up
176. 看	**kàn**	look, see
好看	**hǎokàn**	be good-looking
看看	**kànkan**	take a look
吃吃看	**chīchi kàn**	try and eat, try eating
问问看	**wènwen kàn**	try and ask, try asking
177. 起	**qǐ**	rise, begin (can't be used alone)
对不起	**duìbuqǐ**	"excuse me"
起来	**-qilai**	(verb ending that means "in the VERBing")
看起来	**kànqilai**	in the looking
学起来	**xuéqilai**	in the learning
178. 轻	**qīng**	be light (not heavy)
年轻	**niánqīng**	be young
179. 出	**chū**	out, go out
出生	**chūshēng**	be born
180. 还	**hái**	still
还可以	**hái kéyi**	still be O.K., not too bad
还是	**hái shi**	still is
还是···好了	**hái shi...hǎole**	it would be better if...

A. SENTENCES

一、你们的女儿长大了，也长高了。她很好看！

二、那个年轻人还是学生，还没有名片。

三、好像左边的位子比较好，您先在那儿坐坐看吧。

四、这个地方看起来不太好看，可是住起来还可以。

五、她是女的，不过看起来好像是男的。

六、何先生、何太太的女儿是在中国出生的，儿子是在美国出生的。

七、那个饭店，里面、外面都很好看，可是饭吃起来真难吃。

八、我不知道这个地方对不对，你还是先问问看吧。

九、我不知道那个东西在哪里，我先找找看吧。

十、王大海今年22岁，还年轻，很多事他还不知道。

B. CONVERSATIONS

一、

美国人： 你是哪里人?

中国人： 我在西安出生，在成都长大的。

美国人： 你看起来很年轻。你还没有三十岁吧?

中国人： 还没有。我今年二十九。

二、

李太太： 方小姐，今天您就住在我这里吧!

方小姐： 好，真谢谢您!

李太太： 方小姐，您的东西都带来了吗?

方小姐： 都带来了。不过，您别叫我"方小姐"，好吗? 我叫方文明，还是叫名字好了!

李太太： 好，好。您还没吃饭吧? 来，我们先吃一点儿东西吧。这个你吃吃看。

方小姐： 真好吃! 都很好吃。我还真没吃过这么好吃的饭!

李太太： 哪里，哪里。好吃就多吃一点儿。

C. NARRATIVE

林东生是一个美国大学一年级的学生。他在高中学过三年中文，今年在大学上中文二年级。林东生去过中国，他知道中国有很多好看的地方，也有很多很好吃的东西。中文学起来比较难，不过林东生很喜欢学。他还很年轻，还有很多年可以学中文。大三那年他要去北京住一年。林东生一天学两、三个钟头的中文，很忙。他真是一个好学生。

Notes

A1a. In this line, note that the character 长, which is used to write **cháng** "be long," is also used to write **zhǎng** "grow." Previously, we've seen a similar case: 都, which is pronounced **dū** in 成都 **Chéngdū** "Chengdu," but which is also the word **dōu** meaning "both, all." This phenomenon, where two different words have the same written representation, isn't unusual in either Chinese or English. In English such words are called heteronyms; consider the word "minute" in the expressions "a minute of your time" vs. "a minute quantity." In Chinese a character that has two or more different pronunciations and meanings is called a 多音字 **duōyīnzì**. In reading Chinese, it's important to pay careful attention to the context, which will usually help you figure out which word is meant.

A1b. 长高 **zhǎnggāo** "grow tall" is a resultative compound that is grammatically similar to 长大 **zhǎngdà** "grow up."

A4. 这个地方看起来不太好看，可是住起来还可以 "This place doesn't look very nice, but it's O.K. to stay at" (literally, "This place in the looking at not very good-looking, but in the staying at still can").

A7.   饭吃起来真难吃 "the food tastes really awful" (literally, "food in the eating of it really hard to eat").

A8.   我不知道这个地方对不对 "I don't know whether this place is right or not."

B2.   我还真没吃过这么好吃的饭！ "I've really never eaten such good food before!" Instead of meaning "still," as it usually does, the 还 in this sentence expresses emphasis.

C1.   林东生一天学两、三个钟头的中文 "Lin Dongsheng studies two or three hours of Chinese every day." Note that 一天 "on one day" is a common way to express "every day," "each day," or "per day."

C2.   Notice the 的 in 两、三个钟头的中文 "two or three hours of Chinese." The 的 indicates that what precedes the 的 describes what follows the 的.

A Hong Kong girl arrives at her middle school

LESSON 15
Chat at the
Chiang Kai-shek Memorial

PART ONE

Conversation

Situation: The Taiwanese man asks Hammond questions about his children and about where Hammond and his wife work (continued from the previous conversation).

1. **TAIWANESE MAN:**
孩子几岁了？已经上学了吗？
Háizi jǐsuì le? Yǐjīng shàngxuéle ma?
How old are your kids? Already in school?

2. **HAMMOND:**
没有，他们还小。儿子三岁，女儿九个月大，所以还没上学。
Méiyou, tāmen hái xiǎo. Érzi sānsuì, nǚ'ér jiǔge yuè dà, suóyi hái méi shàngxué.
No, they're still small. My son is 3, my daughter is 9 months old, so they're not in school yet.

3. **TAIWANESE MAN:**
你在哪里工作？
Nǐ zài nálǐ gōngzuò?
Where do you work?

4. HAMMOND: 我在美国在台协会服务。
Wǒ zài Měiguo Zài Tái Xiéhuì fúwù.
I work at the American Institute in Taiwan.

5. TAIWANESE MAN: 哦。你太太也上班吗？
Ò. Nǐ tàitai yě shàngbān ma?
Oh. Does your wife work, too?

6. HAMMOND: 她在台北美国学校教书。不过，因为孩子还小，所以
她只能工作半天。
**Tā zài Táiběi Měiguo Xuéxiào jiāoshū. Búguò, yīnwei háizi hái xiǎo, suóyi
tā zhǐ néng gōngzuò bàntiān.**
She teaches at Taipei American School. However, because our kids are still
small, she can only work half-time.

New Vocabulary

上学	**shàngxué**	attend school
没有	**méiyou**	(indicates past negative of action verbs)
所以	**suóyi**	therefore, so
协会	**xiéhuì**	association, society
美国在台协会	**Měiguo Zài Tái Xiéhuì**	American Institute in Taiwan
服务	**fúwù**	serve
上班	**shàngbān**	work, go to work
学校	**xuéxiào**	school
台北美国学校	**Táiběi Měiguo Xuéxiào**	Taipei American School
教	**jiāo**	teach
教书	**jiāoshū**	teach
因为	**yīnwei**	because
能	**néng**	be able to, can

Supplementary Vocabulary

东南	**dōngnán**	southeast
东北	**dōngběi**	northeast
西南	**xī'nán**	southwest
西北	**xīběi**	northwest
航空	**hángkōng**	aviation
航空公司	**hángkōng gōngsī**	airline
下班	**xiàbān**	get off from work
为什么	**wèishemme**	why

Notes on the Conversation

Méiyou to indicate past negative of action verbs

You've already learned **méiyou** "not have, there isn't, there aren't" as the negative form of **yǒu** "have." **Méiyou** can also function, like **méi**, as an auxiliary verb that indicates the past negative of action verbs meaning "did not," "has not," or "have not." This **méiyou** ordinarily occurs before the main verb to which it refers but if the context is clear, as in this conversation, it can occur alone. In many cases, **méi** and **méiyou** are synonymous. However, there are two differences: (1) **méiyou** can occur alone or at the ends of sentences while **méi** cannot; (2) **méiyou** is used all over China while **méi** is more common in the North. Examples: **Huǒchē hái méiyou dào** "The train has not yet arrived," **Wǒ méiyou dài míngpiàn** "I didn't bring name cards," **Tāmen méiyou sòng lǐwù** "They didn't give a gift."

Jiāoshū and Jiāo

When teaching in general is meant, the usual equivalent of the English word "teach" is the verb-object compound **jiāoshū**, which literally means "teach books." For example, **Wǒ xǐhuan jiāoshū** "I like to teach." You could not just say *Wǒ xǐhuan jiāo**, without the addition of the object **shū**, since that would be unclear and sound incomplete. If a specific object is meant, for example, the teaching of a certain subject, level, or person, then the general object **shū** is dropped and the specific object is added. Examples: **Tā jiāo Yīngwén** "She teaches English," **Wáng Lǎoshī jīnnián jiāo yīniánjí le** "Teacher Wang is teaching first grade this year," **Shéi jiāo nǐmen?** "Who is teaching you?" Finally, note that **jiāo** is one of a small group of verbs that can take two objects. Example: **Lǐ Lǎoshī jiāo wǒmen Zhōngwén** "Professor Li is teaching us Chinese."

Yīnwei...suóyi...

Yīnwei means "because" and **suóyi**, when it occurs by itself, means "therefore." The pattern **yīnwei... suóyi...**, literally "because...therefore...," usually translates into English simply as "because." In Chinese, the "because" clause almost always comes first, whereas English word order is more flexible. If the subject of both clauses is the same, **yīnwei** may precede or follow the subject of the first clause; **suóyi** is unmovable and always appears at the beginning of the second clause. Examples: **Tā yīnwei hěn máng, suóyi bù néng lái** "She can't come because she's busy," **Tā yīnwei méi xuéguo Zhōngwén, suóyi bù néng qù Zhōngguo** "He can't go to China because he's never studied Chinese," **Yīnwei Xiǎo Wáng chángcháng chídào, suóyi jīnglǐ hěn bù gāoxìng** "The manager is upset because Little Wang is often late." Notice in the last example that because the subject of the first clause is different from that of the second, the **yīnwei** must be placed before the first subject. Always be careful to distinguish **yīnwei** "because" from **suóyi** "therefore"; don't mix up the two parts of this construction!

Intermediate points of the compass

The intermediate points of the compass are stated in Chinese in the opposite order from English. Chinese takes **nán** "south" and **běi** "north" as the two main points of reference while English takes "east" and "west" as its main points of reference. The terms for the intermediate points can be said alone or with the suffix **biān(r)** added at the end. Examples: **dōngnán** or **dōngnánbiān(r)** "southeast," **dōngběi** or **dōngběibiān(r)** "northeast," **xī'nán** or **xī'nánbiān(r)** "southwest," **xīběi** or **xīběibiān(r)** "northwest."

Reading

New Characters and Words

181.	因	**yīn**	because (can't be used alone)
182.	为	**wèi**	for
	因为	**yīnwei**	because
	为什么	**wèishemme**	why?
183.	所	**suǒ**	that which
	所以	**suóyi**	therefore, so
	因为……所以	**yīnwei...suóyi**	because
184.	作	**zuò**	do, make
	工作	**gōngzuò**	work
185.	校	**xiào**	school
	学校	**xuéxiào**	school
	校长	**xiàozhǎng**	school principal
186.	能	**néng**	be able to, can

A. SENTENCES

一、这是学校的大事，我真不知道我们的校长为什么没有来。

二、台北美国学校不在台北市外边，在台北市里边。

三、你的男朋友在哪儿工作？一个月有多少钱？

四、我因为太忙，所以没能去你们的学校看你们的校长。

五、谢小姐因为下星期一要去香港，比较忙，所以今天不能来。

六、王校长因为在学校里还有一点事，所以先走了。

七、请看，河北省在中国的北边，四川省在中国的西南边。

八、我喜欢中文，可是我不知道为什么中文学起来那么难。

九、你的同屋能不能在饭店里面找一个工作？

十、王大海在他朋友的公司里工作了一、两年，有了一点钱，开了一个小公司。

B. CONVERSATIONS

一、

边太太：你儿子、女儿上学了吗？

方太太：没有，他们还小。儿子三岁，女儿九个月大，所以还没有上学。

边太太：你在哪里工作？

方太太：我在台北美国学校工作。不过，因为儿子、女儿还小，所以我工作半天。

二、

安老师：我们太忙了！为什么我们的工作这么多？

司老师：我们的工作太多是因为学生太多。

安老师：对，对。我们的学生是太多了，工作也太多了，可是钱太少了……

司老师：校长来了，校长来了。我们走吧！

"Everyone is responsible for protecting cultural relics, carving and drawing strictly prohibited, violators will be fined"

C. NARRATIVE

李大海是美国学生，今年住在广东省广州市。因为他上的学校在广州的西南边，工作的地方在广州的东南边，住的地方在广州的西北边，所以他要走很长的路，很忙，很忙。不过广州的什么街在哪儿，什么地方有什么吃的，李大海都知道。所以他在广州的中国朋友都叫他"半个广州人"。

Notes

A1.   大事, literally "big thing," could be translated here as "important issue" or "major event."

A4.   Besides the meaning of "look" or "see," the verb 看 can also sometimes, as here, mean "visit."

A5.   谢小姐因为下星期一要去香港，比较忙，所以今天不能来 "Because Ms. Xie is going to Hong Kong next Monday and (because she) is relatively busy, therefore she can't come today."

A10.   工作了一、两年 "worked for one or two years"

B2.   我们的学生是太多了 "We do have too many students." Normally, there would be no 是 in a sentence with a stative verb like 多. The reason for the 是 here is for emphasis; the speaker is emphatically agreeing with the other speaker, who just made this point.

C1.   他上的学校 "the school he attends"

C2.   工作的地方 "the place where (he) works"

C3.   住的地方 "the place where (he) lives"

C4.   他要走很长的路 "he has to walk a long way" (literally, "he needs to walk a long road")

C5. 广州的什么街在哪儿，什么地方有什么吃的，李大海都知道 "Li Dahai knows the location of all of Guangzhou's streets and where you can get different foods" (literally, "What street of Guangzhou's is where, what place has what things to eat, Li Dahai knows it all.")

C6. 他在广州的中国朋友 "his Chinese friends in Guangzhou"

C7. The expression 半个广州人 translates literally as "half a native of Guangzhou." This means "almost like a native of Guangzhou" or "a semi-native of Guangzhou."

Hong Kong street sign

PART TWO

Conversation 🎧

Situation: The Taiwanese man and Hammond continue talking about each other's families (continued from the previous conversation).

1. TAIWANESE MAN:
你有没有兄弟姐妹？
Nǐ yǒu méiyou xiōngdì jiěmèi?
Do you have brothers or sisters?

2. HAMMOND:
我有一个姐姐。你呢？
Wǒ yǒu yíge jiějie. Nǐ ne?
I have an older sister. And you?

3. TAIWANESE MAN:
我在我们家排行老大。我有一个弟弟，两个妹妹。
Wǒ zài wǒmen jiā páiháng lǎodà. Wǒ yǒu yíge dìdi, liǎngge mèimei.
I'm the oldest in our family. I have a younger brother and two younger sisters.

4. HAMMOND:
他们都住台北吗？
Tāmen dōu zhùzai Táiběi ma?
Do they all live in Taipei?

5. TAIWANESE MAN:
我大妹住在台北。小妹在英国留学。我弟弟移民澳洲了。
Wǒ dàmèi zhùzai Táiběi. Xiǎomèi zài Yīngguo liúxué. Wǒ dìdi yímín Àozhōu le.
My older younger sister lives in Taipei. My little sister is studying in England. My younger brother emigrated to Australia.

6. HAMMOND: 哦，对不起，我还得去办一点事。先走了。
Ò, duìbuqǐ, wǒ hái děi qù bàn yìdiǎn shì. Xiān zǒule.
Oh, sorry, I still have to go do something. I'll be on my way.

7. TAIWANESE MAN: 哦，忘了自我介绍了。我叫郑德天。这是我的名片。
Ò, wàngle zìwǒ jièshaole. Wǒ jiào Zhèng Détiān. Zhè shi wǒde míngpiàn.
Oh, I forgot to introduce myself. My name is Zheng Detian. This is my name card.

8. HAMMOND: 我叫黄文。我也给你一张名片。
Wǒ jiào Huáng Wén. Wǒ yě gěi nǐ yìzhāng míngpiàn.
My name is Huang Wen. I'll also give you a name card.

9. TAIWANESE MAN: 以后有机会再聊吧！
Yǐhòu yǒu jīhui zài liáo ba!
In the future if there's a chance let's chat again!

10. HAMMOND: 好啊。
Hǎo a.
Sure.

New Vocabulary

兄弟	**xiōngdì**	older and younger brothers
姐妹	**jiěmèi**	older and younger sisters
排行	**páiháng**	one's seniority among siblings
老	**lǎo-**	(indicates rank among siblings)
老大	**lǎodà**	oldest (among siblings)
大妹	**dàmèi**	older younger sister
小妹	**xiǎomèi**	younger younger sister
留学	**liúxué**	study as a foreign student
移民	**yímín**	immigrate, emigrate
澳洲	**Àozhōu**	Australia
忘	**wàng**	forget
自我介绍	**zìwǒ jièshao**	introduce oneself
给	**gěi**	give
以后	**yǐhòu**	in the future
机会	**jīhui**	opportunity, chance
聊	**liáo**	chat

Supplementary Vocabulary

父母	**fùmǔ**	parents
祖父	**zǔfù**	paternal grandfather
祖母	**zǔmǔ**	paternal grandmother
外祖父	**wàizǔfù**	maternal grandfather
外祖母	**wàizǔmǔ**	maternal grandmother
澳大利亚	**Àodàlìyà**	Australia
跟	**gēn**	with
聊天	**liáotiān**	chat

Notes on the Conversation

-le...le to indicate completed action

Note the two **le** in the sentence **Wǒ wàngle zìwǒ jièshao le** "I forgot to introduce myself." In sentences with a simple, non-quantified object (like "I bought a car" as opposed to "I bought two cars"), the **-le...le** pattern indicates that the action of the verb has been completed. The first **-le** is attached to the main verb while the second **le** occurs at the end of the sentence. Examples: **Wǒ mǎile chē le** "I bought a car," **Wǒ guānle diànnǎo le** "I turned off the computer," **Tāmen yǐjīng dàole Běijīng le** "They've already arrived in Beijing." The first **-le** in double **le** sentences is sometimes dropped, but we recommend that for now you use both **le**.

The verb gěi

In the sentence **Wǒ yě gěi nǐ yìzhāng míngpiàn** "I also give you a name card," **gěi** functions as a regular verb meaning "give." Notice that **gěi** here has two objects: the indirect object **nǐ** and the direct object **míngpiàn**. You've now encountered these three different usages of **gěi**: (1) as a coverb meaning "for": **Qǐng nǐ gěi wǒ mǎi yíge bēizi** "Please buy a cup for me"; (2) as a postverb meaning "give, for, to": **Duìbuqǐ, wǒmen bù néng màigěi nǐ** "Sorry, we can't sell it to you"; (3) as a main verb meaning "give": **Wǒ jīntiān xiān gěi nǐ èrshikuài, xíng ma?** "I'll give you twenty bucks for today, O.K.?"

Reading

New Characters and Words

187.	哥	**gē**	older brother
	哥哥	**gēge**	older brother
	大哥	**dàgē**	oldest brother
188.	弟	**dì**	younger brother
	弟弟	**dìdi**	younger brother

大弟弟	**dà dìdi**	older younger brother
小弟	**xiǎodì**	little brother
189. 妹	**mèi**	younger sister
妹妹	**mèimei**	younger sister
大妹	**dàmèi**	older younger sister
小妹	**xiǎomèi**	little sister
姐妹	**jiěmèi**	older and younger sisters
190. 忘	**wàng**	forget
191. 家	**jiā**	family, home; (measure for companies, etc.)
我家里	**wǒ jiāli**	in my family
我们家	**wǒmen jiā**	our family
回家	**huíjiā**	return to one's home
一家公司	**yìjiā gōngsī**	a company
192. 给	**gěi**	give; for

A. SENTENCES

一、我大哥今年五十八岁，我大姐五十五岁。
二、哥哥、姐姐、弟弟、妹妹我都没有，可是我有很多好朋友。
三、我差一点儿忘了明天是我弟弟的生日！
四、对不起，您能不能给我那个钟？我要看看。谢谢！
五、你今天去哪家公司？你可别忘了带你的名片。
六、我忘了今天是星期一，那家公司星期一不开门。
七、我家左边有一家公司，右边有一家饭店。
八、我大哥在一家公司工作，很忙，不过我忘了那家公司叫什么。
九、因为星期六我小妹京京要来看我，所以我星期五就不回家了。
十、王大海在他们家是老二，他上面有一个姐姐，下面有一个妹妹。

B. CONVERSATIONS

一、
台湾人：我在我们家是老大。我有一个弟弟、两个妹妹。
美国人：他们都住在台北吗？
台湾人：我大妹住在台北。
美国人：对不起，我忘了我还有一点事，先走了。我姓高，高大文。
　　　　这是我的名片。
台湾人：谢谢您，高先生。我姓何。我也给您我的名片。

二、

林先生　：您贵姓？

谢小姐　：我姓谢。您贵姓？

林先生　：我姓林，这是我的名片。您能给我您的名片吗？

谢小姐　：对不起，我今天忘了带了。下次给您，好吗？

C. NARRATIVE

中国有一个小学生，姓高，名字叫明山，今年十岁。他们家住在西安。高明山不是好学生，学校的老师问他的事，他差不多都不知道，所以老师不太喜欢他。有一天，是星期一，有一位老师问他：

老师　　：高明山，中国有多少人口？你知道不知道？忘了吧？

高明山：我没忘，中国有1,300,000,001个人。

老师　　：不对！上个星期我们不是学过中国有1,300,000,000人吗？

高明山：可是老师，您还不知道吧？星期六我的小妹妹出生了，所以中国的人口多了一个，今天中国有1,300,000,001个人了！

Notes

A3.　我差一点儿忘了明天是我弟弟的生日！ "I nearly forgot that tomorrow is my younger brother's birthday!" Remember that the basic meaning of the verb 差 is "lack." 差一点儿 means "lacking by (only) a little," in other words, "nearly" or "almost." The structure and meaning of 差一点儿 and 差不多 "almost, about" are similar.

A4.　您能不能给我那个钟？ "Can you give me that clock?" Just as in English, this isn't a question asking whether the other person is able to give the speaker a clock, but rather a polite request asking him or her to do so.

A9.　所以我星期五就不回家了 "so Friday I won't be going home (after all, as it now turns out)." The implication of the 就 "then" and the changed situation 了 is that since circumstances have changed, the speaker has changed her or his plans.

C2a.　上个星期我们不是学过中国有1,300,000,000人吗？ "Didn't we learn last week that China has one billion three hundred million people?" This is a rhetorical question being used not to ask a real question but to emphasize a fact.

C2b.　所以中国的人口多了一个 "So China's population has increased by one." The verb 多 here literally means "become more."

LESSON 16
Biographical Information

PART ONE

Conversation 🎧

Situation: John Niu, a young Chinese-American who has just arrived in Beijing to study Chinese medicine, has been invited to have dinner with several of his relatives. Over dinner, he chats with an older cousin of his whom he had never met before.

1. AMERICAN: 表姐，你们家住在哪儿啊？
   Biǎojiě, nǐmen jiā zhùzai nǎr a?
   Cousin, where does your family live?

2. CHINESE: 我们住在通县，在北京城的东边儿。
   Wǒmen zhùzai Tōng Xiàn, zài Běijīng chéngde dōngbianr.
   We live in Tong County, to the east of Beijing city.

3. AMERICAN: 哦。你们家都有什么人啊？
   Ò. Nǐmen jiā dōu yǒu shémme rén a?
   Oh. Who all is there in your family?

4. CHINESE: 我和你表姐夫，还有一个孩子。
   Wǒ hé nǐ biǎojiěfu, hái yǒu yíge háizi.
   My husband and me, and also one child.

5. AMERICAN: 男孩儿女孩儿啊？多大了？
   Nánháir, nǚháir a? Duō dàle?
   Is it a boy or a girl? How old?

6. CHINESE: 呃，女孩儿，今年九岁了。

E, nǚháir, jīnnián jiǔsuì le.

Uh, a girl, nine years old.

7. AMERICAN: 表姐，您在哪儿工作啊？

Biǎojiě, nín zài nǎr gōngzuò a?

Cousin, where do you work?

8. CHINESE: 呃，我在幼儿园工作。

E, wǒ zài yòu'éryuán gōngzuò.

Uh, I work in a kindergarten.

9. AMERICAN: 表姐夫呢？

Biǎojiěfu ne?

And your husband?

10. CHINESE: 你表姐夫原来在一家工厂工作。因为身体不太好，所以呢，现在改行了，做点儿小买卖。

Nǐ biǎojiěfu yuánlái zài yìjiā gōngchǎng gōngzuò. Yīnwei shēnti bú tài hǎo, suóyi ne, xiànzài gǎihángle, zuò diǎnr xiǎo mǎimài.

My husband used to work in a factory. Because his health isn't very good, he's now switched jobs and is in business for himself.

New Vocabulary

表姐	**biǎojiě**	older female cousin of different surname
县	**xiàn**	county
和	**hé**	and
表姐夫	**biǎojiěfu**	husband of older female cousin of different surname
还	**hái**	in addition
男孩儿	**nánháir**	boy
女孩儿	**nǚháir**	girl
幼儿园	**yòu'éryuán**	kindergarten
原来	**yuánlái**	originally, formerly
工厂	**gōngchǎng**	factory
身体	**shēnti**	body
改行	**gǎiháng**	change one's line of work
买卖	**mǎimài**	buying and selling, business
做买卖	**zuò mǎimài**	do or engage in business

Supplementary Vocabulary

口	**kǒu**	(measure for people)
从前	**cóngqián**	in the past, formerly

Notes on the Conversation

Choice-type questions with choice implied

There are several ways to indicate choice in Chinese. While there are explicit words for "or" which will be introduced later, one of the most common ways to indicate alternatives is simply by listing them, one directly after another. Such questions are called choice-type questions with choice implied. Examples: **Nánháir nǚháir?** "A boy or a girl?," **Nǐ yào zhèige yào nèige?** "Do you want this one or do you want that one?," **Zhèr hǎo nàr hǎo?** "Is it better here (in China) or there (in America)?"

....

Suóyi ne

Note the phrase **suóyi ne, ...** "therefore, ..." The particle **ne** is here a pause filler after the **suóyi**. Using it gives speakers more time to plan the rest of their utterance and makes their speech seem smoother, since a pause after **suóyi** would sound abrupt and awkward. Here are some other common examples of **ne** as a pause filler after introductory expressions: **Xiànzài ne, ...** "Now, ...," **Kěshi ne, ...** "But, ...," **Búguò ne, ...** "However, ..."

....

Reading

New Characters and Words

193.	表	**biǎo**	(indicates cousins of a different surname)
	表哥	**biǎogē**	older male cousin of different surname
	表姐	**biǎojiě**	older female cousin of different surname
	表弟	**biǎodì**	younger male cousin of different surname
	表妹	**biǎomèi**	younger female cousin of different surname
194.	县	**xiàn**	county
195.	城	**chéng**	city
	北京城	**Běijīng chéng**	the city of Beijing
	城里	**chéngli**	in the city
	城里头	**chéng lǐtou**	in the city
	长城	**Cháng Chéng**	Great Wall
196.	原	**yuán**	original (can't be used alone)
	原来	**yuánlái**	originally, formerly
	太原	**Tàiyuán**	Taiyuan (capital of Shanxi Province)
197.	厂	**chǎng**	factory
	工厂	**gōngchǎng**	factory
198.	现	**xiàn**	appear; current, present
	现在	**xiànzài**	now

A. SENTENCES

一、中国有两千多个县。

二、我原来是工人，在太原的一家工厂工作，可是现在老了，不工作了。

三、我表弟原来在长城饭店工作，现在他开公司了。

四、您知道不知道那个工人现在是不是还在那家工厂工作？

五、我们家有五口人，我们一家五口都住在广东省台山县。

六、我们很喜欢现在住的地方。

七、我知道长城饭店在北京城里头，不过我忘了在什么路上。

八、我们家原来住在台中县，现在住在台中市了。

九、那家工厂原来在北京城里头，现在在北京城外头了。

十、王大海在中国有两个表哥，在台湾还有一个表弟、一个表妹。

B. CONVERSATIONS

一、

表妹：表姐，你们家住在哪儿？

表姐：我们住在大兴县，在北京城的南边儿。

表妹：那，你们家都有什么人？

表姐：我们家有三口人：你表哥、你二表姐还有我。

表妹：表姐，您在哪儿工作？

表姐：我原来在一家工厂工作。因为他们给的钱太少，所以呢，现在在一家比较小的公司工作，可是钱很多。

二、

关小文：何老师，去年这个学校学中文的学生多不多？

何老师：我原来在第43中学工作，所以不知道。

关小文：现在在这里学中文的学生是男生多？是女生多？

何老师：好像一半一半吧。

C. NARRATIVE

高文公先生是南京人。他家里有三口人：高先生、高太太，还有一个儿子小明。高家一家三口都住在南京市东山街五十五号。高先生开工厂，他的工厂在南京城外头。我忘了那个地方叫什么名字，好像叫南口县。高先生原来在一家美国公司工作。他在那儿工作了五、六年，可是因为他们给的钱太少，所以他开了这家工厂。高先生开工厂差不多一年半了。高先生的表弟林明原来也在这家工厂工作，可是现在他去南京市里的一家公司工作了。

Notes

A1.   It's not so easy to count the total number of counties in China, since besides the traditional counties, the term 县 also encompasses so-called autonomous counties, county-level cities, and yet other administrative divisions that are equivalent to counties. Furthermore, the total number tends to change every few years. But it's safe to say there are well over two thousand counties in China.

A4.   那个工人现在是不是还在那家工厂工作？ A literal translation would be: "That worker, is it or is it not the case that he/she is now still working at that factory?" In smoother English, we could say: "Is that worker now still working at that factory?"

A5.   一家五口 "all five of us in our family" (literally, "whole family five members"). The number 一 can sometimes mean "whole." Other examples are 一天 "the whole day long" and 一路 "the whole road—all along the way."

B2.   是男生多？是女生多？ "Are there more male students or female students?" (literally, "Is it that male students are many? Is it that female students are many?")

C1.   开工厂 "operate a factory," "run a factory"

C2.   开工厂差不多一年半了 "has been operating a factory for about a year and a half." The implication is that Mr. Gao is still operating the factory now (or as of the time of the writing of this passage). In sentences indicating duration of time, a sentence-final particle 了 at the end of the sentence indicates that the action of the verb has been continuing for a period of time up to and including the present.

Forbidden City, Beijing

PART TWO

Conversation

Situation: Lisa Olsen, who is studying in Beijing, has been invited to a dinner banquet. Next to her is seated a Chinese woman whom she has never met before.

1. **OLSEN:**

    您好!

    Nín hǎo!

    How are you?

2. **CHINESE WOMAN:**

    您好! 您会说中国话呀!

    Nín hǎo! Nín huì shuō Zhōngguo huà ya!

    How are you? You can speak Chinese!

3. **OLSEN:**

    会一点儿。

    Huì yìdiǎnr.

    I know a little.

4. **CHINESE WOMAN:**

    哦, 您说得不错嘛! 是在哪儿学的?

    Ò, nín shuōde bú cuò ma! Shi zài nǎr xuéde?

    Oh, you really speak quite well! Where did you learn?

5. **OLSEN:**

    原来我在美国学过一点儿。现在在北京语言文化大学继续学。

    Yuánlái wǒ zài Měiguo xuéguo yìdiǎnr. Xiànzài zài Běijīng Yǔyán Wénhuà Dàxué jìxù xué.

    I learned some in America before. Now I'm continuing my study of it at Beijing Language and Culture University.

6. **CHINESE WOMAN:**   您会写中国字儿吗？
   Nín huì xiě Zhōngguo zìr ma?
   Do you know how to write Chinese characters?

7. **OLSEN:**   我认识几百个中国字。有的也会写，有的不会。
   Wǒ rènshi jǐbǎige Zhōngguo zì. Yǒude yě huì xiě, yǒude bú huì.
   Some I can also write, others I can't.

8. **CHINESE WOMAN:**   您还会其他的语言吗？
   Nín hái huì qítāde yǔyán ma?
   Do you know any other languages?

9. **OLSEN:**   我以前会说一点儿西班牙语，可是现在全忘了。
   Wǒ yǐqián huì shuō yìdiǎnr Xībānyáyǔ, kěshi xiànzài quán wàngle.
   I used to be able to speak a little Spanish, but now I've completely forgotten.

New Vocabulary

会	huì	know how to, can
话	huà	word, language
说话	shuōhuà	speak words, speak
中国话	Zhōngguo huà	spoken Chinese
得	-de	(verb suffix that indicates manner)
不错	bú cuò	"not bad," "quite good"
嘛	ma	(indicates something obvious)
北京语言文化大学	Běijīng Yǔyán Wénhuà Dàxué	Beijing Language and Culture University
继续	jìxù	continue
写	xiě	write
字(儿)	zì(r)	character, word
写字	xiězì	write characters, write
认识	rènshi	recognize
几	jǐ-	a few, several
有的	yǒude	some
其他	qítā	other
以前	yǐqián	before, formerly
西班牙语	Xībānyáyǔ	Spanish (language)
全	quán	completely

Supplementary Vocabulary

英语	**Yīngyǔ**	English (language)
法语	**Fǎyǔ**	French (language)
德语	**Déyǔ**	German (language)
日语	**Rìyǔ**	Japanese (language)
普通话	**Pǔtōnghuà**	Mandarin (language)
汉字	**Hànzì**	Chinese character

Notes on the Conversation

Chinese equivalents of English "know"

Huì is the verb for "know" in the sense of "know how to, have learned how to, can." When pronouncing **huì**, be sure to make the initial **h-** strong and "rough" enough, so that **huì** does not sound like **wèi**. Distinguish **huì** from two other verbs which you've already learned that also often translate as "know": **zhīdao** "know a fact" and **rènshi** "know someone, be acquainted with someone." Contrast the following sentences: **Nǐ huì shuō Zhōngguo huà ma?** "Do you know how to speak Chinese?," **Nǐ zhīdao Chéngdū zài nǎr ma?** "Do you know where Chengdu is?," and **Nǐ rènshi nèige rén ma?** "Do you know that person?"

··

Chinese equivalents of English "can"

In addition to translating as "know how," **huì** can also be translated as "can." Be careful to distinguish it from two other verbs you've had that also often translate as "can"; these are **kéyi**, which means "can" in the sense of "may, be permitted to" and **néng**, which means "can" in the sense of "be physically able to." Contrast the following: **Tā huì shuōhuà ma?** "Can she speak?" (for example, has that baby already learned how to speak?), **Tā néng shuōhuà ma?** "Can she speak?" (for example, is that person physically able to speak after her recent bout of laryngitis), and **Tā kéyi shuōhuà ma?** "Can she speak?" (for example, does she have permission to speak). If you want to say that you speak a certain language, don't say ***Wǒ shuō** or ***Wǒ kéyi shuō**; instead, say **Wǒ huì shuō**.

··

-de after verbs to indicate manner

In the conversation, look at the phrase **nín shuōde bú cuò** "you speak well." The particle **-de** occurring after a verb and before a complement expressing manner indicates the manner in which the action of the verb is, was, or will be performed. More examples: **Nǐ láide tài zǎo** "You came too early," **Xiǎoháir zhǎngde tài kuàile!** "Kids grow up too quickly!," **Wǒ zuótiān yèli shuìde bú tài hǎo** "Last night I didn't sleep very well." If you want to express manner and the main verb of the sentence consists of a verb-object compound, you first state the topic with the verb-object compound in its basic form and then repeat only the verb (not the object), followed by **-de** and the complement expressing manner. Examples: **Tā xiě Zhōngguo zì xiě de hěn hǎokàn** "She writes Chinese characters very attractively," **Tāmen xué Zhōngwén xuéde hěn màn** "They're learning Chinese very slowly," **Wǒmen liáotiān liáode hěn gāoxìng** "We chatted very happily."

··

ma **to indicate an obvious situation**

The particle **ma** occurring at the end of a sentence accompanied by low pitch can indicate that something is obvious to the speaker and that the speaker believes it must also be obvious to the listener. Examples: **Tā bú huì ma!** "She doesn't know how!," **Nàrde dōngxi tǐng guì ma!** "The things there are quite expensive, you know!" While the question particle **ma** which you were introduced to early in this course is accompanied by *high pitch*, the **ma** which indicates an obvious situation is accompanied by *low pitch*. Frequent use of this low-pitch **ma** that indicates an obvious situation is considered by some speakers as effeminate.

Question words used as indefinites

Question words when spoken with light stress and normal (rather than high) pitch may have indefinite rather than question meanings. This is usually clear from the context. Your first example of a question word used as an indefinite is **jǐ-**, which usually means "how many" but can, when used as an indefinite, mean "some" or "several." Contrast these two pairs of sentences: **Nǐ rènshi jǐbǎige Zhōngguo zì?** (question, high pitch) "How many hundred Chinese characters do you know?" vs. **Wǒ rènshi jǐbǎige Zhōngguo zì** (statement, normal pitch) "I know several hundred Chinese characters"; and **Nǐ yǒu jǐkuài qián?** (question, high pitch) "How many dollars do you have?" vs. **Wǒ zhǐ yǒu jǐkuài qián** (statement, normal pitch) "I only have a couple of dollars."

yǒude...yǒude...

The pattern **yǒude...yǒude...** is both common and useful. **Yǒude** alone means "some," for example, **yǒude rén** "some people" or **yǒude zì** "some characters." You can also leave off the noun and what then remains is the pronoun **yǒude** "some." **Yǒude** can be used only before the subject or topic of a sentence; it can't be used in front of the object. **Yǒude** frequently occurs in the pattern **yǒude...yǒude...** "some...some..." or "some...others...." Examples: **Yǒude láile, yǒude méi lái** "Some came, others didn't come," **Yǒude wǒ mǎile, yǒude wǒ méi mǎi** "I bought some, I didn't buy others," **Yǒude rén yǐjīng zhīdao, yǒude hái bù zhīdào** "Some people already know, others don't know yet," **Yǒude dìfang hěn nán, yǒude dìfang bú tài nán** "Some parts were hard, other parts were not too hard."

Reading

New Characters and Words

199.	会	**huì**	know how to, can
200.	说	**shuō**	say, speak
	就是说	**jiù shi shuō**	that is to say
201.	话	**huà**	word, language
	说话	**shuōhuà**	speak words, speak
	中国话	**Zhōngguo huà**	spoken Chinese
	说中国话	**shuō Zhōngguo huà**	speak Chinese
	广东话	**Guǎngdōng huà**	Cantonese dialect
	上海话	**Shànghǎi huà**	Shanghainese dialect

	台湾话	**Táiwān huà**	Taiwanese dialect
202.	写	**xiě**	write
	写字	**xiězì**	write characters, write
	写中国字	**xiě Zhōngguo zì**	write Chinese characters, write Chinese
203.	全	**quán**	completely
204.	得	**děi; -de**	must; (verb suffix that indicates manner)

A. SENTENCES

一、那个美国人会说中国话，可是不会写中国字。

二、他中国话说得很好，不过中国字写得不太好，他还得学几年。

三、你写的中文全对，你的中文写得真好！

四、你说得对，我这儿真的有几百块钱，可是为什么全得给你呢？

五、我的朋友有的是男的，有的是女的。

六、有的中国人在美国住了几十年，中国字差不多全忘了。

七、有的人说中国话很难说，有的人说中国字很难写。你说呢？

八、中国字看起来很好看，不过写起来不太好写。

九、老王会写几百个字，小何会写几十个，我会写几个。你呢？你会
　　写几个？

十、王大海说他得走了，好像他家里还有一点儿事。

B. CONVERSATIONS

一、

北京人：您会说中国话！

美国人：会一点儿。

北京人：您说得很好。是在哪儿学的？

美国人：原来我在美国学过一点儿，现在在北京的一个学校学。

北京人：您会写中国字儿吗？

美国人：我会几百个中国字。有的会写，有的不会。

北京人：您还会说什么话？

美国人：我学过一点儿广东话，可是现在全忘了。

二、

李明山：大安，这个地方是不是你的学校？

何大安：对，这就是台北美国学校。

李明山：这里的学生都会中文吗？

何大安：有的会说，也会写；有的会说，不会写；还有的不会说也不
　　　　会写。

C. NARRATIVE

住在我们家后面的林老太太可真喜欢说话！上个星期日七点钟我去看她，她说她儿子现在在一个学校学日文。她说她儿子是很好的儿子，也是很好的学生，日文差不多全会说了，日文的字也会写不少了。她还说她女儿也是好女儿，会说很多地方的话——台湾话、广东话、台山话、上海话都说得很好。差不多九点钟我说："林老太太，对不起，我还有事儿，得走了，"不过她不要我走，她说她还有很多的话还没说。九点半我说："林老太太，对不起，现在我真得走了，"不过林老太太还要说话！十点多钟她还要说话，我很不高兴，走了。在她家外面的大街上，她说请我下个星期日还来。有人说女人都很喜欢说话，我不知道这个话对不对，不过我知道林老太太这个人真的太喜欢说话了！

Hong Kong street sign

Notes

A6.　几十年 "several tens of years" or "several decades."

A9.　我会写几个。你呢？你会写几个？ "I can write a few. How about you? How many can you write?" Notice the two different meanings of 几个. Always pay careful attention to the context.

B2.　有的……有的……还有的…… "Some...others... and still others...."

More Biographical Information

PART ONE

Conversation 🎧

Situation: Eric Bigelow is speaking with one of his professors on the campus of Capital University of Economics and Business in Beijing.

1. **CHINESE PROFESSOR:** 你什么时候到北京的？
   Nǐ shémme shíhou dào Běijīngde?
   When did you arrive in Beijing?

2. **BIGELOW:** 我是今年二月份到的。
   Wǒ shi jīnnián èr yuèfen dàode.
   I arrived in February of this year.

3. **CHINESE PROFESSOR:** 你一个人来的吗？
   Nǐ yíge rén láide ma?
   Did you come alone?

4. **BIGELOW:** 不，和我爱人一起来的。
   Bù, hé wǒ àirén yìqǐ láide.
   No, I came together with my wife.

5. **CHINESE PROFESSOR:** 你在哪儿学的中文？是不是以前在中国学过？
   Nǐ zài nǎr xuéde Zhōngwén? Shì bu shi yǐqián zài Zhōngguo xuéguo?
   Where did you learn Chinese? Had you learned it in China before?

6. BIGELOW: 开始是在美国学的，后来又在台湾学了一段儿时间。
Kāishǐ shi zài Měiguo xuéde. Hòulái yòu zài Táiwān xuéle yíduànr shíjiān.
At first I studied it in the States. Later I studied for a while in Taiwan.

7. CHINESE PROFESSOR: 难怪你的汉语讲得这么好。
Nánguài nǐde Hànyǔ jiǎngde zhèmme hǎo.
No wonder you speak Chinese so well.

8. BIGELOW: 哪里，哪里。还差得很远呢！
Náli, náli. Hái chàde hěn yuǎn ne!
Not at all. I still have a long way to go!

New Vocabulary

时候	**shíhou**	time
月份	**yuèfen**	month
一个人	**yíge rén**	by oneself, alone
和	**hé**	with
一起	**yìqǐ**	together
开始	**kāishǐ**	in the beginning
后来	**hòulái**	afterward, later
又	**yòu**	again
段(儿)	**duàn(r)**	section, segment, period
难怪	**nánguài**	no wonder
讲	**jiǎng**	speak, say
远	**yuǎn**	be far away

Supplementary Vocabulary

开始	**kāishǐ**	begin
那么	**nèmme**	like that, so
有的时候	**yǒude shíhou**	sometimes
讲话	**jiǎnghuà**	speak, talk

Notes on the Conversation

Shi...-de to express the details concerning known past actions

The **shi...-de** pattern indicates the details (such as time, place, with whom, by what means, etc.) of known past actions. For example, **Wǒ shi hé wǒ àirén yìqǐ lái de** "I came together with my husband." When using **shi...-de**, you and your interlocutor are already aware of the fact that something has happened in the past; what you don't know is under what circumstances the past action took place. Examples: **Nǐ shi zuótiān dàode ma?** "Did you arrive yesterday?," **Wǒ bú shi zuótiān dàode, wǒ shi jīntiān dàode** "I didn't arrive yesterday, I arrived today." In rapid speech, the **shi** part of the **shi...-de** pattern in a positive sentence is often omitted, so instead of saying **Wǒ shi gēn tā yìqǐ qùde** "I went together with him," many Chinese would simply say **Wǒ gēn tā yìqǐ qùde**. But in a negative sentence with **bú shi...-de**, the **shi** can never be dropped.

....

Hé...yìqǐ and gēn...yìqǐ

Hé...yìqǐ "together with..." is a useful and common pattern for expressing that you have undertaken or will undertake some action together with someone else. Examples: **Wǒ hé nǐ yìqǐ qù** "I'll go together with you," **Wǒ shi hé wǒ àirén yìqǐ láide** "I came together with my husband." Besides **hé...yìqǐ**, you can also use **gēn** "with" in the related pattern **gēn...yìqǐ**, which has the same meaning and is used in the same way. Example: **Wǒmen gēn tāmen yìqǐ zǒu ba!** "Let's go together with them!"

....

Nánguài

The pattern **nánguài...** means "no wonder (that)...." The **nánguài** is placed directly before the sentence about which the speaker wants to express "no wonder." Examples: **Xiǎo Wángde tàitai shi Měiguo rén, nánguài tāde Yīngwén nèmme hǎo** "Little Wang's wife is American, no wonder his English is so good," **Tā shi gāozhōng Zhōngwén lǎoshī, nánguài tāde Hànyǔ jiǎngde nèmme hǎo** "She is a high school Chinese teacher, no wonder she speaks Chinese so well," **Zhèrde fàn zhēn hǎochī, nánguài nǐ měitiān dōu lái zhèr chī wǔfàn!** "The food here is really good, no wonder you come here every day to eat lunch!"

....

Reading

New Characters and Words

205.	到	**dào**	arrive, reach; to
	到……去	**dào...qù**	go to
	到……来	**dào...lái**	come to
	还不到	**hái bú dào**	have not yet reached
206.	时	**shí**	time; hour, o'clock; when (written Chinese)
207.	候	**hòu**	wait (can't be used alone)
	时候	**shíhou**	time
	什么时候	**shénme shíhou**	what time? (pronounced **shémme shíhou**)
	有的时候	**yǒude shíhou**	sometimes
208.	始	**shǐ**	begin (can't be used alone)
	开始	**kāishǐ**	begin; in the beginning
209.	和	**hé**	and; with
	和……一起	**hé...yìqǐ**	together with
210.	又	**yòu**	again

A. SENTENCES

一、我表哥谢文和的工作可真好！钱那么多，事儿又那么少！

二、老路星期一来找我，星期二又来找我，星期三又来找我……我开始有一点儿不喜欢他了。

三、因为她开始工作了，所以现在比较忙了。

四、我第一次到中国去是我高一那年，今年又要去了，真高兴！

五、我有的时候和我的女朋友一起吃饭，有的时候一个人吃饭。

六、公司星期一到星期五九点开门，五点半关门；星期六九点开门，十二点关门。

七、王太太还没来，我也不知道她什么时候来。

八、小金的男朋友没有钱又不好看，可是人好，所以小金那么喜欢他。

九、这个太好吃了，所以我吃了那么多。

十、王大海看起来很年轻，有一次有一个女同学问他，是不是还不到二十岁？

B. CONVERSATIONS

一、

中国人：你什么时候到北京的？

美国人：我是今年二月到的。

中国人：你一个人来的吗？

美国人：不，和我太太一起来的。

中国人：你在哪儿学的中文？是不是在中国学过？

美国人：开始是在美国学的。我大学三年级那年又在台湾学了几个月。

中国人：你的中国话说得真好！

美国人：哪里，哪里。我的中文还很差呢。

二、

住在美国的中国人：你的中文说得这么好，什么时候开始学的？

美国人　　　　　：我大一那年就开始了。

住在美国的中国人：去过中国吗？

美国人　　　　　：去过十几次了，我上个月去了，下个月又要去了。

C. NARRATIVES

一、在中国，七月中到八月三十一号，学生不上学。我在那个时候和
我的高中同学去过很多地方。我们去过天津、西安、上海和南
京，也去过山西、湖北、四川、广东、广西和海南。

二、李安国老先生是四川人，说的是一口四川话。他原来不住在台
湾，他原来住在四川。他是一九四九年和家人一起到台湾去的，
住在台北，到现在有六十多年了。开始，他不太喜欢台湾，可是
现在喜欢了。有的时候有人问他是什么地方的人，他就说："我是
四川人，不过我在台湾住了这么多年了，你也能说我现在是半个
台湾人了！"

Notes

A2.　我开始有一点儿不喜欢他了 "I began to not like him so much anymore" or "I began to somewhat dislike him." The pattern 有一点儿 occurs before some verbs to indicate that something is "a little" something or "somewhat" something. The meaning is usually negative.

A8.　小金的男朋友没有钱又不好看 "Little Jin's boyfriend has no money and he's also not good-looking" or "Little Jin's boyfriend neither has money nor is good-looking." Here 又, literally "again," is best translated "and also" or "and in addition."

C1.　七月中 "mid July"

C2.　说的是一口四川话 means literally "what he speaks is a mouthful of Sichuan speech." In more idiomatic English, we could translate this as "he speaks Sichuan dialect." 口, literally "mouthful," can serve as a measure for languages and dialects.

PART TWO

Conversation 🎧

Situation: An American college student who is studying Chinese decides to try out his Mandarin on the waitress at a Chinese restaurant in Massachusetts.

1. AMERICAN: 请问，你是从中国来的吗？
   Qǐng wèn, nǐ shi cóng Zhōngguo láide ma?
   Excuse me, are you from China?

2. WAITRESS: 是啊。你去过中国吗？你的中国话说得挺棒嘛！
   Shì a. Nǐ qùguo Zhōngguo ma? Nǐde Zhōngguo huà shuōde tǐng bàng ma!
   Yes. Have you been to China? You really speak Chinese very well!

3. AMERICAN: 哪里。你家在中国什么地方？
   Náli. Nǐ jiā zài Zhōngguo shémme dìfang?
   Thanks. Where in China is your home?

4. WAITRESS: 西安。是个古城。你听说过吗？
   Xī'ān. Shì ge gǔ chéng. Nǐ tīngshuōguo ma?
   Xian. It's an ancient city. Have you heard of it?

5. AMERICAN: 听说过。来美国之前，你在什么单位工作？
   Tīngshuōguo. Lái Měiguo zhīqián, nǐ zài shémme dānwèi gōngzuò?
   Yes, I have. Where did you work before you came to the U.S.?

6. WAITRESS: 我大学毕业以后，在一个中学教了几年书（哦。），然后就
   申请来美国念研究生了。
   **Wǒ dàxué bìyè yǐhòu, zài yíge zhōngxué jiāole jǐnián shū (Ò.), ránhòu jiù
   shēnqǐng lái Měiguo niàn yánjiūshēng le.**
   After graduating from college, I taught for a few years at a middle school (Oh.),
   then I applied to come to the States to attend graduate school.

7. AMERICAN: 哦，是这样。那么，你觉得美国怎么样？

Ò, shi zhèiyang. Nèmme, nǐ juéde Měiguo zěmmeyàng?

Oh, so that's how it was. So what do you think of America?

8. WAITRESS: 不错。美国挺富裕，大多数人工作都很努力，就是治安差了点儿（哦。）。

Bú cuò. Měiguo tǐng fùyu, dà duōshù rén gōngzuò dōu hěn nǔlì, jiù shi zhì'ān chàle dianr (Ò.).

Not bad. America is very prosperous and the majority of people work very hard; the only thing is there's a little too much crime (Oh.).

New Vocabulary

从	**cóng**	from
棒	**bàng**	be great, wonderful
古	**gǔ**	be ancient
听说	**tīngshuō**	hear of, hear it said that
……之前	**...zhīqián**	before, ago
毕业	**bìyè**	graduate
……以后	**...yǐhòu**	after
申请	**shēnqǐng**	apply
念	**niàn**	study
研究	**yánjiū**	research
研究生	**yánjiūshēng**	graduate student
这样	**zhèiyang**	this way, like this
觉得	**juéde**	feel
富裕	**fùyu**	be prosperous
多数	**duōshù**	the majority
努力	**nǔlì**	be diligent, work hard
就	**jiù**	only
治安	**zhì'ān**	public order, public security
差	**chà**	be lacking, deficient

Supplementary Vocabulary

那样儿	**nèiyang(r)**	that way, like that
……以前	**...yǐqián**	before, ago
……之后	**...zhīhòu**	after

Notes on the Conversation

Phrase + **yǐqián/zhīqián** and phrase + **yǐhòu/zhīhòu**

There is a pair of words in Chinese for "before" or "ago": **yǐqián** and **zhīqián**; and there is a pair of words for "after": **yǐhòu** and **zhīhòu**. The difference between the members of each pair is in part stylistic (the series beginning in **yǐ-** is considered by some speakers to be less formal while that beginning in **zhī-** is considered somewhat more formal) and in part simply a matter of personal preference. Whichever word is used, it is (in the meaning of "before" or "after" some event) placed at the *end* of the clause to which it belongs, unlike in English where we place the words "before" and "after" at the *beginning* of the clause. Examples: **Wǒ lái zhèr yǐqián jiù tīngshuōguo** "I had heard about it before I came here," **Tā chīle fàn yǐhòu jiù qù túshūguǎn xuéxí** "After eating, he went to the library to study," **Chén Xiānsheng liǎngge yuè zhīhòu yào jiéhūnle** "Mr. Chen is going to get married in two months."

Bìyè

The verb **bìyè** "graduate" is somewhat complicated. In English, we say "graduate *from*" some school or institution, but in Chinese, most speakers don't use **cóng** but rather say the name of the school or institution followed directly by the verb **bìyè**. For example, **Tā jiějie shi Běidà bìyède** "Her sister graduated from Beijing University." More examples: **Nǐ shi něige dàxué bìyède?** "What college did you graduate from?" **Nǐ shi něinián dàxué bìyède?** "What year did you graduate from college?" **Nǐ dàxué bìyè yǐhòu yào zuò shémme?** "What do you want to do after you graduate from college?"

Backchannel comments

In conversation, when Chinese listen to someone else speak, they frequently punctuate the speaker's language with backchannel comments like **Ò** "Oh" and **Zhèiyang** "So that's how it is." Other common backchannel comments include **Èi** "Uh-huh," **Ng** "Yeah," **Shì** "It is thus," **Shìde** "Yes," and **Duì** "Correct." The basic meaning of backchannel comments is simply "I hear you, I'm listening, I understand," not necessarily "I agree with you." Many misunderstandings and failed business deals have resulted from the misinterpretation of backchannel comments! To facilitate comprehension, we recommend you make judicious use of backchannel comments. This is especially important on the telephone, where there is a lack of visual clues. Appropriate use of backchannel comments can make you sound more natural and can serve to assure your interlocutor that you're following what the speaker is saying.

Reading

New Characters and Words

211.	从	**cóng**	from
	从······来	**cóng...lái**	come from
212.	前	**qián**	in front, front
	以前	**yǐqián**	before, formerly
	······以前	**...yǐqián**	before
	前边	**qiánbian**	in front; front
	前面	**qiánmian**	in front; front

	前头	**qiántou**	in front; front
	从前	**cóngqián**	in the past, formerly
	前天	**qiántiān**	day before yesterday
	前年	**qiánnián**	year before last
213.	后	**hòu**	in back, back
	以后	**yǐhòu**	in the future
	……以后	**...yǐhòu**	after
	后边	**hòubian**	in back, back
	后面	**hòumian**	in back, back
	后头	**hòutou**	in back, back
	后来	**hòulái**	afterwards, later
	后天	**hòutiān**	day after tomorrow
	后年	**hòunián**	year after next
214.	之	**zhī**	(written-style particle, often equivalent to 的)
	……之前	**...zhīqián**	before, ago
	……之后	**...zhīhòu**	after, in
215.	听	**tīng**	listen, hear
	听说	**tīngshuō**	hear of, hear it said that
	好听	**hǎotīng**	be nice to listen to, pretty (of music, etc.)
216.	觉	**jué**	feel (can't be used alone)
	觉得	**juéde**	feel

A. SENTENCES

一、前天我听说你的表姐要从广州来看你。

二、小林来这家公司之前，在哪里工作？

三、你听我说，从前，在中国有一个老人，住在山里头，他一百二十岁了，可是看起来好像六十几岁。

四、你听谁说我有两个哥哥？我就有一个哥哥！

五、我觉得这里的中国饭不好吃，以后我们不要来这家饭店了。

六、你是谁？你从什么地方来？你到什么地方去？

七、那个中国学生说他到了美国之后，去了很多地方，真的学了不少东西。

八、前边、后边都有人坐，没有位子了，我们走吧。

九、上大学以前，我没学过中文。我是上大学以后开始学中文的。

十、王大海，为什么你中国话说得那么好，可是中国字写得那么差呢？

B. CONVERSATIONS

一、

美国人：请问，你是从中国来的吗？

中国人：是。你去过中国吗？你的中国话说得很好！

美国人：哪里。你家在中国什么地方？

中国人：西安。你听说过吗？

美国人：听说过。来美国之前，你在哪里工作？

中国人：来美国以前，我在一家工厂工作。

二、

美国学生：请问，您是从北京来的吗？

住在美国的北京人：是的。有什么事儿？

美国学生：您说的中国话听起来真好听！

住在美国的北京人：谢谢你！你是美国人，你的中文说得也不差！

C. NARRATIVES

一、我来中国以前，不会说中国话，也不会写中国字。"一二三"、"你好"、"谢谢"我都不会。可是来了三年之后，中国话差不多都会说了，中国字写得也不差。我还有一个中国女朋友，北京人，人很好，她说的北京话可真好听。我觉得中国真好！

二、从前有一个姓王的，叫王大。因为王大很喜欢吃饭，所以很多人都叫他"吃饭大王"。后来王大老了，看起来好像一个钟那么大。他得在家里，不能工作，也不能到街上去看看，所以他的朋友也就很少了。

Notes

A3.   你听我说 "Listen" (literally, "Listen to me speak")

A7.   学了不少东西 "learned lots of things"

C2.   吃饭大王 "great king of eating." This involves word play, since the person's name is 王大, which is the exact reverse of 大王 "great king."

LESSON 18
"How Do I Get to the Beijing Hotel?"

PART ONE

Conversation 🎧

Situation: Patricia Nguyen, who is studying Chinese at a study abroad program in Beijing, asks a pedestrian how to get to the Beijing Hotel.

1. NGUYEN:
劳驾，去北京饭店怎么走？
Láojià, qù Běijīng Fàndiàn zěmme zǒu?
Excuse me, how do I get to the Beijing Hotel?

2. PEDESTRIAN:
北京饭店，是吗？一直往前走，过了天安门就到了。
Běijīng Fàndiàn, shi ma? Yìzhí wàng qián zǒu, guòle Tiān'ānmén jiù dàole.
The Beijing Hotel? Go straight ahead, it's right after Tiananmen.

3. NGUYEN:
离这儿很远吗？
Lí zhèr hěn yuǎn ma?
Is it very far from here?

4. PEDESTRIAN:
离这儿不太远。
Lí zhèr bú tài yuǎn.
It's not too far from here.

5. **NGUYEN:** 大概要多久？

Dàgài yào duō jiǔ?

About how long will it take?

6. **PEDESTRIAN:** 走路的话，大概要二十分钟左右，或者您打个的更快，五分钟就到了。

Zǒulùde huà, dàgài yào èrshifēn zhōng zuǒyòu, huòzhě nín dǎ ge dī gèng kuài, wǔfēn zhōng jiù dàole.

If you walk, it will probably take about twenty minutes, or if you take a cab, it will be even faster, you'll be there in five minutes.

7. **NGUYEN:** 好，谢谢您。

Hǎo, xièxie nín.

O.K., thanks.

8. **PEDESTRIAN:** 不客气。

Bú kèqi.

You're welcome.

New Vocabulary

劳驾	**láojià**	"excuse me"
北京饭店	**Běijīng Fàndiàn**	Beijing Hotel
走	**zǒu**	go, walk
一直	**yìzhí**	straight
往	**wàng**	to, toward
过	**guò**	pass, go by
离	**lí**	be distant from, from
大概	**dàgài**	probably, about
走路	**zǒulù**	walk
左右	**zuǒyòu**	about, approximately
或者	**huòzhě**	or
打的	**dǎdī**	take a taxi
更	**gèng**	even more, more
快	**kuài**	be fast

Supplementary Vocabulary

近	**jìn**	be close, near
南	**nán**	south
西	**xī**	west
开	**kāi**	drive (a vehicle)

北	**běi**	north
东方	**dōngfāng**	east, the East
西方	**xīfāng**	west, the West
南方	**nánfāng**	south, the South
北方	**běifāng**	north, the North
东方人	**Dōngfāng rén**	Asian
西方人	**Xīfāng rén**	Westerner
南方人	**nánfāng rén**	Southerner
南方话	**nánfāng huà**	southern speech
北方人	**běifāng rén**	Northerner
北方话	**běifāng huà**	northern speech

Notes on the Conversation

Qù...zěmme zǒu?

The pattern for asking "How does one get to such-and-such a place?" is **Qù** + name of place + **zěmme zǒu?** This literally means "go to (name of place) how to go?" Frequently there will be a polite phrase like **láojià** or **qǐngwèn** before the **qù**. Examples: **Láojià, qù Wàijiāobù zěmme zǒu?** "Excuse me, how do you get to the Foreign Ministry?," **Láojià, qù Cháng Chéng Fàndiàn zěmme zǒu?** "Excuse me, how does one get to the Great Wall Hotel?," **Qǐngwèn, qù Táidà zěmme zǒu?** "Excuse me, how do you get to National Taiwan University?"

....

Wàng to express movement toward a certain direction

The coverb **wàng** "to, toward" expresses movement toward a certain direction. It is followed by a localizer and a verb. Example: **wàng qián zǒu** "go toward the front, walk ahead." Sometimes this **wàng** may be pronounced **wǎng**; both pronunciations are correct. More examples: **Qǐng nǐ xiān wàng dōng zǒu, ránhòu zài wàng xī zǒu** "Please first walk toward the east, and then walk toward the west," **Tā zhǐ huì wàng qián kāi, hái bú huì wàng hòu kāi** "He can only drive straight ahead, he can't yet drive backwards," **Xiān wàng zuǒ kàn, zài wàng yòu kàn!** "First look toward the left, and then look toward the right!"

....

Lí to express distance from

The coverb **lí** literally means "be separated from." There are two common patterns with **lí**: **lí...yuǎn** "be far from..." and **lí...jìn** "be close to...." Although **lí** is used most commonly to indicate physical distance, it is sometimes used abstractly, for example, to indicate how distant in time something is or was. Examples: **Zhōngguo lí Měiguo hěn yuǎn** "China is far from America," **Jiānádà lí Měiguo hěn jìn** "Canada is close to America." More examples: **Nǐ jiā lí zhèr yuǎn ma?** "Is your home far from here?," **Hángzhōu lí Shànghǎi bù yuǎn yě bú jìn** "Hangzhou is neither far from nor close to Shanghai," **Xiànzài lí shàngkè hái yǒu shífēn zhōng** "Now there are still ten minutes from the time class starts." *Attention:* Be careful not to confuse **lí** "be separated from" with **cóng**, which simply means "from (one place)." When you want to express distance between two points, you must use **lí**. If you want to express origin or direction, you should use **cóng**. Compare: **Wǒ jiā lí nǐ jiā bú tài yuan** "My home isn't very far from your home" vs. **Cóng wǒ jiā dào nǐ jiā zěmme zǒu?** "How do you get from my home to your home?"

Conditional clauses with <u>-de huà</u>

The addition of **-de huà** (literally, "the words that...") at the end of a clause emphasizes that the clause is conditional. This pattern is often used after **yàoshi** and other adverbs meaning "if"; or it can also be used alone, as in this conversation. Examples: **Zǒulùde huà, dàgài yào yíge zhōngtóu zuǒyòu** "If you walk, it will probably take about an hour," **Yàoshi dǎdīde huà, dàgài yào shífēn zhōng zuǒyòu** "If you take a cab, it will probably take about ten minutes."

<u>Zuǒyòu</u>

The place word **zuǒyòu**, literally "to the left or right of," means "approximately, about" and is placed after a numerical expression to indicate an approximate quantity. Distinguish **zuǒyòu** from **chàbuduō** and **dàyuē**, which have approximately the same meaning but are placed before the numerical expression. Examples: **Yào èrshifēn zhōng zuǒyòu** "It will take about 20 minutes," **Táiběide rénkǒu yǒu sānbǎiwàn zuǒyòu** "The population of Taipei is about three million," **Cóng Běijīng dào Chángchéng hěn kuài, zhǐ yào yíge zhōngtóu zuǒyòu** "It's very fast to get from Beijing to the Great Wall; it takes only approximately one hour."

Reading

New Characters and Words

217.	怎	**zěn**	how (can't be used alone)
	怎么	**zěnme**	how (pronounced **zěmme**)
	去……怎么走	**qù...zěnme zǒu**	how do you get to…
218.	往	**wǎng**	to, toward
	往东走	**wàng dōng zǒu**	go toward the east
	往西开	**wàng xī kāi**	drive toward the west
219.	离	**lí**	be distant from, from
220.	远	**yuǎn**	be far away
	离……很远	**lí...hěn yuǎn**	be far from
221.	近	**jìn**	be close, near
	离……很近	**lí...hěn jìn**	be close to
222.	概	**gài**	approximate, general (can't be used alone)
	大概	**dàgài**	probably, about

A. SENTENCES

一、 先生，请问，去天安门怎么走？离这儿还远吗？

二、 你往前走差不多一刻钟，过了北京饭店就到了。

三、 小李的家离我的家很近，可是老王的家离我的家很远。

四、 我要是知道那么远的话，我大概就不走路来了！

五、 北方人说北方话，南方人说南方话。

六、 他是西方人，不过他有很多朋友是东方人。

七、 大学离我的家不远，走半个钟头左右就可以到。

八、 我的公司离我住的地方很近，走一刻钟就可以到。

九、 我的生日是八月三号，今天是三月八号，所以离我的生日还很
远。

十、 王大海说他很不高兴，因为他的生日过了，朋友都没给他东西；
我说他们大概太忙了，所以忘了。

B. CONVERSATIONS

一、

美国人： 请问，去北京饭店怎么走？

北京人： 北京饭店是吗？往前走，过了天安门就到了。

美国人： 离这儿还远吗？

北京人： 离这儿比较远。走路的话，大概要半个钟头左右吧。

美国人： 好，谢谢您！

二、

东方人： 你的中国话说得太好了！

西方人： 哪里，哪里。我的中文不好，还差得很远……

"Long live the People's Republic of China"

"Long live the great unity of the world's peoples"

C. NARRATIVES

一、有一位老先生姓钱。他是北方人，可是说的是一口南方话。我前天问他天安门怎么走？他先说得往东走，后来又说不对，得往西走。我问他天安门离北京饭店远不远。他说天安门离北京饭店很近，可是又说北京饭店离天安门很远！钱老先生大概忘了天安门在哪儿了吧。

二、我家住在北京西长安街55号，离天安门、北京饭店都很近。我家的后面是南长街。从南长街往北走不远有一家饭店名字叫海南大饭店。我觉得那家饭店还可以，不太贵，他们的海南饭也很好吃。我很喜欢和我们公司的同事在那家饭店吃中饭。你的美国朋友谢小姐可以住在那里。要是谢小姐不要住那家，南长街还有很多其他的饭店可以去看看。

Notes

C1a. 说的是一口南方话 means literally "what he speaks is a mouthful of southern speech." In more idiomatic English, we could translate this as "he speaks southern dialect" or just "he speaks southern."

C1b. In the clause 他先说得往东走, the character 得 is pronounced **děi** and means "must."

C2a. 从南长街往北走不远有一家饭店名字叫海南大饭店 "Going north from Nanchang Street, not far away there is a hotel named the Hainan Hotel."

C2b. 吃中饭 "eat lunch." Be sure to distinguish 吃中饭 from 吃中国饭 "eat Chinese food"!

Taipei street sign

PART TWO

Conversation

Situation: Linda Fuentes, a graduate student who has spent the past year conducting research in Beijing, calls for a cab to take her from the Foreign Experts Building at Beijing Foreign Studies University to Capital Airport.

1. DISPATCHER: 您好！友谊宾馆汽车公司。
   Nín hǎo! Yǒuyì Bīnguǎn Qìchē Gōngsī.
   Hello. Friendship Hotel Taxi Company.

2. FUENTES: 喂？你好。我要一辆车去首都机场。
   Wéi? Nǐ hǎo. Wǒ yào yíliàng chē qù Shǒudū Jīchǎng.
   Hello? Hi. I'd like a car to go to Capital Airport.

3. DISPATCHER: 您现在在哪儿？
   Nín xiànzài zài nǎr?
   Where are you now?

4. FUENTES: 在北京外国语大学的专家楼。
   Zài Běijīng Wàiguóyǔ Dàxuéde zhuānjiā lóu.
   In the Foreign Experts Building at Beijing Foreign Studies University.

5. DISPATCHER: 几个人？
   Jǐge rén?
   How many people?

6. FUENTES: 就我一个人。
   Jiù wǒ yíge rén.
   Just me alone.

7. DISPATCHER:

什么时候要车？

Shémme shíhou yào chē?

What time would you like the car?

8. FUENTES:

现在就要。

Xiànzài jiù yào.

Right now.

9. DISPATCHER:

行。您贵姓？

Xíng. Nín guìxìng?

All right. What's your last name?

10. FUENTES:

我是美国人，我的中文姓名是傅琳达。

Wǒ shi Měiguo rén, wǒde Zhōngwén xìngmíng shi Fù Líndá.

I'm an American, my Chinese name is Fù Líndá.

11. DISPATCHER:

好的。车子十分钟以后就到。您在北外专家楼门口儿等吧。

Hǎode. Chēzi shífēn zhōng yǐhòu jiù dào. Nín zài Běiwài zhuānjiā lóu ménkǒur děng ba.

All right. The car will be there in ten minutes. Wait at the entrance to the Foreign Experts Building at BFSU.

New Vocabulary

友谊	yǒuyì	friendship
宾馆	bīnguǎn	guest house, hotel
友谊宾馆	Yǒuyì Bīnguǎn	Friendship Hotel
汽车	qìchē	car, vehicle
喂	wéi	"hello" (on the telephone)
辆	liàng	(for land vehicles)
首都	shǒudū	capital
机场	jīchǎng	airport
首都机场	Shǒudū Jīchǎng	Capital Airport
外国	wàiguo	foreign country
外国语	wàiguoyǔ	foreign language
北京外国语大学	Běijīng Wàiguoyǔ Dàxué	Beijing Foreign Studies
专家	zhuānjiā	expert
楼	lóu	building (with two or more floors)
专家楼	zhuānjiā lóu	(Foreign) Experts Building
姓名	xìngmíng	first and last name
好的	hǎode	"all right," "O.K."
车子	chēzi	car, vehicle
北外	Běiwài	(abbreviation for Beijing Foreign Studies University)
门口(儿)	ménkǒu(r)	doorway, entrance

Supplementary Vocabulary

外国人	**wàiguo rén**	foreigner
外国话	**wàiguo huà**	foreign language
出租	**chūzū**	rent out
出租汽车	**chūzū qìchē**	taxi

Notes on the conversation

The measure for vehicles <u>liàng</u>

Liàng is the measure for all kinds of land vehicles that end in **-chē**. Examples: **yíliàng chē** "a car," **zhèiliàng qìchē** "this automobile," **nèiliàng qìchē** "that car," **jǐliàng chēzi?** "how many cars?," **něiliàng chūzū qìchē?** "which taxi?"

Pivot sentences

The sentence **Wǒ yào yíliàng chē qù Shǒudū Jīchǎng** "I want a car to go to Capital Airport" is an example of a so-called pivot sentence. This sentence is actually composed of the following two sentences: **Wǒ yào yíliàng chē** "I want a car" + **Chē qù Shǒudū Jīchǎng** "The car goes to Capital Airport." In the first sentence **chē** is the object, while in the second sentence **chē** is the subject. When the two sentences are combined, the second **chē** is deleted and the first **chē** acts as a "pivot," serving simultaneously as the object of the first sentence and as the subject of the second sentence. Other common verbs in pivot sentences besides **yào** include **qǐng**, **yǒu**, and **zhǎo**. More examples: **Wǒ qǐng nǐ chī wǔfàn** "I'd like to invite you for lunch," **Wǒ yǒu ge péngyou xìng Lǐ** "I have a friend who is surnamed Li," **Wǒmen zhǎo yíge tóngxué gēn wǒmen yìqǐ qù** "We're looking for a classmate to go together with us."

Reading

New Characters and Words

223.	汽	**qì**	steam, vapor, gas
224.	车	**chē**	vehicle (car, taxi, bus, bicycle)
	车子	**chēzi**	car, vehicle
	汽车	**qìchē**	car, vehicle
	汽车公司	**qìchē gōngsī**	car company, taxi company
225.	首	**shǒu**	head; chief, capital (can't be used alone)
226.	机	**jī**	opportunity; machine (can't be used alone)
	机会	**jīhui**	opportunity, chance
227.	场	**chǎng**	place (can't be used alone)
	机场	**jīchǎng**	airport
	首都机场	**Shǒudū Jīchǎng**	Capital Airport
228.	等	**děng**	wait, wait for

A. SENTENCES

一、听说坐汽车去机场要一个钟头左右。

二、我们明天七点要坐老何的车子去首都机场。

三、要是有机会的话，我要到上海去看我的一个外国朋友。

四、一九二八年到一九四九年，中国的首都在南京，不在北京。

五、您是外国人，请您写您的中文姓名，还有您的外国姓名。

六、我觉得外国话都很难学，也很难听，你觉得呢？

七、她是中国人，在金门出生的，可是她的先生是外国人。

八、有的住在美国的中国人叫美国人"外国人"。

九、"首都汽车公司：八时开门，五时半关门"

十、王大海要我们半个钟头以后到北外门口等他。

B. CONVERSATIONS

一、

汽车公司的人：您好！北京汽车公司。

外国人　　　　：你好。我要个车去首都机场。

汽车公司的人：您现在在哪儿？

外国人　　　　：在北京大学。

汽车公司的人：几个人？

外国人　　　　：就我一个人。

汽车公司的人：什么时候要车？

外国人　　　　：现在就要。

汽车公司的人：行。您贵姓？

外国人　　　　：我是美国人，我的中文姓名是司开来。

汽车公司的人：好的。您在北大门口儿等吧。

二、

车太太：女儿，你在你的大学有机会说中国话吗？

女儿　：有，说中国话的机会很多。

车太太：那么，有没有机会学写中国字？

女儿　：也有，不过学中国字的机会比较少。

C. NARRATIVES

一、我家离首都机场很近，从这儿坐半个钟头的车就可以到首都机场。我住在东山街四十五号，真的不难找，我的姓名写在大门上。

二、王先生从美国带来的车子真好看。现在在中国有美国汽车的人还
　　不太多，所以王先生很高兴。王先生在首都机场工作，以前因为
　　家离工作的地方太远，所以他一个星期就回家一次。现在有了汽
　　车，他可以开车回家，开半个多钟头就可以到家了。

Notes

A6a.　我觉得外国话都很难学，也很难听 "I feel that foreign languages are all hard to learn, and also don't sound nice." The two 难 in this sentence are rather different. The first one means "be difficult" while the second one means "be unpleasant." Compare 难吃 "be unpleasant to eat, bad-tasting" and 难看 "be unpleasant to look at, ugly."

A6b.　你觉得呢？ "What do you think?" (literally, "And you feel...?").

A9.　This line is from a sign and was composed in written-style Chinese. In spoken-style Chinese, this would be said as 八点开门，五点半关门.

A10.　王大海要我们半个钟头以后到北外门口等他 "Wang Dahai wants us to go to the entrance to Beijing Foreign Studies University to wait for him in half an hour." Here, 半个钟头以后 literally means "after half an hour," but when describing future events, we would usually translate 以后 into English as "in...."

B2.　说中国话的机会很多 "There are many opportunities to speak Chinese" (literally, "Opportunities to speak Chinese are many").

C1.　我的姓名写在大门上 "My name is written on the front door." Notice how the postverb construction 写在 "write on" or (as in this sentence) "be written on" is used. Also, note that 大门 means "front door" (literally, "big door" or "main door").

C2a.　王先生从美国带来的车子看起来真好看 "The car that Mr. Wang brought from the U.S. looks really nice." Private individuals would not normally be allowed to import vehicles into China, unless they worked in foreign embassies or had special connections.

C2b.　他一个星期就回家一次 "He returns home only once a week" (literally, "He one week only returns home one time").

Hong Kong street sign

Calling for a Taxi to the Airport

PART ONE

我半个小时以前打电话要过车，怎么到现在还没来？

Conversation 🎧 LISTEN

Situation: Almost half an hour has passed but the taxi has still not arrived, so Fuentes – who is becoming increasingly worried about missing her flight – decides to get up and call the taxi company again to ask why her cab isn't yet there (continued from the previous conversation).

1. **DISPATCHER:** 你好！友谊宾馆汽车公司。
   Nǐ hǎo! Yǒuyì Bīnguǎn Qìchē Gōngsī.
   Hello. Friendship Hotel Taxi Company.

2. **FUENTES:** 喂？我半个小时以前打电话要过一辆车。你们说十分钟就到，怎么到现在还没来啊？
   Wéi? Wǒ bàn'ge xiǎoshí yǐqián dǎ diànhuà yàoguo yíliàng chē. Nǐmen shuō shífēn zhōng jiù dào. Zěmme dào xiànzài hái méi lái a?
   Hello? Half an hour ago I called and requested a cab. You said it would arrive in ten minutes. How come it still hasn't come until now?

3. **DISPATCHER:** 对不起，现在是上下班时间，交通比较拥挤。车，我们已经派去了，请您再耐心等一会儿。
   Duìbuqǐ, xiànzài shi shàngxiàbān shíjiān, jiāotōng bǐjiào yōngjǐ. Chē wǒmen yǐjīng pàiqule, qǐng nín zài nàixīn děng yìhuǐr.
   I'm sorry, it's rush hour now and traffic is quite congested. We've already dispatched the cab, please be patient and wait a bit longer.

4. FUENTES: 还要等多久啊？
Hái yào děng duō jiǔ a?
How much longer do I have to wait?

5. DISPATCHER: 您别着急，我想一会儿就会到。
Nín bié zháojí, wǒ xiǎng yìhuǐr jiù huì dào.
Don't worry, I think it will be there soon.

6. FUENTES: 麻烦您快一点儿，好吗？我快要来不及了！
Máfan nín kuài yidianr, hǎo ma? Wǒ kuài yào láibujíle!
Please try to hurry, will you? Soon I'll be late!

7. DISPATCHER: 好，我马上通知司机尽快赶到。
Hǎo, wǒ mǎshàng tōngzhī sījī jìnkuài gǎndào.
O.K., I'll immediately notify the driver to rush there as fast as he can.

New Vocabulary

小时	xiǎoshí	hour
打	dǎ	hit
电话	diànhuà	telephone
打电话	dǎ diànhuà	make a telephone call
要	yào	request
怎么	zěmme	how come, why
交通	jiāotōng	traffic
拥挤	yōngjǐ	be crowded
派	pài	dispatch, send
派去	pàiqu	dispatch, send out
耐心	nàixīn	be patient
一会儿	yìhuǐr	a while
要	yào	need to, should
着急	zháojí	worry, get excited
会	huì	be likely to, will
麻烦	máfan	trouble, disturb
马上	mǎshàng	immediately, right away
通知	tōngzhī	notify
司机	sījī	driver, chauffeur
尽快	jìnkuài	as fast as possible
赶	gǎn	rush, hurry
赶到	gǎndào	rush or hurry to a place

Supplementary Vocabulary

决定	**juédìng**	decide
法子	**fázi**	means, method, way
上	**shàng**	go to, come to

Notes on the Conversation

Dǎ diànhuà

Dǎ diànhuà is the expression for "make a telephone call." **Dǎ** by itself means "hit" while **diànhuà** literally means "electric speech," this being the term that came to be used after the importation of the telephone into China in the 19th century. If the person to whom the call is being made is mentioned, this is done with the coverb **gěi** "give, to, for" followed by the appropriate noun or pronoun. Negative **bù** or **méi** precedes the **gěi**. Examples: **Qǐng nǐ gěi tā dǎ diànhuà** "Please call her on the telephone," **Wǒ gěi tā dǎle hǎojǐcì diànhuà, kěshi méi rén zài** "I called him quite a few times but there was nobody there," **Wǒ méi gěi tā dǎ diànhuà** "I didn't call her on the telephone."

Different meanings of the verb yào

Pay attention to the different meanings of the verb **yào**. The first **yào** in this conversation means "request," the second **yào** means "need to, should," and the third **yào** means "be going to, will." You've encountered **yào** previously with the meanings "want (to)," "need," "cost," and "take." Compare: **Nǐ yào shémme?** "What do you want?," **Zhèige yào duōshǎo qián?** "How much does this cost?," **Wǒ yào qù Zhōngguo le!** "I'm going to go to China!," **Wǒ yě yào kàn!** "I want to see it, too!," **Wǒ yàoguo liǎngliàng chē** "I requested two cars," **Hái yào děng duō jiǔ?** "How much longer do we have to wait?"

Resultative compounds

In this conversation, **pàiqu** "dispatch, send out" is composed of the verb **pài** "send" plus the resultative ending **-qu** ("go"), which indicates motion away from the speaker. Also notice in this lesson the resultative compound **láibují** "not be able to make it in time." In earlier lessons you learned **gǎocuò** "get wrong," composed of the action verb **gǎo** "get" and the resultative verb ending **-cuò** "wrong"; and **zhǎngdà** "grow up." All of these verbs are examples of resultative verbs, which are composed of an action verb followed by a resultative ending which indicates the result of the action. For example, **zhǎngdà** "grow with the result that one becomes big, grow up" is composed of the action verb **zhǎng** "grow" plus the resultative ending **-dà** "big." Some resultative compounds are composed of verbs indicating direction or motion plus the resultative endings **-lái** "come" or **-qù** "go"; **pàiqu** "dispatch, send out" belongs to this group. In the lessons to come, you'll see many more resultative compounds.

Reading

New Characters and Words

229.	打	**dǎ**	hit, beat
	打的	**dǎdī**	take a taxi
230.	电	**diàn**	electricity; lightning
	电话	**diànhuà**	telephone
	打电话	**dǎ diànhuà**	make a telephone call
231.	班	**bān**	class; shift
	班上	**bānshang**	in a class
	中文班	**Zhōngwén bān**	Chinese class
	上班	**shàngbān**	go to work, work
	下班	**xiàbān**	get off from work
232.	间	**jiān**	between, during (can't be used alone)
	时间	**shíjiān**	time
	上下班时间	**shàngxiàbān shíjiān**	time when one goes to or gets off from work
233.	交	**jiāo**	hand over; intersect
234.	通	**tōng**	through, open; connect
	交通	**jiāotōng**	traffic
	通知	**tōngzhī**	notify
	通县	**Tōng Xiàn**	Tong County

A. SENTENCES

一、要是你觉得走路太远的话，可以打个的，一会儿就到。

二、钱太太家里好像没有电话，我们怎么通知她呢？

三、我在这儿等了一个多小时了，李东山怎么还没来？

四、我一会儿就会给司机打电话，通知他我们今天六点下班。

五、他在电话公司上班，九点上班，五点下班，一天工作八小时。

六、现在是下班时间，交通大概会很不好吧？

七、她在交通大学的中文班上有八个同学：一半是男生，一半是女生。

八、原来的河北省通县现在叫"北京市通州"了。

九、台北市的交通比较差，上下班时间车子太多。

十、王大海说他半个小时以前要过车，怎么到现在还没来？

B. CONVERSATIONS

一、

汽车公司的人：你好！北京汽车公司。

外国人　　　：我半个小时以前打电话要过车，怎么到现在还没来？

汽车公司的人：对不起，现在是上下班时间。

外国人　　　：还要等多长时间？

汽车公司的人：一会儿就会到。

外国人　　　：好吧。

二、

万国明：好像今年北京的交通比较好了。

班安太：不过上下班儿时间还是很差。

万国明：要是打的的话，从北京饭店到首都机场得要一个小时吗？

班安太：要是上下班儿的时候，大概要吧。

C. NARRATIVE

班大明是司机，在上海大饭店上班。他六点上班，九点下班，一天得工作十五个小时，很忙。班先生的车子是美国车，车上还有电话，所以给饭店的汽车公司打电话不难。现在上海市打的的人很多。有的时候班先生在上海大饭店等人，有的时候他得到机场等人。上下班时间，上海的交通不太好。路上车子太多，人也太多，所以班先生很不喜欢在那个时候开车。

"No visitors during working hours"

Notes

A3.　我在这儿等了一个多小时了 "I've been waiting here for more than an hour." 小时 can be said or written, but 钟头 is a spoken word that seldom occurs in standard written Chinese.

A5.　You could say, or write, either 八小时 or 八个小时.

PART TWO

Conversation

Situation: The taxi finally arrives and, after loading the luggage, the driver takes Fuentes to Capital Airport. On arrival, she pays the driver and enters the terminal (continued from the previous conversation).

1. DRIVER:
是您要车到首都机场吗？
Shì nín yào chē dào Shǒudū Jīchǎng ma?
Was it you who requested a cab to Capital Airport?

2. FUENTES:
对，是我。
Duì, shì wǒ.
Yes, it was me.

3. DRIVER:
就这两件行李吗？
Jiù zhèiliǎngjiàn xíngli ma?
Just these two pieces of luggage?

4. FUENTES:
对。从这儿到机场需要多少时间？
Duì. Cóng zhèr dào jīchǎng xūyào duōshǎo shíjiān?
Yes. How long does it take to get from here to the airport?

5. DRIVER:
四十分钟左右吧。糟糕，这儿又堵车了，我们只好换条别的路走了。
Sìshífēn zhōng zuǒyòu ba. Zāogāo, zhèr yòu dǔchē le, wǒmen zhǐhǎo huàn tiáo biéde lù zǒule.
Probably about forty minutes. Darn, there's a traffic jam here again, we'll have to change to a different route.

6. FUENTES: *(when they arrive at the airport):*

多少钱?

Duōshǎo qián?

How much is it?

7. DRIVER: 一百二十八块四。

Yìbǎi èrshibākuài sì.

RMB 128.40.

8. FUENTES: 给您一百五十块。您找我二十块就好了。

Gěi nín yìbǎi wǔshikuài. Nín zhǎo wǒ èrshikuài jiù hǎole.

Here's a hundred fifty dollars. Give me twenty bucks in change and that will be fine.

9. DRIVER: 谢谢。

Xièxie.

Thanks.

10. FUENTES: 再见。

Zàijiàn.

Goodbye.

11. DRIVER: 再见。

Zàijiàn.

Bye.

New Vocabulary

件	jiàn	(measure for luggage, matters)
行李	xíngli	luggage, baggage
需要	xūyào	need
糟糕	zāogāo	"darn it"; be a mess
堵车	dǔchē	be clogged up with cars
只好	zhǐhǎo	have no choice but
换	huàn	change to, exchange
条	tiáo	(for streets, alleys)
别的	biéde	other, another
找	zhǎo	give in change

Supplementary Vocabulary

开车	kāichē	drive a car
应当	yīngdāng	should, ought to
找钱	zhǎoqián	give (someone) change
轻	qīng	be light (not heavy)

重	**zhòng**	be heavy
公斤	**gōngjīn**	kilo
米	**mǐ**	meter
半天	**bàntiān**	"half the day," a long time
最后	**zuìhòu**	in the end, finally
师傅	**shīfu**	master; driver
塞车	**sāichē**	be clogged up with cars

Notes on the Conversation

Specifier + number + measure + noun

You've seen before the pattern specifier + measure + noun, for example, **zhèijiàn xíngli** "this piece of luggage." You've also seen the pattern number + measure + noun, for example, **liǎngjiàn xíngli** "two pieces of luggage." In this conversation you learn a new pattern where these two old patterns have been combined. The new pattern is specifier + number + measure + noun, for example, **zhèiliǎngjiàn xíngli** "these two pieces of luggage." More examples: **zhèisānzhāng zhuōzi** "these three tables," **nèibáge rén** "those eight people," **něiliǎngliàng chē?** "which two cars?," **měishíge yuè** "every ten months," **"péngyou" zhèiliǎngge zì** "these two characters in the word 'friend.'"

....

cóng…dào…

The pattern **cóng…dào…** "from…to…" is a common pattern for expressing the beginning and ending points when talking about places, directions, destinations, times, and dates. Examples: **Cóng Běijīng dào Tiānjīn bú tài yuǎn** "From Beijing to Tianjin isn't too far," **Wǎnfàn shi cóng jǐdiǎn dào jǐdiǎn?** "Dinner is from what time until what time?," **Tā cóng 1981 nián dào 1987 nián zài Běidà xuéxí** "From 1981 to 1987 she studied at Beijing University," **Tā měitiān cóng zǎoshang dào wǎnshang yìzhí dōu hěn máng** "He's busy every day all the time from morning to evening."

....

Zhǐhǎo

The adverb **zhǐhǎo** "have no choice but, can only" is commonly used to indicate that no alternative is available and you must choose a less desirable course of action. Examples: **Wǒmen zhǐhǎo míngtiān zài lái** "We've no choice but to come again tomorrow," **Túshūguǎn yǐjīng guānle, wǒmen zhǐhǎo huí sùshè** "The library has already closed, we've no choice but to return to our dorm," **Xiǎo Wáng bú zài, wǒmen zhǐhǎo gěi tā liú ge tiáozi** "Little Wang isn't here, the only thing we can do is leave him a note."

....

Huàn

The verb **huàn** means "change, exchange." **Huàn lù** means "change roads." Here are some other expressions with **huàn**: **huàn chē** "change buses," **huàn qián** "change money," **huàn fángjiān** "change rooms," **huàn gōngzuò** "change jobs," **huàn rén** "change people," **huàn nánpéngyou** "change boyfriends," **huàn nǚpéngyou** "change girlfriends," **huàn lǎoshī** "change teachers."

....

Height and weight

Learn the stative verb **zhòng** "be heavy." To ask how much a person weighs say **Nǐ duō zhòng?** "How heavy are you?" To answer questions about weight, use the measure **gōngjīn** "kilo." For example, **Wǒ liùshisāngōngjīn** "I weigh 63 kilos" (no verb is needed here). You already know the stative verb **gāo** "be tall." To ask how tall someone is, ask **Nǐ duō gāo?** "How tall are you?" To answer questions about height, use the appropriate number followed by the measure **mǐ** "meter." For the number of centimeters, simply read off one digit after another, in telephone number style. For example, **Wǒ yìmǐ bā'èr** "I'm one meter eighty-two."

Reading

New Characters and Words

235.	件	**jiàn**	(for pieces of luggage, matters, etc.)
	一件事	**yíjiàn shì**	a matter, a thing (abstract)
236.	行	**xíng**	be all right, be O.K.
	行李	**xíngli**	luggage, baggage
237.	需	**xū**	need (can't be used alone)
	需要	**xūyào**	need
238.	只	**zhǐ**	only
	只好	**zhǐhǎo**	have no choice but, can only
239.	换	**huàn**	change, change to, exchange
	换车	**huàn chē**	change buses, change trains
	换工作	**huàn gōngzuò**	change jobs
	换钱	**huàn qián**	change money
	换人	**huàn rén**	change (to other) people
240.	条	**tiáo**	(for long and narrow things)
	条子	**tiáozi**	note (written on a strip of paper)

A. SENTENCES

一、先生，对不起，您好像还没找钱给我呢！

二、这件行李怎么这么轻？是不是里头没有东西？

三、我开车开了半天了，我们换个人开，行不行？

四、李先生，我有一件事需要找您，您现在有没有时间？

五、你行李太多了！去外国好像一个人只能带两件行李。

六、你的男朋友给你的条子上写了什么？

七、这条路车子太多了，我们只好换一条别的路走了。

八、请问，从西安开车到成都需要多长时间？

九、要是需要换钱的话，是不是在机场就可以换？

十、这件事儿，要是王大海也不行，我们只好换人。

B. CONVERSATIONS

一、

司机　：是您要车到首都机场吗？

外国人：对，是我。

司机　：就这两件行李吗？

外国人：对。从这儿到机场需要多少时间？

司机　：一个小时左右吧。这条路车子太多，我们只好换条别的路走
　　　　了。

外国人：多少钱？

司机　：一百二十八块四。

外国人：给您一百五十块。您找我二十块就好了。

司机　：谢谢！

外国人：没事儿。

二、

外国人：司机先生，您看，
　　　　路上车子这么多，
　　　　我们是不是换条别
　　　　的路走比较好？

司机　：您要换别的路也
　　　　行，不过现在是下
　　　　班儿时间，走别的
　　　　路也差不多。

Hong Kong taxi

C. NARRATIVES

一、你说有几个中国？从1949年到现在，北京说："只有一个中国，没有两个中国。"从1949年到现在，台北也说："只有一个中国，没有两个中国。"

二、我是美国大三的学生。我很高兴，下个月就要去北京大学学中文了。我要去中国住一年，所以得带很多东西。不过，机场的人说去外国，一个人只能带两件行李，所以我只好少带东西。中国离美国很远；从我家到北京需要二十四个小时左右，时间太长了！有很多事我还不知道：怎么从机场到北京大学？在哪儿换钱？怎么打电话回家？可是，我去以前大概可以问我这边的中国同学吧。

Notes

B2a. 司机先生, literally "driver sir," is a very polite way to refer to a cab driver or chauffeur.

B2b. 我们是不是换条别的路走比较好？ "Might it be better if we took a different road?" (literally, "As for us, is it or is it not a situation where changing to a different road to go on would be relatively better?"). 是不是 is often used in this manner to make polite suggestions.

B2c. 您要换别的路也行 "If you want to change to another road that also would work" or, in better English, "We could change to a different road."

B2d. 走别的路也差不多 "Going by way of another road would be about the same."

Lost in Beijing

PART ONE

Conversation 🎧

Situation: Cindy Han, a Chinese language student in Beijing, is looking for the Peace Hotel and asks a pedestrian for directions.

1. HAN:

对不起，请问，去和平宾馆怎么走？

Duìbuqǐ, qǐng wèn, qù Hépíng Bīnguǎn zěmme zǒu?

Excuse me, how do you get to the Peace Hotel?

2. FIRST CHINESE PEDESTRIAN:

对不起，我不是本地人，我也不太清楚。那儿有一位交通警，您去问他吧。

Duìbuqǐ, wǒ bú shi běndì rén, wǒ yě bú tài qīngchu. Nàr yǒu yíwèi jiāotōngjǐng, nín qù wèn tā ba.

Sorry, I'm not from here, I'm not sure either. Over there is a traffic policeman, why don't you go ask him.

3. HAN:

(asks another pedestrian):

劳驾，请问，去和平宾馆怎么走？

Láojià, qǐng wèn, qù Hépíng Bīnguǎn zěmme zǒu?

Pardon me, how do you get to the Peace Hotel?

4. SECOND CHINESE PEDESTRIAN:	从这儿一直往前走。过了第二个红绿灯，往北拐。再走差不多五分钟就到了。

Cóng zhèr yìzhí wàng qián zǒu. Guòle dì'èrge hónglǜdēng, wàng běi guǎi. Zài zǒu chàbuduō wǔfēn zhōng jiù dàole.

From here keep going straight. When you pass the second traffic light, turn to the north. Go another five minutes or so and you'll be there.

5. HAN:	谢谢。

Xièxie.

Thanks.

6. SECOND CHINESE PEDESTRIAN:	不用谢。

Bú yòng xiè.

Don't mention it.

New Vocabulary

和平宾馆	**Hépíng Bīnguǎn**	Peace Hotel
本地	**běndì**	this place, here
清楚	**qīngchu**	be clear, clear about
交通警	**jiāotōngjǐng**	traffic police
红	**hóng**	be red
绿	**lǜ**	be green
灯	**dēng**	light, lamp
红绿灯	**hónglǜdēng**	traffic light
拐	**guǎi**	turn
不用	**bú yòng**	not need to, don't need to
谢	**xiè**	thank
不用谢	**bú yòng xiè**	"don't mention it"

Supplementary Vocabulary

路口	**lùkǒu**	intersection
转	**zhuǎn**	turn
警察	**jǐngchá**	police, policeman, policewoman
交通警察	**jiāotōng jǐngchá**	traffic police
颜色	**yánsè**	color
黑	**hēi**	be black
白	**bái**	be white
蓝	**lán**	be blue
黄	**huáng**	be yellow

红色	**hóngsè**	the color red
蓝色	**lánsè**	the color blue
黑色	**hēisè**	the color black
白色	**báisè**	the color white
绿色	**lùsè**	the color green
黄色	**huángsè**	the color yellow

Notes on the Conversation

Chinese equivalents of English "ask"

Wèn means "ask" in the sense of asking someone a question. For example, **Nǐ yàoshi bù dǒngde huà, yào wèn lǎoshī a!** "If you don't understand, you should ask the teacher!" If the sense is politely asking or requesting someone to do something (as in "Ask him to come again tomorrow") or inviting someone to some event (as in "Ask her over to dinner"), then you can't use **wèn** but must use **qǐng** "invite" instead, for example, **Qǐng tā míngtiān zài lái** "Ask him to come again tomorrow" or **Qǐng tā dào wǒmen jiā lái chī fàn** "Ask her over to our house for dinner." If a superior asks an inferior to do something, then **qǐng** is considered too polite and **jiào** "tell (someone to do something)" or **ràng** "have (someone do something)" are used instead, for example, **Lǎoshī jiào wǒmen zuò zuòyè** "The teacher asked us to do our homework."

Sign on building in Beijing housing development

Bú yòng xiè

Bú yòng xiè "don't need to thank, don't mention it, you're welcome" is very common. Besides the verb **xiè** "thank," this expression is made up of **bú** "not" and **yòng**, an auxiliary verb meaning "need to" (as in **Wǒ yòng qù ma?** "Do I need to go?"). The negative **bú yòng** is much more common than the affirmative **yòng**. **Bú yòng** can also be used with verbs besides **xiè**. Examples: **Nǐ bú yòng shuō** "You don't need to say it," **Nǐ bú yòng gěi tā qián** "You don't need to give her money," **Nǐ bú yòng gēn wǒ qù** "You don't have to go with me," **Bú yòng zhǎo** "Keep the change."

Color terms

Most of the various color terms are stative verbs, so that **hóng**, for example, means "to be red." To transform these stative verbs into nouns, **-sè** "color" is added, for example, **hóngsè** "the color red." To make adjectives out of the forms with **-sè**, a **-de** can be added, for example, **hóngsède xíngli** "red-colored luggage." To ask "What color is it?," say **Shì shémme yánsède?** Color stative verbs work differently from other stative verbs in that to say that something is a certain color, such as green, you say that it is "a green one." For example, in English we can say "The grass is green" but in Chinese, if you say **Cǎo hěn lù**, that stresses the intensity of the color green (as in "The grass is *really* green!"). If you simply wish to comment that "The grass is green," then the normal way to say this in Chinese is **Cǎo shi lùde**. Similarly, "The sky is blue" is **Tiān shi lánde**.

Reading

New Characters and Words

241.	平	píng	even, balanced, flat; calm, peaceful
	和平	hépíng	peace
242.	本	běn	root; this (can't be used alone)
	本地	běndì	this place, here
	本地人	běndì rén	person from "this area," local person
	日本	Rìběn	Japan
	日本人	Rìběn rén	Japanese person
	日本话	Rìběn huà	Japanese language
243.	直	zhí	straight
	一直	yìzhí	straight
244.	分	fēn	minute; cent, fen (unit of currency)
	一分钟	yìfēn zhōng	one minute
	一分钱	yìfēn qián	one cent, one penny, one fen
245.	清	qīng	clear; Qing (Dynasty) (can't be used alone)
246.	楚	chǔ	clear (can't be used alone)
	清楚	qīngchu	be clear, be clear about

A. SENTENCES

一、您往前走，一直走到前面那个路口，就到和平饭店了。

二、从1928年一直到1949年，北京不叫"北京"，叫"北平"。

三、小妹妹，你真有钱！你说，你那儿有几分钱？

四、（电话里）平小姐，我十分钟就到您那儿，您等我一下！

五、本地的日本饭真好吃，也不贵。

六、明明，你听我说，这个路口车很多，我们得先左右看一下。

七、对不起，我写得不太清楚，这是一个"平"字，不是"半"。

八、我问你，要是一个人一分钟能写三十个字的话，那么十分钟能写多少字？

九、日本的首都叫东京；听说东京人说的日本话真好听。

十、王大海需要换钱，可是他不太清楚到什么地方去换钱。

B. CONVERSATIONS

一、

钱海文：请问，和平饭店离这儿有多远？

王金平：对不起，我不是本地人，我也不太清楚。

钱海文： 请问，和平饭店离这儿有多远？
安中天： 要走差不多十分钟吧。
钱海文： 一直走就可以到吗？
安中天： 不是，你得在下一个路口往东走。
钱海文： 我知道了，谢谢！

二、
高老师： 请问，机场在哪里？
林小明： 对不起，我不是本地人，这个我不太清楚。您问那位先生吧。
高老师： 先生，请问机场在哪里？
山口　 ： 我不是中国人，我是日本人。您说机场？对不起，我也不清楚。
高老师： 先生，请问，您知道不知道机场在哪里？
王京生： 机场，是吗？机场在城外头，离这儿很远。不过，我也要去机场，我车上还有一个位子，你可以和我一起去。

C. NARRATIVES

一、前天有一个人问我和平饭店在哪里？我因为不是本地人，所以我说对不起，我也不清楚。今天又有两个人问我和平饭店在哪里。为什么这么多人要找这家饭店呢？

Beijing street sign

二、楚先生的儿子不是一个好学生，很多事他都不知道。他就知道一年有十二个月，一个月有三十天，别的事他都不太清楚。你问他这个月是几月？他说是一号了。你问他今天几号了？他说是星期一。你问他今年是哪年？他说他忘了。你问他为什么不知道？他说学校里的老师没说。

Notes

A2a.   从⋯⋯一直到⋯⋯ is a common pattern that means "from...straight up to..." or "from...all the way until... ."

A2b.   In 1928, the government of the Republic of China moved the capital of China from Beijing to Nanjing. Since Beijing 北京 literally means "Northern Capital," it was decided to change the name Beijing to Beiping 北平, meaning "Northern Peace."

A10.   他不太清楚到什么地方去换钱 "He wasn't very clear about where he should go to change money." Note that the stative verb 清楚 "be clear about..." can be followed by a clause.

B1.   Observe what Qian Haiwen asks: 和平饭店离这儿有多远？ "How far away from here is the Peace Hotel?" Be sure you understand and can use the pattern: A离B有多遠？ "How far away from B is A?"

Taipei street sign

PART TWO

Conversation 🎧 LISTEN

Situation: Rick Price wants to visit the Summer Palace in Beijing. He asks a pedestrian which bus to take.

1. PRICE: 对不起，请问，去颐和园坐几路车？
   Duìbuqǐ, qǐng wèn, qù Yíhéyuán zuò jǐlù chē?
   Excuse me, to get to the Summer Palace, what bus number do you take?

2. PEDESTRIAN: 颐和园啊？我得想想。您先坐三二三路公共汽车，然后
   换一一一路电车，坐到终点站就是颐和园了。
   Yíhéyuán a? Wǒ děi xiángxiang. Nín xiān zuò sān-èr-sān-lù gōnggòng qìchē, ránhòu huàn yāo-yāo-yāo-lù diànchē, zuòdao zhōngdiǎn zhàn jiù shi Yíhéyuán le.
   The Summer Palace? Let me think. First take bus number 323, and then transfer to street car number 111. Take it to the last stop, which is the Summer Palace.

3. PRICE: 那，我坐到哪儿换一一一路呢？
   Nà, wǒ zuòdao nǎr huàn yāo-yāo-yāo-lù ne?
   And where do I transfer to 111?

4. PEDESTRIAN: 坐到动物园换车。
   Zuòdao Dòngwùyuán huàn chē.
   You transfer at Zoo.

5. PRICE: 谢谢。
   Xièxie.
   Thanks.

6. PEDESTRIAN: 不客气。车来了！快上车吧。
Bú kèqi. Chē láile! Kuài shàngchē ba.
You're welcome. (sees the bus coming) The bus is coming! Get on quick.

New Vocabulary

颐和园	**Yíhéyuán**	Summer Palace
路	**lù**	(for bus routes)
想想	**xiángxiang**	think a bit
公共	**gōnggòng**	public
公共汽车	**gōnggòng qìchē**	public bus, bus
电车	**diànchē**	street car, tram
终点	**zhōngdiǎn**	final or terminal point
站	**zhàn**	station, stop
终点站	**zhōngdiǎn zhàn**	last station, last stop
动物	**dòngwù**	animal
动物园	**dòngwùyuán**	zoo
上车	**shàngchē**	get on a vehicle

Supplementary Vocabulary

车站	**chēzhàn**	bus stop; bus station
不必	**búbì**	don't need to, not be necessary
养	**yǎng**	raise, keep
只	**zhī**	(measure for most animals)
猫	**māo**	cat
鸟	**niǎo**	bird
鱼	**yú**	fish

Notes on the Conversation

Xiān...ránhòu...

The paired adverb pattern **xiān...ránhòu...** "first...then..." is commonly used for indicating the order in which two actions occur. There is often, but not always, a **zài** "again, then" after the **ránhòu**. Examples: **Xiān chīfàn, ránhòu zài qù mǎi dōngxi** "First eat and then go shopping," **Xiān xué shuōhuà, ránhòu zài xué xiězì** "First learn speaking, then learn writing," **Xiān zuò gōnggòng qìchē, ránhòu zài huàn diànchē** "First take the bus, then change to a street car."

Búbì

Búbì "don't need to" is a common way to express the negative of **děi** "must" (*bù děi isn't possible, nor can *bì be said alone in this sense). Contrast these two sentences: **Nǐ děi qù** "You must go" and **Nǐ búbì qù** "You don't need to go." Instead of **Nǐ búbì qù**, you could also say **Nǐ bú yòng qù**, with the same meaning.

Measures for animals

Most animals take the measure **zhī**, so you would say **yìzhī gǒu** "a dog," **yìzhī māo** "a cat," and **yìzhī niǎo** "a bird" However, the word **yú** "fish" takes **tiáo**, so then you would say **yìtiáo yú** "a fish." Instead of **yìzhī gǒu**, there are also some speakers who use the measure **tiáo** "long and thin strip of something" and say **yìtiáo gǒu** "one dog, a dog."

Reading

New Characters and Words

247.	共	**gòng**	altogether
	公共	**gōnggòng**	public
	公共汽车	**gōnggòng qìchē**	public bus, bus
	一共	**yígòng**	in all
248.	站	**zhàn**	station, stop
	车站	**chēzhàn**	bus stop
249.	然	**rán**	thus (can't be used alone)
	然后	**ránhòu**	afterward, then
	先……然后	**xiān...ránhòu**	first...then
250.	动	**dòng**	move
251.	物	**wù**	thing, matter
	动物	**dòngwù**	animal
252.	园	**yuán**	garden, park (can't be used alone)
	动物园	**dòngwùyuán**	zoo

Beijing bus stop

A. SENTENCES

一、65路公共汽车是从北京西站到动物园的。

二、我们先去北京大学看一位老师，然后去北京动物园看动物。

三、从北京西站到天安门坐什么车好？坐公车好？坐电车好？打的好？

四、广州动物园里头一共有多少动物，谁知道？

五、你要是太忙了，没时间从家里打电话，就等一会儿从公共电话打
　　给我也行。

六、请问，去动物园要坐几站？

七、前面那个车站是公车站？是电车站？我是外国人，我不太清楚。

八、我的同屋下个月要先去香港，然后去台湾，一共要走差不多一个
　　星期。

九、请问，去动物园是坐公共汽车比较好呢？是坐电车比较好呢？

十、王大海很喜欢和他的女朋友一起去动物园看动物，听说他们去年
　　一共去了十几次。

B. CONVERSATIONS

一、

外国人：对不起，请问，去长城大饭店坐几路车？

中国人：长城大饭店，是吗？您先坐二〇三路公共汽车，然后换一一
　　　　六路电车。

外国人：那，我坐到哪儿换一一六路呢？

中国人：坐到电话公司换车。

外国人：谢谢！

中国人：没事儿。车来了，上车吧！

二、

关明山：请问，去北京动物园要坐几路公共汽车？

边海清：我看看。去动物园……坐27路、601路都行。

关明山：在哪儿上车？

边海清：前面就是车站。

关明山：那，在哪儿下车呢？

边海清：在动物园站下车。那站就叫"动物园"。

关明山：谢谢您！

边海清：不谢，不谢。

C. NARRATIVES

一、 我的男朋友很喜欢去动物园。他一个星期要去一、两次。他说他很喜欢动物，有时候他觉得人没有动物好呢。我问他为什么这么说，他说他也不太清楚。今天我原来要和他一起去饭店吃一点东西，可是他说十点钟又要带我去动物园了！

二、 今天六点半，我的儿子小安就说他要去动物园。我说："我今天带你去动物园，可是我们得先去买一点儿东西，然后去动物园，好不好？"小安听了很不高兴，因为他不能等。我们只好不买东西，去动物园了。今天是星期天，很多车往动物园去，所以交通不太好。在公共汽车站等车的人也很多，上了公共汽车，也没有位子坐。不过小安很高兴！

Notes

A1. 65路公共汽车是从北京西站到动物园的 "Public bus number 65 is from Beijing West Railway Station to Zoo." The pattern 是……的 here emphasizes that "that's the way it is." Though the following wouldn't normally be said, the underlying structure of the previous sentence could be analyzed as this: 65路公共汽车是从北京西站到动物园的公共汽车 "Public bus number 65 is a public bus that goes from Beijing West Railway Station to Zoo."

A3. 公车 "public bus, bus" is a common abbreviation of 公共汽车.

B2. 不谢 "You're welcome" (literally, "Don't thank") is a common response to expressions of thanks. It is often said twice, as here.

C1. 有时候他觉得人没有动物好 "Sometimes he feels people aren't as good as animals." The pattern A 没有 B C means "A is/are not as C as B." The "kernel" of this sentence is: 人没有动物好 "People aren't as good as animals" (literally, "People don't have animals good").

C2. 今天六点半，我的儿子小安就说他要去动物园 "Today at 6:30 my son, Little An, already said he wanted to go to the zoo." This 就 means "as early as" a given time.

By Bus and Street Car to the Summer Palace

PART ONE

Conversation 🎧

Situation: Price gets on the bus and buys a ticket from the conductress (continued from the previous conversation).

1. CONDUCTRESS: 有买票的吗？没票的买票！
Yǒu mǎi piàode ma? Méi piàode mǎi piào!
Is anybody buying a ticket? Those who don't have a ticket, buy a ticket!

2. PRICE: 一张到动物园儿的。
Yìzhāng dào Dòngwùyuánrde.
One ticket to Zoo.

3. CONDUCTRESS: 您是在哪儿上的？
Nín shi zài nǎr shàngde?
Where did you get on?

4. PRICE: 刚上的。
Gāng shàngde.
I just got on.

5. CONDUCTRESS: 五毛。
Wǔmáo.
Fifty cents.

6. PRICE: 给您钱。到动物园儿麻烦您叫我一下。
Gěi nín qián. Dào Dòngwùyuánr máfan nín jiào wo yixia.
Here's the money. When we get to Zoo, please call me.

7. CONDUCTRESS: 行。
Xíng.
O.K.

New Vocabulary

票	**piào**	ticket
没	**méi**	not have
上	**shàng**	get on
刚	**gāng**	just now, just
叫	**jiào**	call (someone)

Supplementary Vocabulary

聪明	**cōngming**	be smart
笨	**bèn**	be stupid
懒	**lǎn**	be lazy
用功	**yònggōng**	be hardworking, studious
干净	**gānjìng**	be clean
脏	**zāng**	be dirty
整齐	**zhěngqí**	be in order, neat
乱	**luàn**	be disorderly, messy
售票员	**shòupiàoyuán**	ticketseller, conductor
刚刚	**gānggāng**	just now, just
不但	**búdàn**	not only
而且	**érqiě**	moreover, and, also
生气	**shēngqì**	get angry
开玩笑	**kāi wánxiào**	joke around, play a prank
说笑话(儿)	**shuō xiàohua(r)**	tell a joke
希望	**xīwàng**	hope

Notes on the Conversation

The two meanings of méi

Note the **méi** "not have" in **méi piàode** "one who doesn't have a ticket." **Méi** is an abbreviated form of **méiyou**; a fuller form of **méi piàode** would be **méiyou piàode rén**. You've actually seen this use of **méi** to mean **méiyou** before in **méi yìsi** "not be interesting," **méi guānxi** "never mind," and **méi shì** "it's nothing." So now you should realize that there are actually two **méi**: the one that indicates past negative of action verbs (**Wǒ méi qù** "I didn't go), and the one that means "not have" or "there is/are not." Also note that while **méiyou** can occur at the end of a sentence or question, the abbreviated form **méi** ordinarily can't.

The adverb gāng

Gāng "just now, just" is a common and useful adverb that refers to the immediate past, or to a past action that occurred or was to occur immediately prior to some other past action. There is usually no **-le** at the end of verbs occurring after **gāng**. To negate a sentence with **gāng**, place **bú shi** before the **gāng**; don't use **méi**. Examples: **Tā gāng dào** "He just arrived," **Wǒ gāng yào zǒu, tā jiù láile** "I was just about to leave when she came," **Nǐ gāng cóng Měiguo lái, dàgài hái bù xíguàn** "You just came from America, probably you aren't used to it yet," **Wǒ bú shi gāng láide, wǒ yǐjīng láile yíge duō zhōngtóu le!** "I didn't just come, I've been here for over an hour!"

Búdàn...érqiě...

The pattern **búdàn...érqiě...** "not only...but also..." is a common and useful pattern that emphasizes the information contained in the second part of the sentence (the part that follows the **érqiě**). The meanings of the two parts of the sentence must logically build upon and reinforce each other; the two parts must either both be positive or else both be negative. Sometimes **búdàn** can occur with **hái** instead of **érqiě**. Examples: **Xiǎo Zhèng búdàn cōngming, érqiě hěn yònggōng** "Little Zheng is not only smart but also very hard-working," **Tā búdàn lǎn, érqiě hěn bèn** "He's not only lazy, but also very stupid," **Wǒmen búdàn shi tóngshì, érqiě yě shi péngyou, duì bu dui?** "We're not only colleagues, but also friends, right?," **Tā búdàn huì shuō Guóyǔ, hái huì shuō qítāde wàiyǔ** "He not only can speak Mandarin, he can also speak other foreign languages."

READING

New Characters and Words

253.	买	mǎi	buy
254.	卖	mài	sell
	买卖	mǎimài	buying and selling, business
255.	票	piào	ticket
256.	张	zhāng	(for flat objects like tables, name cards)
257.	刚	gāng	just now, just
	刚刚	gānggāng	just now, just
258.	毛	máo	ten cents, dime

A. SENTENCES

一、以前北京的公车票一张只要五毛钱，可是现在好像要一块了。

二、美国人说"十五分钱"，中国人说"一毛五分钱"。

三、我刚刚给你一张我的名片，你还说我没给你！

四、王小姐，我没叫您，我叫的是文小姐。她今天在不在？

五、听说买票得到公共汽车公司去买了，不能在公车上买了，
　　是真的吗？

六、我刚从机场来，为什么现在又要去机场呢？

七、张南生，毛老师刚叫了你的名字，你怎么还不去？

八、我没钱买公共汽车票，一毛都没有，只好走路。

九、我刚买了两张车票，来，给你一张，我们一起坐车。

十、大海刚卖了他的汽车，他说以后要坐公车、电车。

B. CONVERSATIONS

一、

公车小姐：有买票的吗？没票的买票！

外国人　：一张到动物园儿的。

公车小姐：您是在哪儿上的？

外国人　：刚上的。

公车小姐：一块。

外国人　：给您钱。

二、

毛太太：老张！这几天买卖还行吧？

老张　：不是很好，不过还可以。

毛太太：我买一张公车票。

老张　：好，五毛钱。

毛太太：谢谢你！

老张　：没事儿。

Hong Kong gas station

C. NARRATIVES

一、我表姐小平下个月从香港来美国，她要我给她买一张从我家到 Chicago的票。我买了以后，她说我买的时间不好，所以我只好去换票。我买了第二张票以后，她还是不高兴，说我买的票太贵。我以后不给她买票了。

二、我们都叫老毛"五毛"。他去哪儿都只带五毛钱。老毛以前说是因为没钱，可是他现在是买卖人，很有钱了。不知道为什么，老毛还是只带五毛钱！

Notes

A3. 我刚刚给你一张我的名片，你还说我没给你！ "I just gave you one of my name cards, and you actually say that I didn't give you any!" This 还 expresses emphasis and can be translated as "even," "still," or "actually."

A4. 我叫的是文小姐 "The one I called (for) is Ms. Wen."

A8. 我……一毛都没有 "I don't have even a dime."

C2. 他去哪儿都只带五毛钱 "Wherever he goes, he only takes along 50 cents." When question words are followed by 都, they often take on an indefinite sense of "wherever," "whoever," "whatever," etc.

Hong Kong MTR station

PART TWO

Conversation 🎧

Situation: Price prepares to get off the bus but discovers he has misplaced his ticket. He tells the conductress he can't find his ticket (continued from the previous conversation).

1. PRICE:

快到了吧？

Kuài dàole ba?

I suppose we're almost there?

2. CONDUCTRESS:

早着呢，还有四站。到时候我叫您。喂，下一站就是动物园儿了。您该准备下车了。

Zǎozhe ne, hái yǒu sìzhàn. Dào shíhou wǒ jiào nín. Wèi, xiàyízhàn jiù shi Dòngwùyuánr le. Nín gāi zhǔnbèi xiàchēle.

It's still early, there are still four stops. When the time comes, I'll call you. *(after a while)* Hey, the next station is Zoo. You should prepare to get off.

3. PRICE:

好，谢谢您。

Hǎo, xièxie nín.

O.K., thank you.

4. CONDUCTRESS:

(to all passengers):

下车的同志请出示车、月票。

Xiàchēde tóngzhì qǐng chūshì chēyuèpiào.

Comrades who are getting off, please show your individual or monthly tickets.

5. PRICE:

(about to get off the bus, searching for his ticket):

对不起，我的票找不着了。

Duìbuqǐ, wǒde piào zhǎobuzháole.

I'm sorry, I can't find my ticket.

6. CONDUCTRESS: 没关系，我记得您买过票了。以后可得小心点儿！

Méi guānxi, wǒ jìde nín mǎiguo piào le. Yǐhòu kě děi xiǎoxīn diǎnr!

That's all right, I remember you bought a ticket. In the future you really should be more careful!

New Vocabulary

早	**zǎo**	be early
着	**-zhe**	(indicates continuous aspect)
呢	**ne**	(indicates continuous aspect)
喂	**wèi**	"hey"
该	**gāi**	should
准备	**zhǔnbèi**	prepare, plan
下车	**xiàchē**	get off a vehicle
同志	**tóngzhì**	comrade
出示	**chūshì**	show, produce
车票	**chēpiào**	bus ticket
月票	**yuèpiào**	monthly ticket
找着	**zhǎozháo**	look for and find, find
记得	**jìde**	remember
小心	**xiǎoxīn**	be careful

Supplementary Vocabulary

睡着	**shuìzháo**	fall asleep
找到	**zhǎodào**	look for and find, find
听	**tīng**	hear, listen
懂	**dǒng**	understand
听懂	**tīngdǒng**	hear and understand
看	**kàn**	read
看懂	**kàndǒng**	read and understand

Notes on the Conversation

The suffix -zhe to indicate continuous aspect

In this line of the conversation, note **zǎozhe ne** "it's continuing being early" or "it's still early." The verb suffix **-zhe** can be attached to various kinds of verbs to indicate continuous aspect, that is, that some action or state (in this case "earliness") is continuing over a period of time. This **-zhe** sometimes corresponds to the "-ing" form of the verb in English. Sentence-final particle **ne** is often added at the end of the sentence to further emphasize the continuous aspect. More examples: **Mén hái kāizhe ne** "The door is still open," **Tāmen dōu hái zài fángjiānli zuòzhe ne** "They're all still sitting in the room."

....

Tóngzhì

The gender-neutral term **tóngzhì** "comrade" (literally, "same aspiration") was introduced to China with the advent of Communism in the early years of the twentieth century. From the 1950s through the 1980s, **tóngzhì** was used commonly throughout China, supplanting the more traditional terms **xiānsheng**, **tàitai**, and **xiáojie**. In recent years, due to the opening of Chinese society and influence from Taiwan and Hong Kong, where the traditional terms continued to be used, **xiānsheng** and (to a lesser extent) **tàitai** and **xiáojie** have made a come-back. While the word **tóngzhì** is now used less commonly than before, it is still used to refer to people in the Communist Party and is sometimes encountered on other occasions as well. In recent years, **tóngzhì** has gained an additional meaning of "gay person" or "homosexual." Compare the following words that all begin with the same syllable **tóng-**: **tóngshì** "colleague," **tóngwū** "roommate," **tóngxué** "classmate," **tóngzhì** "comrade."

....

Potential resultative compounds

A resultative compound like **zhǎozháo** "find" in the middle of which has been added the infix **-de-** means "be able to... ." A resultative verb in the middle of which has been added the infix **-bu-** means "not be able to... ." Examples: **zhǎo** "look for," **zhǎozháo** "look for and find," **zhǎodezháo** "be able to find," **zhǎobuzháo** "be unable to find"; **kàn** "see," **kàndào** "see," **kàndedào** "be able to see," **kànbudào** "be unable to see." The affirmative and negative potential resultative compounds can be used together to form affirmative-negative questions, for example, **Nǐ kàndedào kànbudào?** "Are you able to see it?" Pay careful attention to the difference between negative potential resultative compounds (for example, **zhǎobudào** "couldn't find") and resultative compounds with **méi** (for example, **méi zhǎodào** "didn't find"). The former indicate inability while the latter simply indicate that some action didn't take place. Although **néng** and **kéyi** can also be used to express ability and inability, potential resultative compounds are particularly common and idiomatic in Chinese, and you should make an effort to incorporate them into your speech.

....

READING

New Characters and Words

259.	早	**zǎo**	be early
	早上	**zǎoshang**	in the morning
	早饭	**zǎofàn**	breakfast
260.	着	**-zháo; -zhe**	(action of verb is realized); (continuous aspect)
261.	记	**jì**	remember; record
	记得	**jìde**	remember
262.	心	**xīn**	heart, mind
	小心	**xiǎoxīn**	be careful
	中心	**zhōngxīn**	center

263.	准	**zhǔn**	be accurate
264.	备	**bèi**	prepare (can't be used alone)
	准备	**zhǔnbèi**	prepare, get ready; plan, intend

A. SENTENCES

一、老毛，你现在就要走了吗？还早着呢，多坐一会儿吧。

二、请您别准备早饭，我知道吃早饭比较好，可是我们家里早上不吃早饭。

三、从1929年在中国北方找到的"北京人"可以知道，很早以前，那个地方就有人住了。

四、这条路车子太多了，你要记得，走路要很小心！

五、你的名片我记得我有两张，可是不知道为什么，现在找不着了。

六、我们还吃着早饭呢，请她等一会儿，还早着呢。

七、我准备九月先去香港，然后去台湾。

八、有中国人的地方就听得到中国话，吃得到中国饭。

九、你要是找不着小张的话，可以给他写一个条子。他会看中文吧？

十、大海前天给他的女朋友准备了早饭，可是不太好吃，她不喜欢。

B. CONVERSATIONS

一、

外国人　　：到了吧？

公车小姐：早着呢，还有五站，到时候我叫您。（过了几分钟以后）这位先生，下一站就是动物园儿了，您要准备下车了。

外国人　　：好，谢谢您……对不起，我的票找不着了！

公车小姐：我记得您买过票了，以后可得小心点儿。

外国人　　：好的，真对不起。

二、

姐姐：弟弟，你怎么还没去上学？

弟弟：早着呢，我还有时间吃早饭呢。

姐姐：东西都准备好了吗？

弟弟：都准备好了。

姐姐：弟弟，今天第一天上学，你得小心一点儿。别忘了在第五站下车。你听到了吗？

弟弟：听到了，我会记得的。

C. NARRATIVE

北京有一个地方叫"京广中心","京"是"北京"的京,"广"是"广州"的广,在北京市的东边。这个地方北京人都知道,从1990年开到现在有20多年了。京广中心很高也很大,里面有一家很好的饭店、几十家公司,还有卖东西的地方和人住的地方,所以有的人说京广中心是"城里面的城"。不过在京广中心住很贵,一个月大概要一万五千块到两万五千块。不少外国买卖人在京广中心开了公司,也在那儿上班,也在那儿住。京广中心交通还行,外头就有很多车站,离北京站也不远,早上五、六点钟打的去首都机场也只要半小时左右就到了。有一家美国大学开的中文中心离京广中心比较近。要是你是外国人,住在京广中心的话,你大概可以在那儿学中文。

Notes

A1a.　你现在就要走了吗？ "You're leaving right now?" The pattern 就要……了 means "be about to…," so 你现在就要走了吗？ literally means "You now are about to leave?"

A1b.　还早着呢,多坐一会儿吧 "It's still early, why don't you sit a while longer?" The phrase 多坐一会儿 literally means "more sit a while."

A3a.　In this sentence, be sure you understand that the coverb 从 "from" does not go with the year "1929" that follows it (as would often be the case in other sentences), but rather 从 goes with the noun 北京人 that comes later in the sentence. So the "skeleton" of the first phrase is: 从"北京人"可以知道 "from 'Peking Man' we can know that… ."

A3b.　很早以前,那个地方就有人住了 "Long ago, there were already people living in that place." 很早以前 "long ago, a long time ago" is a common and useful phrase that you should memorize as a "chunk." The 就 later in this sentence means "as early as then" or "already."

Taipei bus advertisement

A3c. Here, 北京人 refers to "Peking Man," that is, fossils from the early human known as *Homo erectus pekinensis* that were discovered in the vicinity of Beijing in 1923.

A4. 要 is a verb of many meanings. In 你要记得, the verb 要 indicates necessity, so we could translate this phrase as "you need to remember" or "you should remember."

A6. 我们还吃着早饭呢，请她等一会儿，还早着呢 "We're still eating breakfast; ask her to wait a while, it's still early." In both the first and the last clauses of this sentence, the combination of 着 plus 呢 indicates continuous aspect, in other words, that the action of eating and the state of being early are still continuing and have not yet been completed.

A7. Although the meaning of 准备 is often "prepare" or "get ready," in this sentence it means "plan" or "intend."

A8. 有中国人的地方就听得到中国话，吃得到中国饭 "Wherever there are Chinese people, you can hear the Chinese language and you can eat Chinese food" (literally, "Places where there are Chinese people, can hear Chinese speech, can eat Chinese food").

B1. 过了几分钟以后 "after a few minutes had passed"

B2. 我会记得的 "I'll remember." This 会 means "will." In the speech and writing of many Chinese, especially those from southern mainland China and Taiwan, this 会 that means "will" is often followed at the end of the sentence by an optional 的.

C1. 京广中心交通还行，外头就有很多车站 "Transportation at the Jingguang Center is fairly convenient, there being many bus stops right outside." The 就 in 外头就有 here means "as close as that" or "that close."

LESSON 22
A Weather Forecast

PART ONE

Conversation 🎧

Situation: Holly Young, an English teacher in Taipei, has just gotten up. She walks into the living room of the apartment she and her Taiwanese friend, Su Ning, share and asks Su what the weather forecast is.

1. YOUNG:　早！今天天气预报怎么说？
　　　　　Zǎo! Jīntiān tiānqi yùbào zěmme shuō?
　　　　　Good morning! What's the weather forecast for today?

2. SU:　　*(looking at the weather forecast in the newspaper):*

　　　　　我看看。今天上午是晴天，下午可能会变成阴天。
　　　　　Wǒ kànkan. Jīntiān shàngwǔ shi qíngtiān, xiàwǔ kěnéng huì biànchéng yīntiān.
　　　　　Let me see. This morning will be clear, this afternoon it's possible it will become cloudy.

3. YOUNG:　哦。
　　　　　Ò.
　　　　　Oh.

4. SU: *(continues summarizing the weather forecast):*

从明天开始会越来越热。今天最高温度是二十八度，最低温度是二十四度。

Cóng míngtiān kāishǐ huì yuè lái yuè rè. Jīntiān zuì gāo wēndù shi èrshibādù, zuì dī wēndù shi èrshisìdù.

Starting tomorrow it's going to get hotter and hotter. Today's high will be 28 degrees, the low will be 24 degrees.

5. YOUNG: *(hears sound of thunder and rain):*

诶？好像打雷了！是不是要下雨？哎呀！已经下了，还下得不小诶！

Éi? Hǎoxiàng dǎléile! Shì bu shi yào xiàyǔ? Āiyà! Yǐjīng xiàle, hái xiàde bù xiǎo ei!

Huh? I think I heard thunder. Is it going to rain? Gosh! It's already started raining, and pretty heavily, too!

6. SU: 所以说，天气预报也只是预报而已，不一定准！

Suóyi shuō, tiānqi yùbào yě zhǐ shi yùbào éryǐ, bù yídìng zhǔn.

That's why weather forecasts are merely forecasts, and not necessarily accurate.

New Vocabulary 🎧

早	**zǎo**	"good morning"
天气	**tiānqi**	weather
预报	**yùbào**	forecast
天气预报	**tiānqi yùbào**	weather forecast
晴天	**qíngtiān**	fine day, sunny day
可能	**kěnéng**	be possible
变成	**biànchéng**	change into, become
阴天	**yīntiān**	cloudy or overcast weather
越来越……	**yuè lái yuè…**	more and more…
热	**rè**	be hot
最	**zuì**	most
温度	**wēndù**	temperature
度	**dù**	degree (of temperature)
低	**dī**	be low
诶	**éi**	(introduces questions)
打雷	**dǎléi**	thunder
雨	**yǔ**	rain
下雨	**xiàyǔ**	rain
哎呀	**āiyà**	"oh," "gosh"

所以说	**suóyi shuō**	so, therefore
……而已	**...éryǐ**	...and that's all
一定	**yídìng**	definitely
准	**zhǔn**	be accurate

Supplementary Vocabulary

天	**tiān**	sky
云	**yún**	cloud
闪电	**shǎndiàn**	lightning strikes

Notes on the Conversation

Cóng...kāishǐ

Cóng means "from" and **kāishǐ** means "begin." The pattern **cóng...kāishǐ** means "beginning from..." or "starting from... ." A time expression is often inserted in between **cóng** and **kāishǐ**. Examples: **cóng míngtiān kāishǐ** "starting from tomorrow," **cóng xià xīngqī kāishǐ** "starting next week," **cóng míngnián wǔyuè yīhào kāishǐ** "starting on May 1 of next year."

....

Yuè lái yuè...

The common and useful pattern **yuè lái yuè...** means "more and more..." In English, this pattern is often translated by two adjectives ending in "-er." If the verb or adjective is negative, the Chinese can sometimes be translated by "less and less." Examples: **Nǐde Hànyǔ yuè lái yuè hǎo!** "Your Chinese is getting better and better!," **Zuìjìn wēndù yuè lái yuè gāo** "Recently the temperature has been getting higher and higher," **Wǒ yuè lái yuè bù xǐhuan ta** "I dislike him more and more," **Tā yuè lái yuè huì zuò Zhōngguo cài le** "He can cook Chinese food better and better."

....

Éryǐ

Éryǐ can occur at the end of a sentence to express "and that's all" or "nothing more." **Éryǐ** may be used alone or in combination with a preceding adverb like **zhǐ** "only" or **jiù** "only." Examples: **Tiānqi yùbào zhǐ shi yùbào éryǐ** "Weather forecasts are only forecasts and that's all," **Wǒ zhǐ yǒu yìbǎikuài éryǐ** "I have only one hundred dollars and that's all," **Wǒmen bù yídìng zhēn xiǎng mǎi shémme, zhǐ shi kànkan éryǐ** "We don't necessarily really want to buy something, we're just looking, that's all."

....

READING

New Characters and Words

265.	越	**yuè**	exceed; more
	越来越……	**yuè lái yuè**	more and more
	越南	**Yuènán**	Vietnam

越南文	**Yuènánwén**	written Vietnamese language
越南话	**Yuènán huà**	spoken Vietnamese language
越南人	**Yuènán rén**	Vietnamese person

266. 最   **zuì**   most

     最近   **zuìjìn**   recently; in the near future

     最后   **zuìhòu**   in the end, finally

267. 温   **wēn**   warm, mild

     最高温   **zuì gāowēn**   highest temperature

     温州   **Wēnzhōu**   (city in Zhejiang Province)

268. 低   **dī**   be low

     最低温   **zuì dīwēn**   lowest temperature

269. 度   **dù**   degree (of temperature)

     温度   **wēndù**   temperature

     最高温度   **zuì gāo wēndù**   highest temperature

     最低温度   **zuì dī wēndù**   lowest temperature

270. 定   **dìng**   settle, determine

     一定   **yídìng**   definitely

     不一定   **bù yídìng**   not necessarily

A. SENTENCES

一、你的中文说得越来越准，可是我的中文好像越来越差！

二、你最喜欢吃什么？最不喜欢吃什么？

三、你会不会觉得最近温度好像越来越低了？

四、本地的最高温大概几度？最低温几度？

五、我们不一定得去动物园，你不要去我们就不去了！

六、这个我以前还真没听说过，不可能吧！

七、小心！有一个小动物离你越来越近了！

八、我开始上班以后，不知道为什么，越来越没钱。

九、那个人不一定是中国人，可能是越南人吧。

十、王大海那个人真好，早上看到人，一定说"早，您好"。

B. CONVERSATIONS

一、

王先生：李开来，早！

李先生：王定和，早！你最近还好吧？

王先生：我最近越来越忙。

李先生：可是你最近钱越来越多，不是吗？

王先生：不是。我越来越忙，不过钱越来越少！

李先生：那你可能得换一个工作！

二、

温州人：你知道中国去年的GDP是多少吗？

上海人：我只知道中国的GDP最近几年越来越高，可是说真的，我不太清楚去年是多少。

C. NARRATIVES

一、有一个外国人在中国住了很长时间了，中文原来很好，不过不知道为什么，他的中文最近越来越差。他的中国同事说"请坐"，他听成了"请走"，他觉得同事大概不喜欢外国人。他要问他的中国朋友"你最近好不好？"，可是他不小心，说成了"你最近老不老？"。"左"字他看成了"右"字，"十"字他写成了"千"字。最后他觉得中文太难太难了，就回国去了。

二、中国一共有多少姓？北京有一个"姓名中心"，那儿的人说他们最近找到了四千一百多个中国人的姓。他们说北京人姓王的最多，姓张的第二多，姓李的第三多。王、张、李这三个姓都是中国人的"大姓"。他们还说，十个北京人里头就有一个姓王。有一位中国大学老师说，最近在中国，三个字的姓名越来越多。原来在中国三个字的姓名很多，可是从1960年到1990年出生的中国人，两个字的姓名的比较多。不过，从差不多2000年开始，三个字的姓名又多起来了。最后那位老师还说，中国人有的时候说"两个姓李的人五百年以前是一家人"，这么说不一定对。

"Diligently study the new traffic regulations"

Notes

A3.   你会不会觉得 literally means "Would you be likely to feel that...?" However, in actual use, it's just an equivalent of English "Do you feel that...?"

A5.   你不要去我们就不去了 here means "If you don't want to go, then we won't go!"

A6.   这个我以前还真没听说过 "This I really have never heard of before." The 还 here means "really," "even," or "actually" and serves to strengthen the negative sense of the verb.

A10.   早上看到人 means "In the morning when he sees people." 看到 means "see" (someone or something).

C1.   "左"字他看成了"右"字，"十"字他写成了"千"字 "He read the character for 'left' as the character for 'right,' and he wrote the character for 'ten' as the character for 'thousand.'" Notice how characters are quoted in Chinese: "左"字 "the character **zuǒ**," etc.

C2a.   多起来了 here means "became many" or "increased."

C2b.   两个姓李的人五百年以前是一家人 "Five hundred years ago, two people with the surname Li were members of the same family." This is commonly said and believed but, as this narrative points out, it isn't really true.

Detail of a Taoist temple in Penghu, Taiwan

PART TWO

Conversation 🎧

Situation: Oliver Kerr is chatting with a Chinese classmate on the campus of Beijing Foreign Studies University one fine October morning.

1. KERR:

北京的天气不错嘛！不冷也不热，挺舒服。

Běijīngde tiānqi bú cuò ma! Bù lěng yě bú rè, tǐng shūfu.

Hey, the weather in Beijing isn't bad! It's neither cold nor hot, quite comfortable.

2. CHINESE CLASSMATE:

也就是秋天还可以。夏天热得要死。冬天又干又冷，很少下雪。

Yě jiù shi qiūtiān hái kéyi. Xiàtiān rède yào sǐ. Dōngtiān yòu gān yòu lěng, hěn shǎo xiàxuě.

Fall is pretty good. Summers are extremely hot. Winters are both dry and cold, and it seldom snows.

3. KERR:

那，春天呢？

Nà, chūntiān ne?

Well, what about the spring?

4. CHINESE CLASSMATE:

如果不是风沙太大就好了。要想在北京玩儿，也就是秋天最合适。

Rúguǒ bú shi fēngshā tài dà jiù hǎole. Yào xiǎng zài Běijīng wánr yě jiù shi qiūtiān zuì héshì.

If there weren't so much wind and sand it would be O.K. If you want to have a good time in Beijing, the fall is best.

5. KERR:

这么说，我来得正是时候了。
Zhèmme shuō, wǒ láide zhèng shi shíhou le.
Then I've come at just the right time.

6. CHINESE CLASSMATE:

对。
Duì.
Right.

New Vocabulary

父亲	**fùqin**	father
冷	**lěng**	be cold
舒服	**shūfu**	be comfortable
秋天	**qiūtiān**	fall, autumn
夏天	**xiàtiān**	summer
死	**sǐ**	die
冬天	**dōngtiān**	winter
干	**gān**	be dry
很少	**hěn shǎo**	seldom
雪	**xuě**	snow
下雪	**xiàxuě**	snow
春天	**chūntiān**	spring
如果	**rúguǒ**	if
风	**fēng**	wind
沙	**shā**	sand, gravel
风沙	**fēngshā**	wind and sand; blowing sand
要	**yào**	if
玩(儿)	**wán(r)**	play, have a good time
合适	**héshì**	be appropriate
这么说	**zhèmme shuō**	saying it like this; then
正	**zhèng**	just

Supplementary Vocabulary

季节	**jìjié**	season
太阳	**tàiyáng**	sun
出太阳	**chū tàiyáng**	the sun comes/is out

Notes on the Conversation

Bù...yě bù...

The pattern **bù...yě bù...** means "neither...nor... ." Examples: **Jīntiān tiānqi bù lěng yě bú rè** "Today the weather is neither cold nor hot," **Wǒde péngyou bù duō yě bù shǎo** "My friends are neither many nor few," **Tā shuō Zhōngwén bù nán yě bù róngyi** "He said that Chinese was neither hard nor easy."

Stative verb + -de + yào sǐ

Rède yào sǐ literally means "be hot to the extent that one is going to die" or "so hot you're going to die," in other words, "extremely hot." This **-de**, which expresses extent ("so...that..."), is often attached to stative verbs. The expression **...yào sǐ** "...going to die" is used in informal speech for unpleasant matters. More examples: **Wǒ lèide yào sǐ** "I'm extremely tired," **Tā zuìjìn mángde yào sǐ** "She's been extremely busy recently," **Kuài yào kǎoshìle, wǒ jǐnzhāngde yào sǐ!** "Soon we'll be testing, I'm incredibly nervous!"

Yòu...yòu...

With affirmative verbs, the paired adverb pattern **yòu...yòu...** means "both...and... ." This pattern indicates that several states or actions exist at the same time. Therefore, the two expressions that come after the two **yòu** must logically be able to complement each other and can't contradict each other. For example, you could say **yòu hǎo yòu piányi** "both good and cheap" but you could not normally say *yòu hǎo yòu guì "both good and expensive." More examples: **Nèige xuésheng yòu cōngming yòu yònggōng** "That student is both smart and diligent," **Tā shuōhuà yòu kuài yòu bù qīngchu** "She speaks both fast and unclearly," **Tā yòu bú huì shuō Zhōngguo huà, yòu bú huì xiě Zhōngguo zì** "He can neither speak Chinese nor write it."

Conditional sentences with rúguǒ...jiù...

This pattern, which means "if...then...," is a common way to express a condition. For example, **Rúguǒ xiàxuě, wǒ jiù bú qù** "If it snows, I (then) won't come." **Rúguǒ...jiù...** is equivalent in meaning to **yàoshi...jiù...**, except that the pattern with **yàoshi** is more colloquial and is used mainly in Northern China. The pattern with **rúguǒ**, on the other hand, can be written as well as spoken and is common throughout the Chinese-speaking world. More examples: **Rúguǒ tā lái, wǒ jiù bù lái** "If she comes, (then) I won't come," **Rúguǒ nǐ bù xǐhuan, wǒ jiù bù mǎi** "If you don't like it, (then) I won't buy it," **Rúguǒ xiàyǔde huà, wǒmen jiù bú qù** "If it should rain, (then) we won't go."

Reading

New Characters and Words

271.	气	**qì**	gas, air
	天气	**tiānqi**	weather
	生气	**shēngqì**	get angry
272.	冷	**lěng**	be cold
273.	热	**rè**	be hot

274.	死	**sǐ**	die
275.	干	**gān**	be dry
276.	正	**zhèng**	just

A. SENTENCES

一、有的人比较喜欢热的天气，有的人比较喜欢冷的天气。

二、那儿的天气不冷也不热，就是太干了。

三、今天外面真是冷得要死。

四、你们来得正是时候，不冷也不热。

五、广州的天气要是不这么热就好了。

六、那个地方不是热得要死就是冷得要死，怎么能住呢？

七、现在是七月，天气怎么这么冷？这儿七月很少这么冷。

八、这条路又难走，车子又多，我们换条别的路走吧。

九、你说你不是学生，这么说，你是老师吧？

十、王大海又要去动物园了。他的女朋友很少生气，不过这次她真的生气了。

B. CONVERSATIONS

一、

方国兴：小王，早！

王外山：小方，早！今天天气好吗？

方国兴：太热了，真是热得要死！

王外山：你知道现在外面有多少度？

方国兴：我也不太清楚，可是听说今天最高气温是四十一度。

二、

金小姐：何小姐，你来得正是时候！

何小姐：是吗？为什么呢？

金小姐：我们这里十月的天气最好。

何小姐：那太好了。我上次来真是热死了。

金小姐：你上次是什么时候来的？

何小姐：好像是七月吧。

C. NARRATIVES

一、我觉得最近几年，本地的天气越来越好。从前这儿不是太冷就是太热。一月冷得要死，八月又热得要死，天气也很干。可是现在很少那么干，温度不高也不低，天气不冷也不热。正好！

二、我们都知道，有的人很喜欢生气，还有的人很少生气。我有一个
朋友，老毛，他很少生气。不过，要是老毛生气的话，他可真的
会生很大的气。老毛是一个……等一下儿，什么事儿？是不是老
毛生气了？我们小心一点儿，离他远点儿比较好。走吧！

Notes

B1. The character 兴 is a 多音字 **duōyīnzì** "character with multiple pronunciations." You learned it previously with the pronunciation **xing** as in 高兴. However, in personal and geographical names, 兴 is usually pronounced **xīng**. Therefore, the personal name 方国兴 should be pronounced **Fāng Guóxīng**.

C1. 从前这儿不是太冷就是太热 "Formerly, if it wasn't too cold here then it was too hot" or "It used to be that it was either too cold here or else it was too hot." Learn the pattern 不是A就是B "if it isn't A, then it's B" or "it's either A or B."

C2a. 生很大的气 "get very angry"

C2b. 等一下儿，什么事儿？ "Wait a second, what's the matter?"

C2c. 离他远点儿比较好 "it would be better to get further away from him"

A park in Taipei

Talking about the Weather in Your Hometown

PART ONE

Conversation 🎧

Situation: Eileen Thompson is in Taipei for several days, staying at the Japanese-style home of her Taiwanese friend, Wu Xiaoling. The two women are chatting when Thompson sees heavy fog right outside the screen door.

1. **THOMPSON:** 今天早上怎么又有雾！好像是从纱窗飘进来的样子。

    Jīntiān zǎoshàng zěmme yòu yǒu wù? Hǎoxiàng shi cóng shāchuāng piāojìnláide yàngzi.

    How come there's fog again this morning? It seems like it floated in through the window screen.

2. **WU:** 嗯。阳明山冬天常常是这样子。空气很潮湿，也常下毛毛雨。其实，现在就在下，但是因为有雾，所以看不出来。

    M. Yángmíng Shān dōngtiān chángcháng shi zhèiyangzi. Kōngqì hěn cháoshī, yě cháng xià máomáoyǔ. Qíshí, xiànzài jiù zài xià, dànshi yīnwei yǒu wù, suóyi kànbuchūlái.

    Yeah. Yangming Mountain is often like this in the winter. The air is humid and it often drizzles. Actually, it's drizzling right now, but because of the fog, you can't tell.

3. THOMPSON: 我运气真是不好。上次来台湾碰上大台风。这次天天下雨，根本没办法出门！

Wǒ yùnqi zhēn shi bù hǎo. Shàngcì lái Táiwān pèngshang dà táifēng. Zhèicì tiāntiān xiàyǔ, gēnběn méi bànfǎ chūmén!

I'm really unlucky. When I came to Taiwan last time, I encountered a big typhoon. This time it's been raining every day, so I can't go out at all!

New Vocabulary

雾	wù	fog
纱窗	shāchuāng	screen window
飘	piāo	float
来	-lái	(indicates motion toward speaker)
进来	jìnlái	come in
飘进来	piāojìnlái	float in
嗯	m	(indicates agreement)
阳明山	Yángmíng Shān	Yangming Mountain
这样子	zhèiyangzi	this way, like this
空气	kōngqì	air
潮湿	cháoshī	be humid
毛毛雨	máomáoyǔ	light rain
下毛毛雨	xià máomáoyǔ	drizzle
其实	qíshí	actually
在	zài	(indicates progressive aspect)
但是	dànshi	but
出来	chūlái	come out
看出来	kànchūlái	know something by looking
运气	yùnqi	luck
碰	pèng	bump, run into
碰上	pèngshang	run into, encounter
台风	táifēng	typhoon
根本	gēnběn (+ NEGATIVE)	(not) at all
办法(儿)	bànfǎ(r)	way of doing something, method
出门	chūmén	go outside

Supplementary Vocabulary

进去	**jìnqu**	go in
出去	**chūqu**	go out
那样子	**nèiyangzi**	that way, like that

Notes on the Conversation

Hǎoxiàng...-de yàngzi

The pattern **hǎoxiàng...-de yàngzi** means "seem like the appearance of..." or "seem as though..." or "seem like...." A sentence is placed between **hǎoxiàng** and the **-de yàngzi**; **hǎoxiàng** can precede or follow the subject. Examples: **Hǎoxiàng wù cóng shāchuāng piāojìnláide yàngzi** "It seems as though the fog floats in through the window screen," **Hǎoxiàng tā xiànzài bú zàide yàngzi** "It seems she's not here now," **Hǎoxiàng zhèiyàng bǐjiào hǎokànde yàngzi** "It would seem to look better like this."

Directional verbs

In the conversation for this lesson, note the verbs **piāojìnlái** "float in" and **kànbuchūlái** "be unable to tell something by looking." Also note the four important verbs **jìnlái** "come in," **jìnqu** "go in," **chūlái** "come out," and **chūqu** "go out." All of these verb forms are examples of directional verbs. A directional verb is a resultative compound verb composed of a base verb indicating direction or motion to which is attached one of two resultative endings: either **-lái**, which indicates motion toward the speaker, or **-qù**, which indicates motion away from the speaker. For example, take the base verb **jìn** meaning "enter." If we attach to it the resultative ending **-lái**, then we can create the directional verb **jìnlái** "come in." The negatives of the above are all with **méi**: **méi jìnlái** "didn't come in," **méi jìnqu** "didn't go in," **méi chūlái** "didn't come out," and **méi chūqu** "didn't go out." Sometimes resultative compounds composed of directional verbs can themselves function as resultative endings and be attached onto other verbs. That is the case with the verbs **piāojìnlái** and **kànchūlái**, where the verb endings **jìnlái** and **chūlái** themselves function as verb endings that are attached to the base verbs **piāo** "float" and **kàn** "look." Finally, the infixes **-de-** or **-bu-** can be inserted between the base verb and the verb ending of directional verbs to indicate whether the result indicated by the resultative ending can or cannot be achieved, for example, **jìndequ** "able to go in," **chūbulái** "can't come out."

Zài as auxiliary verb to indicate progressive aspect

Look at the phrase in the conversation **xiànzài jiù zài xià** "(light rain) is falling right now." The auxiliary verb **zài** when used before a main verb frequently indicates progressive aspect, that is, that an action is in progress. The meaning is similar to English "be" followed by "VERB + -ing." The action can be present, past, or future, depending on the context. More examples: **Tā zài chīfàn** "She's eating," **Nǐ zài zuò shémme ne?** "What are you doing?," **Wǒ zài xuéxí ne!** "I'm studying!"

Reduplication of measures and nouns to indicate "every"

Certain measures and nouns may be reduplicated to mean "every." For example, the measure **tiān** "day" when reduplicated as **tiāntiān** gains the meaning "every day." A few other measures and nouns operate similarly. More examples: **nián** "year" → **niánnián** "every year," **rén** "person" → **rénrén** "everybody."

The noun suffix -fǎ(r)

The noun **bànfǎ(r)** "way or method of doing something" is composed of the verb **bàn** "do" plus the noun suffix **-fǎ(r)**, which means "way" or "method." Numerous other verbs may also be followed by the suffix **-fǎ(r)** to create nouns. The expression **méi bànfǎ(r)** "have no way to do something" is frequently used in an idiomatic way to mean "no way" or "there's nothing that can be done." More examples: **Duìbuqǐ, méi bànfǎr** "Sorry, there's nothing that can be done," **Wǒ shízài méi bànfǎr** "There was really nothing I could do," **Wǒmen yídìng yào xiǎng ge bànfǎ a!** "We've got to think of a way!" Here are some other verbs that you've learned to which **-fǎ** has been added to create nouns: **kànfǎ** "way of looking at things," **shuōfǎ** "way of speaking," **xiǎngfǎ** "way of thinking," **xiěfǎ** "way of writing."

Reading

New Characters and Words

277.	样	**yàng**	kind, variety; way, manner
	样子	**yàngzi**	way, appearance
	这样	**zhèyang**	this way, like this
	这样子	**zhèyangzi**	this way, like this
	那样	**nàyang**	that way, like that
	那样子	**nàyangzi**	that way, like that
	怎么样	**zěnmeyàng**	how, in what way (pronounced **zěmmeyàng**)
	好像……的样子	**hǎoxiàng...-de yàngzi**	it seems like...
278.	进	**jìn**	enter
	请进	**qǐng jìn**	"please come in"
	进来	**jìnlái**	come in
	进去	**jìnqu**	go in
	走进来	**zǒujìnlái**	come walking in
	走进去	**zǒujìnqu**	go walking in
279.	雨	**yǔ**	rain
	下雨	**xiàyǔ**	to rain
	毛毛雨	**máomáoyǔ**	light rain
	下毛毛雨	**xià máomáoyǔ**	drizzle
280.	但	**dàn**	but
	但是	**dànshi**	but
	不但	**búdàn**	not only
281.	其	**qí**	its, his, her, their
	其他	**qítā**	other

282. 实   shí   real, solid, true
     其实   qíshí   actually
     实在   shízài   really, truly

A. SENTENCES

一、其他的人都出来了，只有小何还没出来。你进去看看，好吗？

二、今天外头不但冷，听说还会下大雨，你别出去了。

三、您六十岁了？实在看不出来！看您的样子，最多四十五岁吧。

四、其实，外面正在下雨，但是因为是毛毛雨，所以看不出来。

五、你进来坐坐吧，外头实在太冷了。不但冷，还在下雨呢。

六、我看不太清楚，但是外面看起来好像在下毛毛雨的样子。

七、林进明天天早上六点钟就出门。你呢？你几点出门？

八、这班学生里头只有一个同学天天都来，其他的有的时候来，有的
    时候不来。

九、好像要下雨的样子，我们进去吧！

十、因为下雨了，所以我们都要回家，只有王大海一定要去动物园。

B. CONVERSATIONS

一、

谢太太：是不是又要下雨了？

边太太：对。其实，现在就在下，但是因为是毛毛雨，所以你可能看
        不出来。

谢太太：我这次来台北，天天都下雨，都不能出门！

边太太：对。不但这样，天气也很冷。下次我们去台中吧。

二、

钱大安：小李，是你吗？请进！最近怎么样？

李平 ：还是老样子。小钱，你看，下雨了！下得越来越大了。我真
        不喜欢这样儿的天气。

钱大安：但是我喜欢。我最喜欢下雨。

李平 ：真的吗？那我得问你，你喜欢下大雨？喜欢下毛毛雨？

钱大安：下大雨，下毛毛雨我都喜欢。

C. NARRATIVES

一、这个地方又干又热，很少下雨，也很少会冷。最高温差不多四十度，最低温差不多二十五度，天天都是这样。最近两个月一次也没下雨。看样子，明后天也不会下雨。但是有人说明天会下大雨。可能吗？实在看不出来。我们等等看吧！

二、有一次，一个住在美国的中国人和他的美国朋友一起去买东西。那个中国人找到了他要的东西，最后问他的美国朋友："好吃吗？"美国人说："这个可不能吃！"中国人说："我不是要吃，我是要知道这个东西卖多少钱。你们美国话'多少钱'不是叫'HAO CHI MA'吗？"过了一会儿，他又说："对不起，其实，我要说的是'HAO MA CHI'，不是'HAO CHI MA'，我外国话不好，我要问卖东西的人'多少钱'"。

Notes

A3. 看您的样子 "looking at your appearance" or, in better English, "from the way you look"

A6. 我看不太清楚，但是外面看起来好像在下毛毛雨的样子 "I can't see very clearly, but outside, from looking at it, it appears to be drizzling." Note 看不太清楚; this is the negative potential resultative compound 看不清楚 "can't see clearly" with an additional 太 infixed into it, meaning 看不太清楚 "not be able to see too clearly" or "can't see very clearly."

A7. 林进明天天早上六点钟就出门 "Lin Jinming goes out every morning at 6:00, that early." The 就 here means "that early" or "as early as that."

A8. 这班学生里头只有一个同学天天都来 "In this class of students there is only one classmate who comes every day." Note the 都 after 天天.

B1. 是不是又要下雨了？ "Is it going to rain again?" Normally, 又 is used for past events, for example, 老毛又生气了 "Old Mao got angry again." However, for events that take place on a regular basis such as rain, 又 can be used when discussing the future.

C1a. 很少下雨，也很少会冷 "It seldom rains, and it'll seldom get cold."

C1b. 最近两个月一次也没下雨 "The last two months it hasn't rained even once." The pattern 一次也没 + VERB means "didn't VERB even once."

C1c. 看样子 "the way it looks" (literally, "looking at appearance")

C1d. 明後天 means "tomorrow or the day after tomorrow." 明 is here an abbreviation for 明天.

C2a. 这个可不能吃 "This you certainly can't eat." Remember that 可 can function as an adverb meaning "certainly, indeed."

C2b. 过了一会儿 "after a while"

PART TWO

Conversation 🎧

Situation: In a park in Beijing, a local Chinese man sees what appears to him to be an overseas Chinese man reading a foreign magazine. He decides to sit down and strike up a conversation.

1. CHINESE: 你好！
   Nǐ hǎo!
   Hi!

2. AMERICAN: 你好！
   Nǐ hǎo!
   Hello!

3. CHINESE: 请问，你是中国人吗？
   Qǐng wèn, nǐ shi Zhōngguo rén ma?
   Excuse me, are you Chinese?

4. AMERICAN: 我是华裔的美国人。
   Wǒ shi Huáyìde Měiguo rén.
   I'm Chinese-American.

5. CHINESE: 哦，你是美籍华人。诶，你家在美国什么地方？
   Ò, nǐ shi Měijí Huárén. Éi, nǐ jiā zài Měiguo shémme dìfang?
   Oh, you're an American Chinese. So, where in the U.S. do you live?

6. AMERICAN: 在美国西岸，加州，离旧金山不远。
   Zài Měiguo xī'àn, Jiāzhōu, lí Jiùjīnshān bù yuǎn.
   On the U.S. west coast, California, not far from San Francisco.

7. CHINESE:　　那儿的气候怎么样？

Nàrde qìhou zěmmeyàng?

What's the climate like there?

8. AMERICAN:　挺不错的。冬天比北京暖和，也没有这儿这么干燥；而且夏天还比这儿凉快。可以说是冬暖夏凉。

Tǐng bú cuòde. Dōngtiān bǐ Běijīng nuǎnhuo, yě méiyou zhèr zhèmme gānzào; érqiě xiàtiān hái bǐ zhèr liángkuai. Kéyi shuō shi dōng-nuǎn-xià-liáng.

Pretty nice. Winters are warmer than in Beijing, and not as dry as here; and summers are cooler than here. You could say it's "warm in the winter and cool in the summer."

9. CHINESE:　那，你来北京这么久了，现在已经习惯北京的气候了吧？

Nà, nǐ lái Běijīng zhèmme jiǔ le, xiànzài yǐjīng xíguàn Běijīngde qìhou le ba?

Well, you've been in Beijing so long, by now you must be used to Beijing's climate?

10. AMERICAN:　嗯，刚来的时候，不太适应。现在差不多了。

M, gāng láide shíhou, bú tài shìyìng. Xiànzài chàbuduōle.

Yeah, when I had just come, I wasn't very much used to it. Now it's pretty much O.K.

New Vocabulary

美籍华人	**Měijí Huárén**	Chinese person with U.S. nationality
西岸	**xī'àn**	west coast
加州	**Jiāzhōu**	California
气候	**qìhou**	climate
比	**bǐ**	compare
暖和	**nuǎnhuo**	be warm
干燥	**gānzào**	be dry
凉快	**liángkuai**	be comfortably cool
冬暖夏凉	**dōng-nuǎn-xià-liáng**	"warm in winter, cool in summer"
习惯	**xíguàn**	be accustomed to
……的时候	**...-de shíhou**	at the time when...
适应	**shìyìng**	adapt, get used to
差不多	**chàbuduō**	not lack much, be good enough

Supplementary Vocabulary

东岸	**dōngàn**	east coast
澳门	**Àomén**	Macao
风景	**fēngjǐng**	scenery
美	**měi**	be beautiful
晚	**wǎn**	be late
难过	**nánguò**	be sad

Notes on the Conversation

Bǐ to express unequal comparison

In Chinese, as in English, there are equal comparisons ("this one is as good as that one") and unequal comparisons ("this one is better than that one"). **Bǐ** can be used to indicate unequal comparisons. As a regular verb, **bǐ** means "compare," for example, **Nǐ bié gēn rénjia bǐ** "Don't always compare (yourself) to others." Strictly speaking, **bǐ** has this same meaning when used as a coverb in a sentence like **Tā bǐ wǒ gāo** "She is taller than me"; literally, this sentence means "She compared to me is tall." Some more examples: **Zhèrde xuésheng bǐ nàrde xuésheng cōngming** "The students here are smarter than the students there," **Tā bǐ wǒ huì wánr** "He knows how to have fun more than I do," **Tā bǐ wǒ zǎo láile yíge zhōngtóu** "She came an hour earlier than I."

How to indicate something isn't as something as something else

The very common pattern **A méiyou B nèmme** (or **zhèmme**) **C** means "A isn't as C as B is." This pattern is what is normally used as the negative of the pattern with **bǐ** that is introduced above. Compare the following two sentences: **Zhèige bǐ nèige hǎo** "This one is better than that one" and **Zhèige méiyou nèige nèmme hǎo** "This one isn't as good as that one." In general, if you're talking about something close to you, **zhèmme** is used; otherwise, **nèmme** is used. Example: **Zhōngwén méiyou Rìwén nèmme nán** "Chinese isn't as hard as Japanese." More examples: **Tā méiyou wǒ zhèmme gāo** "She isn't so tall as I am," **Wǒ méiyou tā nèmme cōngming** "I'm not as smart as she is."

Four-character expressions

There exist in both spoken and written Chinese a great number of four-character expressions, which are called **chéngyǔ** in Chinese. These often allude to famous stories or events in Chinese history, or may be direct quotations from famous works of Chinese literature. Chinese speakers frequently use **chéngyǔ**, since they often sum up succinctly a meaning which it would take many words of ordinary spoken Chinese to express and, moreover, they convey the impression that you're a learned and eloquent person. **Dōng-nuǎn-xià-liáng**, which literally means "winter warm summer cool," is your first example of a **chéngyǔ**. Familiarity with **chéngyǔ** is useful in gaining credibility in Chinese society; nothing impresses Chinese more than an aptly used **chéngyǔ** coming from the mouth of a foreigner!

...-de shíhou(r) to indicate "when"

The pattern **...-de shíhou(r)** at the end of a clause means "at the time when..." or "when..." or "while....." Examples: **Tā gàosu wǒde shíhou, yǐjīng tài wǎnle** "When she told me, it was already too late," **Wǒ tīngbudǒngde shíhou, zěmme bàn?** "What should I do when I don't understand?," **Měicì kǎoshìde shíhou, tā dōu huì jǐnzhāngde yào sǐ** "Every time when we have tests, he gets incredibly nervous."

Reading

New Characters and Words

283.	岸	**àn**	coast, shore, bank
	东岸	**dōngàn**	east coast
	西岸	**xī'àn**	west coast
	两岸	**liǎng'àn**	the two shores (mainland China and Taiwan)
284.	错	**cuò**	be wrong; mistake
	说错	**shuōcuò**	say something wrong
	不错	**bú cuò**	"not bad," "quite good"
285.	阳	**yáng**	sun (can't be used alone)
	太阳	**tàiyáng**	sun
	出太阳	**chū tàiyáng**	the sun comes out
	阳明山	**Yángmíng Shān**	Yangming Mountain
	贵阳	**Guìyáng**	Guiyang (capital of Guizhou Province)
286.	晚	**wǎn**	be late
	晚上	**wǎnshang**	in the evening
	晚饭	**wǎnfàn**	dinner, evening meal
287.	已	**yǐ**	already (can't be used alone)
288.	经	**jīng**	pass through (can't be used alone)
	已经	**yǐjīng**	already

A. SENTENCES

一、我觉得美国东岸的气候比西岸好，但是小李觉得东岸的气候没有
西岸那么好。

二、对不起，实在对不起，我听错了，所以就说错话了！

三、他已经学了半年的中文了，已经会说不少东西了。

四、今天早上太阳出来的时候实在太美了，你说是不是？

五、我觉得北京饭店不但比和平饭店贵，饭也没有和平饭店的那么好
吃。

六、我小的时候喜欢去阳明山，现在太忙了，已经很多年没去了。

七、今天出大太阳了，明天的天气大概也不错。

八、你的表哥走了，别太难过了，我们早晚都会死……

九、我刚来的时候，不太喜欢东岸的气候，但是现在喜欢了。

十、"大海，你别难过"，王大海的女朋友说："要是你今天晚上一定要
去动物园看动物的话，我可以和你一起去"。

B. CONVERSATIONS

一、

中国人：你家在美国什么地方？

美国人：在美国的西岸，离San Francisco不太远。

中国人：那儿的气候怎么样？

美国人：那儿的气候还不错。比北京好，也没有这儿这么干。

二、

万太太：弟弟，晚饭你要吃什么？

儿子　：我要吃早饭！

万太太：什么？是你说错了？是我听错了？你要吃早饭？！

儿子　：我没说错，你也没听错。我晚上就是喜欢吃早饭。现在美国
　　　　年轻人都是这样，你不知道吗？

C. NARRATIVES

一、我有一个老同事姓高，他是贵阳人。他有一个女儿，名字叫"高
　　兴"。要是有人问她叫什么名字，她就说"高兴"。要是高先生、
　　高太太找女儿的时候，他们就叫："高兴！高兴！"他们家里从
　　早到晚都有人叫："高兴！高兴！高兴！"所以这一家人真的都
　　很高兴。

二、我是北京人，现在给你们说一说我老家北京的气候吧。从三月到
　　五月，北京的天气还不错，不是太冷也不是太热，有时候下一
　　点儿雨。从六月开始，天气越来越热，七月和八月有时候雨也
　　很大。七、八月的时候，最高温度差不多四十度，最低温度差不
　　多二十度。最近几年，北京好像越来越热，有时候热得要死。
　　九月、十月是北京天气最好的时候，人人都喜欢。那个时候不冷
　　也不热，出太阳的时候多。这个时候很多外国人到北京来看天安
　　门、后海、北京动物园、香山和长城，还有很多别的地方。这正
　　是来北京的好时候。从十二月到二月天气又干又冷，很少下雨，
　　那个时候来北京的外国人也比较少。所以说，要是你有机会到北
　　京来，还是九月、十月那个时候来最好！

Notes

A2. 说错话 means "say the wrong thing."

A3. 他已经学了半年的中文了 means "He's already been studying Chinese for half a year." The implication is that he's still studying Chinese now.

A6. The 了 at the end of 已经很多年没去了 indicates that the situation has been continuing for a period of time up to and including the present. An English translation would be "haven't gone (there) for many years."

A8a. 走了 "has gone" is here a euphemism for "has died."

A8b. 早晚 (literally, "early late") is a very common and useful expression that means "sooner or later."

C1. 从早到晚 means "from morning until evening."

C2a. 人人都喜欢 means "everyone likes it." Note the adverb 都 after 人人; it's very common to have a 都 after reduplicated forms like 人人 "everyone," 天天 "every day," or 年年 "every year."

C2b. 后海 is a lake in central Beijing famous for its attractive scenery and lively night life. By day you can take boat rides and shop in the many small boutiques, while at night you can enjoy the many restaurants, pubs, teahouses, and cafes.

Review of Lessons 14–23

Part One: Oral Translation

Instructions: To review the major grammar patterns introduced in the preceding lessons, try interpreting the following English phrases and sentences into spoken Chinese.

MÉIYOU to indicate PAST NEGATIVE of ACTION VERBS

1. She didn't go.
2. I didn't look for it.
3. We didn't move.
4. I didn't guess.
5. They didn't buy it.
6. They didn't sell it.
7. I didn't rest.
8. She didn't wait for me.
9. I didn't turn it on (for example, the electric light switch).
10. The train hasn't departed yet.

JIĀO and JIĀOSHŪ

1. I like to teach.
2. She teaches at a college.
3. She teaches English at a college.
4. He teaches Chinese at a high school.
5. Can you teach me a little Chinese?
6. Who is teaching you English?

-LE...LE in SENTENCES with NON-QUANTIFIED OBJECTS

1. I forgot to introduce myself.
2. She also forgot to introduce herself.
3. I already bought a cup.
4. I already sold my computer.
5. He already turned on the computer.
6. She already turned off her computer.
7. They already ate.

GRADE IN SCHOOL

First give the long form, then give the short form.

1. college first-year/freshman
2. college sophomore
3. college junior
4. college senior
5. high school senior
6. high school junior
7. high school sophomore
8. seventh grade
9. eighth grade
10. ninth grade
11. fifth grade in elementary school
12. third grade in elementary school
13. first grade in elementary school
14. What grade in college?
15. What grade in senior high?
16. What grade in junior high?
17. What grade in elementary school?
18. What year are you in college?

STATIVE VERBS with **HĂO**

1. She/He is quite good-looking.
2. The food there is delicious.
3. It (for example, the music) is very pretty. (="nice to listen to")
4. The food here is awful.
5. The mountains here are very pretty.
6. The teacher's Chinese sounds beautiful. (="very good to listen to")
7. That American student's Chinese sounds terrible!

INTERMEDIATE POINTS of the COMPASS

1. He lives in the northeast.
2. She lives in the southeast.
3. We live in the northwest.
4. They live in the southwest.
5. It's in the northwest of China.
6. It's in the southwest of the U.S.
7. It's in the northeast of the U.S.
8. It's in the southeast of China.
9. They took Northwest Airlines.
10. You should take Southwest Airlines.

YĪNWEI...SUÓYI...

1. I can't go because I'm too busy.
2. She can't come because she doesn't have time.
3. You can't go to China because you didn't study Chinese.
4. I have to go home because I still have something I have to do.
5. I have to leave because it's getting late ("the time is no longer early").
6. She can only work half-time because her children are still small.
7. My daughter doesn't attend school yet because she's still too small.

-QILAI to indicate "IN THE (VERB)-ING"

1. You like very young.
2. He looks quite old.
3. Chinese isn't easy to learn.
4. Chinese is interesting to learn.
5. Computing isn't hard to learn.
6. That job in the doing of it is very easy.
7. Chinese food in the eating tastes quite good.
8. The food in this dining hall tastes good.
9. The food in that dining hall looks tasty but in the eating of it, it's not tasty.

CHINESE EQUIVALENTS of ENGLISH "ask"

1. She asked me where New York was.
2. She asked me to have dinner with her.
3. She asked me to her home.
4. She asked me what my name was.
5. She asked me to ask him what his name was.
6. Ask him to come again tomorrow.
7. I asked her to ask her mother.
8. The teacher asked us to do our homework.
9. If you still don't understand, you should ask the teacher!

XIĀN...RÁNHÒU...

1. First eat and then study.
2. First study and then eat.
3. First eat and then go shopping.
4. First go to Beijing, then go to Shanghai.
5. First take the bus, then change to a train
6. First take a train, then change to a tram.
7. First learn how to speak, then learn how to write.
8. First walk toward the east, then walk toward the west.
9. First learn how to speak Chinese, then learn how to write it.
10. Let's first go study in the library and then go back to our dorm to chat.

BÚDÀN...ÉRQIĚ...

1. He's not only lazy but also stupid.
2. That place is not only rich but also safe.
3. Her dorm is not only messy but also dirty.
4. Little Chen is not only young but also smart.
5. Old Wang is not only smart but also very diligent.
6. The things they sell are not only good but also cheap.
7. Her boyfriend is not only good-looking but also cute.

-ZHE as CONTINUOUS ASPECT SUFFIX

1. It's still early.
2. The door is still open.
3. The computer is still on.
4. The language lab is still open.
5. They're still in my dorm sitting.

POTENTIAL RESULTATIVE COMPOUNDS

1. Can you find it?
2. Yes, I can.
3. No, I can't.
4. Can you fall asleep?
5. Yes, I can.
6. No, I can't.
7. Can one buy them here?
8. Yes, one can.
9. No, one can't.
10. Can you see it?
11. Yes, I can.
12. No, I can't.
13. Can you understand what you hear?
14. Yes, I can.
15. No, I can't.
16. Can you understand what you read?
17. Yes, I can.
18. No, I can't.

CÓNG...KĀISHǏ

1. starting from tomorrow
2. starting from the day after tomorrow
3. starting from next week
4. starting from next Monday
5. starting from next month
6. starting from next year
7. starting from January 1
8. starting from February 15

YUÈ LÁI YUÈ...

1. The weather has been getting hotter and hotter.
2. The weather has been getting colder and colder.
3. There are more and more people.
4. My Chinese is getting better and better.
5. Things are more and more expensive.
6. I feel I've been getting stupider and stupider.
7. You're getting smarter and smarter.
8. Your room is getting cleaner and cleaner.
9. My room is getting messier and messier.
10. I like her/him more and more.
11. I'm more and more hard-working.
12. Chinese is getting easier and easier!

...ÉRYĬ

1. I have only 10 minutes and that's all.
2. I only have $ 100.00 and that's all.
3. I only have one friend and that's all.
4. He has only one girlfriend and that's all.
5. She has only one boyfriend and that's all.
6. A weather forecast is merely a weather forecast and that's all.
7. We're not buying anything, just looking, that's all.

BÙ...YĚ BÙ...

1. You're neither early nor late.
2. Old Gao is neither tall nor short.
3. Here it's neither dry nor humid.
4. Little Li is neither smart nor stupid.
5. She said that Chinese was neither hard nor easy.
6. Today it's neither cold nor hot – it's very comfortable!
7. The things they sell are neither expensive nor cheap.

YÒU...YÒU...

1. That student is both smart and diligent.
2. He's both busy and nervous.
3. In winter it's both dry and cold.
4. In summer it's both hot and humid.
5. He speaks both fast and not clear.
6. She speaks both clearly and slow.
7. She can neither speak nor read Chinese.
8. The things they sell are both good and cheap.
9. The food in that cafeteria is both attractive and delicious.

RÚGUǑ...JIÙ...

1. If it rains, I won't go.
2. If it's too expensive, I won't buy it.
3. If he/she doesn't buy it, I won't buy it either.

4. If you go to China, I want to go also.

5. If he/she goes to Taiwan, I want to go also.

6. If you don't go, I won't go either.

7. What will you do if he/she doesn't marry you?

8. What will you do if he/she divorces you?

9. If you don't understand what you hear, what do you do?

10. If I don't understand what I read, I ask the teacher.

ZÀI as AUXILIARY VERB to indicate PROGRESSIVE ASPECT

1. He's eating.

2. I'm studying.

3. She's speaking.

4. What's she saying?

5. They're writing.

6. What are they writing?

7. She's sleeping.

8. It's raining.

9. It's drizzling.

10. They're looking at you.

REDUPLICATION of MEASURES and NOUNS to indicate "every"

1. They come every day.

2. She has Chinese class every day.

3. We go every year.

4. They come every year.

5. Everyone knows.

6. Everybody can do it.

BǏ to express UNEQUAL COMPARISON

1. I'm taller than he is.

2. He is heavier than I am.

3. This one is cheaper than that one.

4. This one is larger than that one.

5. Japanese is harder than Chinese.

6. Tables are more expensive than chairs.

7. Your car is smaller than mine.

8. Your friends are more numerous than mine.

9. This one is much better than that one.

10. Taipei is hotter than Beijing.

11. The west coast is drier than the east coast.

12. Little Li is much better-looking than Little Wang.

A MÉIYOU B NÈMME/ZHÈMME C

1. I'm not as tall as Little Zheng.

2. I'm not as short as Little Li.

3. I'm not as fat as Old Wang.

4. I'm not as thin as Old Xie.

5. We're not as busy as they are.

6. You're not as smart as I am.

7. You're not as busy as Teacher He.

8. Beijing isn't as humid as Taipei.

9. Your room isn't as messy as my room.

10. He said the place where he lived was not as pretty as here.

11. The computers Mr. Wang sells are not as expensive as those Mrs. Li sells.

...DE SHÍHOU(R)

1. When you came, she had already left.
2. When I heard, it was already too late.
3. When I first came, I couldn't get accustomed to it.
4. What did you do when you didn't understand?
5. When you were in China, did you have many friends?
6. When Mr. Li died, everyone was very sad.
7. When I arrived there, I didn't know that it was Sunday.

Part Two: Written Translation

Instructions: Translate the following 50 sentences into Pinyin and/or characters and hand them in to your instructor. These sentences were designed to review the most important grammar patterns and vocabulary in the preceding lessons.

1. I'm a first-year and she's a junior. What year are you in?
2. My friend was born in China and then grew up in America.
3. Mrs. Zheng, this is a little present which we're giving you.
4. A: How old is her son? B: He's still small. It seems he's seven months old.
5. She's already over 70, but because she eats lots of good things, she looks very young.
6. A: Are you married? B: My older brother is already married; I'm not yet married.
7. That Chinese person said that American food looks good but doesn't taste very good.
8. I have one older sister, she works at Southwest Airlines. Do you have brothers or sisters?
9. Sorry, I forgot to introduce myself. My surname is Huang. I'm a teacher; I teach junior high.
10. A: I suppose your daughter's already in elementary school? B: Yes, she's in second grade.
11. Where did you live before coming to America?
12. You say you have one child, right? A boy or a girl? How old?
13. I've heard that Little Chen knows German, French, and Japanese.
14. A: Did you go by yourself? B: No, I went together with three classmates.
15. A: Can you write Chinese? B: I can write a little, but I don't write it very well.
16. Do you know if that American teacher can speak Standard Chinese (Mandarin)?
17. She lived in Spain for over eleven years; no wonder she speaks Spanish so well.
18. After graduating from high school, she worked for two years, then she applied to college.
19. The university has several thousand students. Some I know, others I don't.
20. A: You speak English very well! Where did you learn it? B: I learned it in kindergarten.
21. Excuse me, how do I get to Taiwan University?
22. We'll come looking for you in half an hour, O.K.?
23. It seems that my home isn't very far from your home.
24. Ms. Li isn't at her desk. Please call her again in ten minutes.
25. Formerly the tourists who came from America almost all stayed at the Beijing Hotel.
26. These two pieces of luggage are mine; those three pieces of luggage are his.
27. Don't get excited, I think Professor Wang is likely to come in just a little while.
28. Keep going straight; after you've passed the French Embassy you'll have arrived.
29. A: How long does it take to get from there to the foreign ministry? B: One hour, more or less.
30. Darn, I forgot! The company is closed today. We've no choice but come again tomorrow.
31. He's not only stupid but also lazy.
32. First take the bus, then take the trolley.
33. When we get to Tiananmen, please call me.

34. She likes red and blue. What colors do you like?
35. I can't fall asleep on trains. Can you fall asleep on trains?
36. Go straight from here and turn left at the first traffic light.
37. You don't need to ask her; she's not very clear about it either.
38. First turn to the east, then turn to the west, and you'll be there!
39. I'm sorry, I can't find my name cards. (don't use **kéyi** or **néng**)
40. At home we raise fish. Do you keep any small animals at home?
41. When Old Wang died, everybody was very sad.
42. The east coast of the U.S. isn't as dry as the west coast.
43. This winter I'm going to Beijing. Is Beijing colder than New York?
44. I'm playing with my computer; Old Sun is sleeping. What are you doing?
45. Macao is hot every day, both hot and humid, so we seldom go outdoors.
46. Recently the weather has been cooler and cooler, more and more comfortable.
47. Starting tomorrow, I'm going to be working at the embassy. I'm so nervous I'm going to die.
48. The weather forecast said that tomorrow the high will be 33° and the low 25°.
49. If it rains tomorrow, we can't go out; but the weather report isn't necessarily accurate.
50. A: My friends are neither many nor few. B: I have only one good friend, that's all. C: I don't have friends at all!

Chinese-English Vocabulary

This Chinese-English vocabulary contains all the Chinese words introduced in the 24 lessons of *Elementary Mandarin Chinese* with English equivalents and indication of where the word was introduced. The first number in parentheses refers to the lesson and the second number refers to the part within the lesson; the letter "R" refers to the reading section. The entries are arranged in alphabetical order of the Pinyin spellings, spelled one syllable at a time, with the vowel **u** preceding **ü**. Syllables are arranged in order of tone, that is, Tone One, Tone Two, Tone Three, and Tone Four followed by neutral tone.

A

āyí 阿姨 aunt (14-1)

à 啊 "oh" (6-2)

a 啊 (softens sentence) (3-1)

āiyà 哎呀 "oh," "gosh" (22-1)

āiyò 哎哟 (indicates surprise) (12-2)

ǎi 矮 be short (not tall) (4-1)

àiren 爱人 spouse, husband, wife (3-2)

ān 安 peace (2-3R)

àn 岸 coast, shore (23-2R)

Àodàlìyà 澳大利亚 Australia (15-2)

Àomén 澳门 Macao (23-2)

Àozhōu 澳洲 Australia (15-2)

B

bā 八 eight (1-2R, 7-1)

bāyuè 八月 August (9-2, 9-2R)

bǎ 把 (for chairs, umbrellas) (11-1)

bàba 爸爸 dad (3-2)

ba 吧 (indicates supposition) (6-1, 6-1R)

ba 吧 (indicates suggestions) (8-1)

bái 白 be white (20-1)

báisè 白色 the color white (20-1)

báitiān 白天 in the daytime (10-1)

-bǎi 百 hundred (8-1, 8-1R)

-bǎiwàn 百万 million (10-2, 10-2R)

bān 班 class; shift (7-1, 19-1R)

bān 搬 move (12-1)

bānjiā 搬家 move one's home (14-2)

bānshang 班上 in a class (7-1, 19-1R)

bàn(r) 半(儿) half (7-1, 8-2R)

bàn yìdiǎnr shì 办一点儿事 take care of some things (3-1)

bànfǎ(r) 办法 way of doing something (23-1)

bàngōngshì 办公室 office (11-1)

bàntiān 半天 "half the day," a long time (19-2)

bàng 棒 be great, wonderful (17-2)

bàoqiàn 抱歉 feel sorry, regret (11-1)

bēibāo 背包 knapsack, backpack (8-1)

bēizi 杯子 cup (8-1)

běi 北 north (1-3R, 18-1)

běibiān(r) 北边(儿) north (12-1, 12-1R)

Běidà 北大 Peking University (11-2)

běifāng 北方 north, the North (18-1)

běifāng huà 北方话 northern speech (18-1)

běifāng rén 北方人 Northerner (18-1)

Běijīng 北京 Beijing (1-3R)

bèi 备 prepare (21-2R)

běn 本 root; this (20-1R)

běndì 本地 this place, here (20-1, 20-1R)

běndì rén 本地人 local person (20-1R)

bèn 笨 be stupid (21-1)

bǐ 比 compare (10-2R, 23-2)

bǐjiào 比较 comparatively, relatively (10-2, 10-2R)

bìyè 毕业 graduate (17-2)

biān 边 side (12-1R)

biànchéng 变成 change into, become (22-1)

biǎo 表 cousin of different surname (16-1R)

biǎodì 表弟 younger male cousin (16-1R)

biǎogē 表哥 older male cousin (16-1R)

biǎojiě 表姐 older female cousin (16-1, 16-1R)

biǎojiěfu 表姐夫 husband of older female cousin (16-1)

biǎomèi 表妹 younger female cousin (16-1R)

bié 别 don't (5-2, 5-2R)

biéde 别的 other, another (19-2)

bīnguǎn 宾馆 guest house, hotel (18-2)

bú cuò 不错 "not bad," "quite good" (16-2, 23-2R)

bú kèqi 不客气 "you're welcome" (4-2)

bú yòng 不用 not need to, don't need to (20-1)

bú yòng xiè 不用谢 "don't mention it" (20-1)

búbì 不必 don't need to, not be necessary (20-2)

búdàn 不但 not only (21-1, 23-1R)

búguò 不过 however (11-1)

búyào 不要 don't (5-2, 10-1R)

bù 不 not (4-1, 4-1R)

bù yídìng 不一定 not necessarily (22-1R)

C

cài 菜 food (11-2)

cèsuǒ 厕所 toilet (12-1)

chà 差 lack (8-2, 8-2R); be lacking (17-2)

chàbuduō 差不多 almost, about (8-2, 8-2R); good enough (23-2)

cháng 常 often (11-2)

cháng 长 be long (8-2, 14-2R)

Cháng Chéng 长城 Great Wall (12-1, 16-1R)

chángcháng 常常 often (10-2)

chǎng 厂 factory (11-2, 16-1R)

chǎng 场 place (18-2R)

cháoshī 潮湿 be humid (23-1)

chē 车 vehicle (8-2, 18-2R)

chēpiào 车票 bus ticket (21-2)

chēzhàn 车站 bus stop, bus station (20-2, 20-2R)

chēzi 车子 car, vehicle (18-2, 18-2R)

chēnghu 称呼 address (5-2)

chéng 城 city (12-1, 16-1R)

chéng 成 become (2-2R)

Chéngdū 成都 Chengdu (2-2R)

chī 吃 eat (11-2, 11-2R)

chīfàn 吃饭 eat food, eat (11-2, 11-2R)

chídào 迟到 arrive late, be late (10-2)

chū 出 out, go out (14-2R)

chū tàiyáng 出太阳 sun comes out (22-2, 23-2R)

chūlái 出来 come out (23-1)

chūmén 出门 go outside (23-1)

chūqu 出去 go out (23-1)

chūshēng 出生 be born (9-2, 14-2R)

chūshì 出示 show, produce (21-2)

chūzhōng 初中 junior high school (14-1)

chūzū 出租 rent out (18-2)

chūzū qìchē 出租汽车 taxi (18-2)

chǔ 楚 clear (20-1R)

chūntiān 春天 spring (22-2)

chuān 川 river (2-3R)

cì 次 time (10-1, 10-1R)

cōngming 聪明 be smart (21-1)

cóng 从 from (17-2, 17-2R)

cóng...lái 从……来 come from (17-2R)

cóngqián 从前 in the past, formerly (16-1, 17-2R)

cuò 错 be wrong; mistake (23-2R)

D

dǎ 打 hit, beat (19-1, 19-1R)

dǎ diànhuà 打电话 make a telephone call (19-1, 19-1R)

dǎdī 打的 take a taxi (18-1, 19-1R)

dǎléi 打雷 thunder (22-1)

dà 大 big, large (1-3R, 14-2)

dà dìdi 大弟弟 older younger brother (15-2R)

dàgài 大概 probably, about (18-1, 18-1R)

dàgē 大哥 oldest brother (15-2R)

dàjiē 大街 main street, avenue (2-3R)

dàmèi 大妹 older younger sister (15-2, 15-2R)

dàshǐguǎn 大使馆 embassy (6-1)

dàxué 大学 university, college (6-1, 11-2R)

dàxuéshēng 大学生 college student (11-2, 11-2R)

dàyuē 大约 approximately, about (10-1)

dài 带 take along, bring (6-2, 6-2R)

dàizi 袋子 bag (8-1)

dānwèi 单位 work unit, organization (6-1)

dàn 但 but (23-1R)

dànshi 但是 but (23-1, 23-1R)

dāngrán 当然 of course (11-1)

dào 到 arrive, reach; to (3-1, 8-2, 17-1R)

-dào 到 arrive at, to (12-1)

dào 道 road, way; Taoism (11-1R)

dào...lái 到……来 come to (17-1R)

dào...qù 到……去 go to (17-1R)

Déguo 德国 Germany (7-1)

Déyǔ 德语 German language (16-2)

-de 得 (verb suffix indicating manner) (16-2, 16-2R)

-de 的 (indicates what precedes describes what follows) (5-2, 5-2R, 6-2)

-de shíhou 的时候 when (23-2)

děi 得 must (4-2, 16-2R)

dēng 灯 light, lamp (20-1)

děng 等 wait, wait for (9-2, 18-2R)

dī 低 be low (22-1, 22-1R)

dǐxia 底下 underneath (12-2)

dì 地 the ground; place (12-1R)

dì 弟 younger brother (15-2R)

dì- 第 (forms ordinal numbers) (10-1, 10-1R)

dìdi 弟弟 younger brother (7-2, 15-2R)

dìfang 地方 place (12-1, 12-1R)

dìzhǐ 地址 address (9-2)

diǎn 点 o'clock (8-2, 8-2R)

diàn 店 shop, store (12-1R)

diàn 电 electricity; lightning (19-1R)

diànchē 电车 street car, tram (20-2)

diànhuà 电话 telephone (19-1, 19-1R)

diànnǎo 电脑 computer (12-2)

dìng 定 settle, determine (22-1R)

dōng 东 east (2-1R, 9-2)

dōngàn 东岸 east coast (23-2, 23-2R)

dōngběi 东北 northeast (15-1)

dōngbiān 东边 east (12-1, 12-1R)

dōngfāng 东方 east, the East (18-1)

Dōngfāng rén 东方人 Asian (18-1)

Dōngjīng 东京 Tokyo (2-1R)

dōngnán 东南 southeast (15-1)

dōng-nuǎn-xià-liáng 冬暖夏凉 "warm in winter cool in summer" (23-2)

dōngtiān 冬天 winter (22-2)

dōngxi 东西 thing (12-2)

dǒng 懂 understand (21-2)

dòng 动 move (20-2R)

dòngwù 动物 animal (20-2, 20-2R)

dòngwùyuán 动物园 zoo (20-2, 20-2R)

dōu 都 all, both (3-2)

dū 都 large city, capital; Du (2-2R)

dǔchē 堵车 be clogged up with cars (19-2)

dù 度 degree of temperature (22-1, 22-1R)

duàn 段 section; period (9-2, 17-1)

duì 对 be correct (7-2, 7-2R)

duìbuqǐ 对不起 "excuse me" (6-1, 14-2R)

duō 多 be many, much, more; how (7-2R, 10-2)

duō dà 多大 how big, how old (7-2, 7-2R)

duō dà niánji 多大年纪 how many years old? (7-2R)

duōshǎo 多少 how much, how many (8-1, 8-1R)

duōshù 多数 the majority (17-2)

E

éi 诶 (introduces questions) (22-1)

èi 欸 "hey, hi" (4-1)

ei 诶 (indicates liveliness) (14-2)

ér 儿 (word suffix) (11-2R)

érqiě 而且 moreover, and, also (21-1)

éryǐ 而已 and that's all (22-1)

érzi 儿子 son (14-2)

èr 二 two (1-1R, 7-1)

èryuè 二月 February (9-2, 9-2R)

F

fázi 法子 means, method, way (19-1)

Fǎguo 法国 France (7-1)

Fǎyǔ 法语 French language (16-2)

fàn 饭 cooked rice, food (11-2, 11-2R)

fàndiàn 饭店 hotel (12-1, 12-1R)

fāng 方 square, open space (12-1R)

fángjiān 房间 room (10-1)

fēn 分 fen, cent; minute (8-1, 8-2, 20-1R)

fēng 风 wind (22-2)

fēngjǐng 风景 scenery (23-2)

fēngshā 风沙 wind and sand; blowing sand (22-2)

fúwù 服务 serve (15-1)

fùmǔ 父母 parents (15-2)

fùqin 父亲 father (7-2)

fùyu 富裕 be prosperous (17-2)

G

gāi 该 should (21-2)

gǎiháng 改行 change one's line of work (16-1)

gài 概 approximate, general (18-1R)

gān 干 be dry (22-2, 22-2R)

gānjìng 干净 be clean (21-1)

gānzào 干燥 be dry (23-2)

gǎn 赶 rush, hurry (19-1)

gǎndào 赶到 rush or hurry to a place (19-1)

gāng 刚 just now, just (21-1, 21-1R)

gānggāng 刚刚 just now, just (21-1, 21-1R)

gǎng 港 harbor (2-3R)

gāo 高 be tall, high (4-1, 4-1R)

gāoxìng 高兴 be happy (5-2, 6-1R)

gāozhōng 高中 senior high school (14-1)

gǎocuò 搞错 get or do something wrong (6-2)

gē 哥 older brother (15-2R)

gēge 哥哥 older brother (7-2, 15-2R)

ge 个 (general measure) (6-1, 6-1R)

gěi 给 give; for, to (5-2, 14-1, 15-2, 15-2R)

gēn 跟 and; with (6-2, 15-2)

gēnběn 根本+ NEGATIVE not at all (23-1)

gèng 更 even more, more (18-1)

gōng 公 public, official (6-2R)

gōng 工 work (11-2R)

gōng 弓 bow (weapon) (9-2)

gōngchǎng 工厂 factory (16-1, 16-1R)

gōnggòng 公共 public (20-2, 20-2R)

gōnggòng qìchē 公共汽车 public bus, bus (20-2, 20-2R)

gōngjīn 公斤 kilo (19-2)

gōngrén 工人 worker, laborer (11-2, 11-2R)

gōngshìbāo 公事包 briefcase, attache case (8-1)

gōngsī 公司 company, firm (6-1, 6-2R)

gōngzuò 工作 work (4-1, 6-1, 15-1R)

gòng 共 altogether (20-2R)

gǒu 狗 dog (12-2)

gǔ 古 be ancient (17-2)

guǎi 拐 turn (20-1)

guān 关 close (9-1, 9-1R)

guānmén 关门 close a door (9-1, 9-1R)

guǎn 管 concern oneself with (12-2)

guǎng 广 broad (2-1R)

Guǎngdōng 广东 Guangdong (2-1R)

Guǎngxī 广西 Guangxi (2-2R)

Guǎngzhōu 广州 Guangzhou (2-1R)

guì 贵 be expensive (6-1R, 8-1)

guìxìng 贵姓 "what's your honorable surname?" (6-1, 6-1R)

Guìyáng 贵阳 Guiyang (23-2R)

Guìzhōu 贵州 Guizhou (6-1R)

guó 国 country (5-1R)

guò 过 pass, go by (18-1)

-guo 过 (indicates experience) (10-1, 10-1R)

H

hái 还 still, in addition (3-2, 14-2R, 16-1)

hái bú dào 还不到 have not yet reached (17-1R)

hái kéyǐ 还可以 still be O.K., not too bad (14-2R)

hái shi 还是 still is (14-2R)

hái shi...hǎole 还是……好了 it would be better if (14-2R)

háizi 孩子 child, children (3-2)

hǎi 海 ocean, sea (2-1R)

Hǎikǒu 海口 Haikou (10-2R)

Hǎinán 海南 Hainan (2-3R)

hángkōng 航空 aviation (15-1)

hángkōng gōngsī 航空公司 airline (15-1)

Hànyǔ 汉语 Chinese language (11-2)

Hànzì 汉字 Chinese character (16-2)

hǎo 好 be good, "all right," "O.K." (3-1R, 3-2, 5-2)

hǎo jiǔ bú jiànle 好久不见了 "long time no see" (3-2)

hǎochī 好吃 be good to eat, delicious (14-1)

hǎode 好的 "all right," "O.K." (18-2)

hǎokàn 好看 be good-looking (14-1, 14-2R)

hǎotīng 好听 be nice to listen to (17-2R)

hǎoxiàng 好像 apparently, it seems to me (10-2, 10-2R)

hǎoxiàng...-de yàngzi 好像……的样子 it seems like (23-1R)

hào 号 day of the month, number (9-2, 9-2R)

Hé 何 He (1-4R)

hé 河 river (2-4R)

hé 和 and; with (16-1, 17-1, 17-1R)

hé...yìqǐ 和……一起 together with (17-1R)

Héběi 河北 Hebei (2-4R)

hēi 黑 be black (20-1)

hēisè 黑色 the color black (20-1)

hěn 很 very (3-2, 3-2R)

hěn shǎo 很少 seldom (22-2)

Hé'nán 河南 Henan (2-4R)

hépíng 和平 peace (9-2, 20-1R)

héshì 合适 be appropriate (22-2)

hóng 红 be red (20-1, 20-1R)

hónglǜdēng 红绿灯 traffic light (20-1, 20-1R)

hóngsè 红色 the color red (20-1)

hòu 候 wait (17-1R)

hòu 后 in back, back (12-2, 17-2R)

hòubian 后边 in back, back (12-2, 17-2R)

hòulái 后来 afterward, later (17-1, 17-2R)

hòumian 后面 in back, back (12-2, 17-2R)

hòunián 后年 year after next (10-1, 17-2R)

hòutiān 后天 day after tomorrow (10-1, 17-2R)

hòutou 后头 in back, back (12-2, 17-2R)

hú 湖 lake (2-4R)

Húběi 湖北 Hubei (2-4R)

Hú'nán 湖南 Hunan (2-4R)

Huáqiáo 华侨 overseas Chinese (11-1)

Huáyì 华裔 person of Chinese descent (5-1)

huà 话 word, language (16-2, 16-2R)

huān 欢 happy (14-1)

huānyíng 欢迎 welcome (4-2, 5-2)

huàn 换 change to, exchange (19-2, 19-2R)

huáng 黄 be yellow (20-1)

huángsè 黄色 the color yellow (20-1)

huí 回 go back to; time (3-1, 12-1, 12-1R)

huíguó 回国 return to one's home country (10-1, 12-1R)

huíjiā 回家 return to one's home (10-1, 15-2R)

huì 会 know how to, can (16-2, 16-2R); likely to, will (19-1)

huǒ 火 fire (8-2)

huǒchē 火车 train (8-2)

huòzhě 或者 or (18-1)

J

jī 机 opportunity; machine (18-2R)

jīchǎng 机场 airport (18-2, 18-2R)

jīhui 机会 opportunity, chance (15-2, 18-2R)

jí 级 rank, grade (14-1)

-jí 及 reach a goal in time (8-2)

jǐ- 几 how many? (7-1, 7-1R); a few (16-2)

jǐge 几个 how many? (7-1, 7-1R)

jǐhào 几号 which day of the month? (9-2)

jǐsuì 几岁 how many years old? (7-2R)

jǐyuè 几月 which month of the year? (9-2, 9-2R)

jì 纪 to record (7-2R)

jì 记 remember; record (21-2R)

jìde 记得 remember (21-2, 21-2R)

jìjié 季节 season (22-2)

jìxù 继续 continue (16-2)

jiā 加 add; plus (8-1)

jiā 家 family; (for companies, factories) (6-1, 10-1, 15-2R)

Jiā'nádà 加拿大 Canada (5-1)

Jiāzhōu 加州 California (23-2)

jiān 间 between, during; space or time in between (19-1R)

jiǎn 减 subtract; minus (8-1)

jiàn 件 (for luggage, matters) (19-2, 19-2R)

jiǎng 讲 speak, say (17-1)

jiǎnghuà 讲话 speak, talk (17-1)

jiāo 交 hand over; intersect (19-1R)

jiāo 教 teach (15-1)

jiāoshū 教书 teach (15-1)

jiāotōng 交通 traffic (19-1, 19-1R)

jiāotōng jǐngchá 交通警察 traffic police (20-1)

jiāotōngjǐng 交通警 traffic police (20-1)

jiào 叫 call, be called (5-1, 5-1R, 5-2, 21-1)

jiào 较 compare (10-2R)

jiē 街 street (2-3R)

jiéhūn 结婚 marry, get married (14-2)

jiě 姐 older sister (4-2R)

jiějie 姐姐 older sister (7-2)

jiěmèi 姐妹 older and younger sisters (15-2, 15-2R)

jièshao 介绍 introduce (5-2)

jīn 金 gold, metal; Jin (2-4R)

jīn 今 now (7-2R)

jīn 津 (abbreviation for Tianjin) (2-2R)

Jīnmén 金门 Quemoy (9-1R)

jīnnián 今年 this year (7-2, 9-2, 7-2R)

Jīnshān 金山 Jinshan (2-4R)

jīntiān 今天 today (9-2)

jǐnzhāng 紧张 be intense, nervous (4-1)

jìn 近 be close, near (18-1, 18-1R)

jìn 进 enter (4-2, 23-1R)

jìnkuài 尽快 as fast as possible (19-1)

jìnlái 进来 come in (23-1, 23-1R)

jìnqu 进去 go in (23-1, 23-1R)

jīng 京 capital (1-3R)

jīng 经 pass through (23-2R)

Jīngdū 京都 Kyoto (2-2R)

jīnglǐ 经理 manager (6-2)

jǐngchá 警察 police (20-1)

jiǔ 久 be long (of time) (10-1)

jiǔ 九 nine (1-2R, 7-1)

jiǔyuè 九月 September (9-2, 9-2R)

jiù 就 precisely, exactly; only; then (7-2, 9-2, 9-2R, 17-2)

jiù shi 就是 be precisely, be none other than (9-2R)

jiù shi shuō 就是说 that is to say (16-2R)

Jiùjīnshān 旧金山 San Francisco (14-2)

jué 觉 feel (17-2R)

juéde 觉得 feel (17-2, 17-2R)

juédìng 决定 decide (19-1)

K

kāi 开 open; depart; drive (9-1, 9-1R, 18-1)

kāi wánxiào 开玩笑 joke around, play a prank (21-1)

kāichē 开车 drive a car (19-2)

kāiguān 开关 switch (12-2)

kāimén 开门 open a door, open (9-1, 9-1R)

kāishǐ 开始 begin; in the beginning (17-1, 17-1R)

kàn 看 look, see; read (14-2R, 21-2)

kànchūlái 看出来 know something by looking (23-1)

kàndǒng 看懂 read and understand (21-2)

kànqilai 看起来 in the looking (14-2)

kéyi 可以 may, can; be O.K. (4-1, 11-1, 11-1R)

kě 可 may, can; but; indeed, certainly (11-1R, 12-1)

kě'ài 可爱 be loveable, cute (7-2)

kěnéng 可能 be possible (22-1)

kěshi 可是 but (5-1, 11-1R)

kè 刻 quarter of an hour (8-2, 8-2R)

kè 课 class (10-2)

kōngqì 空气 air (23-1)

kǒngpà 恐怕 "I'm afraid that"; probably (8-2)

kǒu 口 mouth (measure for people) (10-2R, 16-1)

kuài 块 dollar (monetary unit) (8-1, 8-1R)

kuài 快 soon, quickly; be fast (11-2, 18-1)

kùn 困 be sleepy (4-1)

L

lái 来 come; (motion toward speaker) (5-2, 10-1R, 23-1)

láibují 来不及 not have enough time (8-2)

lán 蓝 be blue (20-1)

lánsè 蓝色 the color blue (20-1)

lǎn 懒 be lazy (21-1)

láojià 劳驾 "excuse me" (18-1)

lǎo 老 be old; (indicates rank among siblings) (4-1, 4-1R, 15-2)

lǎobǎn 老板 boss, owner (11-1)

lǎodà 老大 oldest among siblings (15-2)

lǎoshī 老师 teacher (4-2, 7-1R)

le 了 (changed situation; completed action) (3-2, 4-2R, 6-2)

lèi 累 be tired, fatigued (3-2)

lěng 冷 be cold (22-2, 22-2R)

lí 离 be distant from, from (18-1, 18-1R)

lí...hěn jìn 离······很近 be close to (18-1R)

lí...hěn yuǎn 离······很远 be far from (18-1R)

líhūn 离婚 divorce, get divorced (14-2)

Lǐ 李 Li (1-4R)

lǐ 里 in, inside (12-2, 12-2R)

lǐbài 礼拜 week (9-1)

lǐbài'èr 礼拜二 Tuesday (9-1)

lǐbàijǐ 礼拜几 which day of the week (9-1)

lǐbàiliù 礼拜六 Saturday (9-1)

lǐbàirì 礼拜日 Sunday (9-1)

lǐbàisān 礼拜三 Wednesday (9-1)

lǐbàisì 礼拜四 Thursday (9-1)

lǐbàitiān 礼拜天 Sunday (9-1)

lǐbàiwǔ 礼拜五 Friday (9-1)

lǐbàiyī 礼拜一 Monday (9-1)

lǐbian 里边 in, inside (12-2, 12-2R)

lǐmiàn 里面 in, inside (12-2, 12-2R)

lǐtou 里头 in, inside (12-2, 12-2R)

lǐwù 礼物 gift, present (14-1)

liángkuai 凉快 be comfortably cool (23-2)

liǎng- 两 two (7-1, 7-1R)

liǎng'àn 两岸 the two shores (23-2R)

liàng 辆 (for land vehicles) (18-2)

liáo 聊 chat (15-2)

liáotiān 聊天 chat (15-2)

Lín 林 Lin (1-2R)

líng 零 zero (8-1)

líu 留 leave (11-1)

liúxué 留学 study as a foreign student (15-2)

liù 六 six (1-2R, 7-1)

liùyuè 六月 June (9-2, 9-2R)

-lòng 弄 alley (9-2)

lóu 楼 building; floor (9-2, 18-2)

lù 路 road; Lu; (for bus routes) (2-2R, 9-2, 20-2)

lùkǒu 路口 intersection (20-1)

lǜ 绿 be green (20-1, 20-1R)

lǜsè 绿色 the color green (20-1)

luàn 乱 be disorderly, messy (21-1)

M

m 嗯 (hesitation sound; pause filler; indicates agreement) (10-1, 23-1)

māma 妈妈 mom (3-2)

máfan 麻烦 trouble, disturb (19-1)

Mǎláixīyà 马来西亚 Malaysia (5-1)

mǎshàng 马上 immediately, right away (19-1)

ma 吗 (indicates questions) (3-2, 3-2R)

ma 嘛 (indicates something obvious) (16-2)

mǎi 买 buy (8-1, 21-1R)

mǎimài 买卖 buying and selling, business (16-1, 21-1R)

mài 卖 sell (8-1, 21-1R)

màn zǒu 慢走 "take care" (4-2)

máng 忙 be busy (3-2, 3-2R)

māo 猫 cat (20-2)

máo 毛 ten cents, dime (8-1, 21-1R)

máomáoyǔ 毛毛雨 light rain (23-1, 23-1R)

màoyì 贸易 trade (6-2)

màoyì gōngsī 贸易公司 trading company (6-2)

me 么 (second syllable of several common words) (9-2R)

méi 没 not have; (past negative of action verbs) (6-2, 21-1)

méi guānxi 没关系 "it doesn't matter" (6-2)

méi shì(r) 没事(儿) "it's nothing" (12-1, 12-1R)

méi yìsi 没意思 not be interesting (4-2)

méiyou 没有 not have; there is/are not; (past negative of action verbs) (7-2, 10-2R, 15-1)

měi 美 be beautiful (5-1R, 23-2)

měi- 每 each, every (9-1)

Měiguo 美国 America (5-1, 5-1R)

Měijí Huárén 美籍华人 Chinese-American (23-2)

mèi 妹 younger sister (15-2R)

mèimei 妹妹 younger sister (7-2, 15-2R)

mén 门 door, gate (9-1, 9-1R)

ménkǒu(r) 门口(儿) doorway, entrance (18-2)

men 们 (plural marker for pronouns) (3-2R)

mǐ 米 meter (19-2)

miàn 面 side, surface; face (12-2R)

Mínguó 民国 the Republic (of China) (9-2)

míng 名 name (5-2R)

míng 明 bright (1-3R)

míngnián 明年 next year (9-2)

míngpiàn 名片 business card (6-2, 6-2R)

míngtiān 明天 tomorrow (9-2)

míngzi 名字 name (5-1, 5-2R)

mǔqin 母亲 mother (7-2)

N

nálǐ 哪里 "not at all" (9-1, 12-2R); where (14-2)

nǎ- 哪 which? (5-1R)

nǎbiān 哪边 what side?, where? (12-1R)

nǎge 哪个 which one?, which? (6-1R)

nǎguó 哪国 which country? (5-1R)

nà 那 that; in that case, so (5-2, 8-1R)

nàbiān 那边 that side, there (12-1R)

nàli 那里 there (14-2)

nàyang 那样 that way, like that (23-1R)

nàyangzi 那样子 that way, like that (23-1R)

name 那么 then, in that case, so (9-2R)

nàixīn 耐心 be patient (19-1)

nán 南 south (2-3R, 18-1)

nán 难 be difficult, hard (4-1, 4-1R)

nán- 男 man, male (7-1R)

nánbiān 南边 south (12-1, 12-1R)

nánde 男的 man, male (7-1, 7-1R)

nánfāng 南方 south, the South (18-1)

nánfāng huà 南方话 southern speech (18-1)

nánfāng rén 南方人 Southerner (18-1)

nánguài 难怪 no wonder (17-1)

nánguò 难过 be sad (23-2)

nánháir 男孩儿 boy (16-1)

Nánjīng 南京 Nanjing (2-3R)

nánlǎoshī 男老师 male teacher (7-1, 7-1R)

nánpéngyou 男朋友 boyfriend, male friend (14-1)

nánshēng 男生 male student (7-1, 7-1R)

nánxuésheng 男学生 male student (11-2R)

nǎr 哪儿 where? (3-1, 11-2R)

nàr 那儿 there (11-1, 11-2R)

ne 呢 and how about, what about; (continuous aspect) (3-1, 3-1R, 21-2)

něi- 哪 which? (5-1, 5-1R)

něibiān 哪边 which side?, where? (12-1)

něige 哪个 which one?, which? (6-1R)

něiguó 哪国 which country? (5-1)

nèi- 那 that (5-1, 8-1R)

nèibian(r) 那边(儿) that side, there (12-1)

nèige 那个 that one, that (8-1R)

nèiyang(r) 那样儿 that way, like that (17-2)

nèiyangzi 那样子 that way, like that (23-1)

nèmme 那么 then, in that case; like that, so (8-2, 17-1)

néng 能 be able to, can (15-1, 15-1R)

nǐ 你 you (3-1, 3-1R)

nǐ hǎo 你好 "how are you?," "hi" (3-1, 3-1R)

nǐmen 你们 you (plural) (4-2)

nián 年 year (7-2R, 9-2)

niánjí 年级 grade in school (14-1)

niánji 年纪 age (7-2R)

niánqīng 年轻 be young (14-2, 14-2R)

niàn 念 study (17-2)

niǎo 鸟 bird (20-2)

nín 您 you (polite) (4-2, 6-1R)

Niǔyuē 纽约 New York (14-2)

nǔlì 努力 be diligent, work hard (17-2)

nǚ- 女 woman, female (7-1R)

nǚde 女的 woman, female (7-1, 7-1R)

nǚ'ér 女儿 daughter (14-2)

nǚháir 女孩儿 girl (16-1)

nǚlǎoshī 女老师 female teacher (7-1, 7-1R)

nǚpéngyou 女朋友 girlfriend (14-1)

nǚshēng 女生 female student (7-1, 7-1R)

nǚshì 女士 madam, lady (6-1)

nǚxuésheng 女学生 female student (11-2R)

nuǎnhuo 暖和 be warm (23-2)

O

ò 噢 "oh" (5-2)

P

páiháng 排行 one's seniority among siblings (15-2)

pài 派 dispatch, send (19-1)

pàiqu 派去 dispatch, send out (19-1)

pángbiān 旁边 at or on the side, next to (12-2)

pàng 胖 be fat (12-1)

péixùn 培训 train (11-2)

péng 朋 friend (14-1R)

péngyou 朋友 friend (14-1, 14-1R)

pèng 碰 bump, run into (23-1)

pèngshang 碰上 run into, encounter (23-1)

pí 皮 leather, skin (11-2)

píxié 皮鞋厂 leather shoe (11-2)

piányi 便宜 be cheap (8-1)

piàn 片 flat and thin piece of something (6-2R)

piāo 飘 float (23-1)

piāojìnlái 飘进来 float in (23-1)

piào 票 ticket (21-1, 21-1R)

píng 平 balanced, flat; calm, peaceful (20-1R)

píngcháng 平常 usually, ordinarily (9-1)

Pǔtōnghuà 普通话 Mandarin language (16-2)

Q

qī 七 seven (1-2R, 7-1)

qī 期 period of time (9-1R)

qīyuè 七月 July (9-2, 9-2R)

qí 其 its, his, her, their (23-1R)

qíshí 其实 actually (23-1, 23-1R)

qítā 其他 other (16-2, 23-1R)

qǐ 起 rise, begin (14-2R)

qǐchuáng 起床 get up from bed, rise (9-1)

qì 气 gas, air (22-2R)

qì 汽 steam, vapor, gas (18-2R)

qìchē 汽车 car, vehicle (18-2, 18-2R)

qìchē gōngsī 汽车公司 car company, taxi company (18-2R)

qìhou 气候 climate (23-2)

-qilai 起来 (verb ending) (14-2, 14-2R)

-qiān 千 thousand (8-1, 8-1R)

-qiānwàn 千万 ten million (10-2, 10-2R)

qián 前 in front, front (12-2, 17-2R)

qián 钱 money (8-1, 8-1R)

qiánbian 前边 in front, front (12-2, 17-2R)

qiánmian 前面 in front, front (12-2, 17-2R)

qiánnián 前年 year before last (10-1, 17-2R)

qiántiān 前天 day before yesterday (10-1, 17-2R)

qiántou 前头 in front, front (12-2, 17-2R)

qīng 轻 be light (not heavy) (14-2R, 19-2)

qīng 清 clear; Qing Dynasty (20-1R)

qīngchu 清楚 be clear, be clear about (20-1, 20-1R)

qíngtiān 晴天 fine day, sunny day (22-1)

qǐng 请 "please" (4-2, 4-2R)

qǐng jìn 请进 "please come in" (4-2, 23-1R)

qǐng wèn 请问 "excuse me," "may I ask" (5-1, 5-1R)

qǐng zuò 请坐 "please sit down" (4-2, 4-2R)

qiūtiān 秋天 fall, autumn (22-2)

qù 去 go (3-1, 3-1R)

qùnián 去年 last year (9-2)

quán 全 completely (16-2, 16-2R)

R

rán 然 thus (20-2R)

ránhòu 然后 afterward, then (10-1, 20-2R)

ràng 让 let, cause, make (12-1)

ràng nǐ jiǔ děngle 让你久等了 "made you wait a long time" (12-1)

rè 热 be hot (22-1, 22-2R)

rén 人 person (2-1R, 5-1)

rénkǒu 人口 population (10-2, 10-2R)

rènshi 认识 be acquainted with, know, recognize (5-2, 16-2)

rì 日 day; Japan (9-2R)

Rìběn 日本 Japan (5-1, 20-1R)

Rìwén 日文 Japanese language (9-2R)

Rìyǔ 日语 Japanese language (16-2)

róngyi 容易 be easy (4-1)

rúguǒ 如果 if (22-2)

S

sāichē 塞车 be clogged up with cars (19-2)

sān 三 three (1-1R, 7-1)

sānyuè 三月 March (9-2, 9-2R)

shā 沙 sand, gravel (22-2)

shāchuāng 纱窗 screen window (23-1)

shān 山 mountain (1-3R, 12-1)

Shāndōng 山东 Shandong (2-1R)

Shānxī 山西 Shanxi (2-2R)

shǎndiàn 闪电 lightning strikes (22-1)

shàng 上 above, on top; go to, get on (2-1R, 12-2, 14-1, 19-1, 21-1)

shàngbān 上班 go to work, work (15-1, 19-1R)

shàngbian 上边 on top, on (12-2)

shàngchē 上车 get on a vehicle (20-2)

shàngge xīngqī 上个星期 last week (9-1R)

shàngge yuè 上个月 last month (7-2, 9-2R)

Shànghǎi 上海 Shanghai (2-1R)

shàngkè 上课 have class (10-2)

shàngmian 上面 on top, on (12-2, 2-2R)

shàngtou 上头 on top, on (12-2)

shàngwǔ 上午 morning, A.M. (9-1)

shàngxué 上学 attend school (15-1)

shǎo 少 be few (8-1R, 10-2)

shéi 谁 who, whom (5-2, 9-1R)

shémme 什么 what (5-1)

shēnqǐng 申请 apply (17-2)

shēntǐ 身体 body (16-1)

shén 什 (first syllable of word for "what") (9-2R)

shēng 生 be born, give birth to (1-4R)

shēngqì 生气 get angry (21-1, 22-2R)

shēngrì 生日 birthday (9-2, 9-2R)

shěng 省 province (2-4R)

shī 师 teacher (7-1R)

shīfu 师傅 master; driver (19-2)

shí 时 time; hour, o'clock; when (17-1R)

shí 实 real, solid, true (23-1R)

shí 十 ten (1-2R, 7-1)

shí'èryuè 十二月 December (9-2, 9-2R)

shíhou 时候 time (17-1, 17-1R)

shíjiān 时间 time (8-2, 19-1R)

shítáng 食堂 cafeteria, dining hall (3-1)

shíwàn 十万 hundred thousand (10-2, 10-2R)

shíyàn 实验 experiment (9-1)

shíyànshì 实验室 laboratory (9-1)

shíyīyuè 十一月 November (9-2, 9-2R)

shíyuè 十月 October (9-2, 9-2R)

shízài 实在 really, truly (11-1, 23-1R)

shǐ 始 begin (17-1R)

shǐyòng 使用 use, employ (12-2)

shǐyòng shǒucè 使用手册 operating manual (12-2)

shì 事 matter, thing (abstract) (12-1R)

shì 市 city (2-4R)

shì 是 be (4-1, 5-1R)

shìyìng 适应 adapt, get used to (23-2)

shǒu 首 head; chief, capital (18-2R)

shǒucè 手册 handbook, manual (12-2)

shǒudū 首都 capital (18-2)

Shǒudū Jīchǎng 首都机场 Capital Airport (18-2, 18-2R)

shòu 瘦 be thin, lean, skinny (12-1)

shòupiàoyuán 售票员 ticketseller, conductor (21-1)

shūfáng 书房 study (12-2)

shūfu 舒服 be comfortable (22-2)

shūjià 书架 bookshelf, bookcase (12-2)

shūshu 叔叔 uncle (14-1)

shuì 睡 sleep (9-1)

shuìjiào 睡觉 sleep, go to bed (9-1)

shuìzháo 睡着 fall asleep (21-2)

shuō 说 say, speak (10-1, 16-2R)

shuō xiàohua 说笑话 tell a joke (21-1)

shuōcuò 说错 say something wrong (23-2R)

shuōhuà 说话 speak words, speak (16-2, 16-2R)

sī 司 bureau, department (6-2R)

sījī 司机 driver, chauffeur (19-1)

sǐ 死 die (22-2, 22-2R)

sì 四 four (1-1R, 7-1)

Sìchuān 四川 Sichuan (2-3R)

sìyuè 四月 April (9-2, 9-2R)

sòng 送 give as a present (14-1)

sònggěi 送给 give as a present) (14-1)

sùshè 宿舍 dormitory (3-1)

suì 岁 year of age (7-2, 7-2R)

suóyi 所以 therefore, so (15-1, 15-1R)

suóyi shuō 所以说 so, therefore (22-1)

suǒ 所 that which (15-1R)

T

tā 他 he, him (3-2, 3-2R)

tā 她 she, her (3-2, 3-2R)

tā 它 it (12-2)

tāmen 他们 they, them (3-2, 3-2R)

tāmen 她们 they, them (females only) (3-2R)

tái 台 Taiwan; terrace; (for computers, TV sets) (1-3R, 12-2)

Táiběi 台北 Taipei (1-3R)

Táidōng 台东 Taitung (2-1R)

táifēng 台风 typhoon (23-1)

Táinán 台南 Tainan (2-3R)

Táishān 台山 Taishan (1-3R)

Táiwān 台湾 Taiwan (2-4R, 5-1)

Táizhōng 台中 Taichung (1-4R)

tài 太 excessively, too (4-1, 4-1R)

tàitai 太太 married woman, lady, wife, Mrs. (4-2, 6-1, 6-2)

tàiyáng 太阳 sun (22-2, 23-2R)

Tàiyuán 太原 Taiyuan (16-1R)

táng 糖 candy; sugar (14-1)

tàng 趟 (for runs by trains, buses) (8-2)

táokè 逃课 skip class (10-2)

tiān 天 sky; day (2-2R, 9-1, 22-1)

Tiānjīn 天津 Tianjin (2-2R, 8-2)

tiānqi 天气 weather (22-1, 22-2R)

tiānqi yùbào 天气预报 weather forecast (22-1)

tiáo 条 (for long and narrow things) (19-2, 19-2R)

tiáozi 条子 note (11-1, 19-2R)

tīng 听 hear, listen (17-2R, 21-2)

tīngdǒng 听懂 hear and understand (21-2)

tīngshuō 听说 hear of, hear it said that (17-2, 17-2R)

tǐng 挺 quite, very (4-1)

tǐng...-de 挺······的 very, quite (4-1)

tōng 通 through, open; connect (19-1R)

tōngzhī 通知 notify (19-1, 19-1R)

tóng 同 same (5-2R)

tóngshì 同事 colleague (6-1, 12-1R)

tóngwū 同屋 roommate (5-2, 5-2R)

tóngxué 同学 classmate (5-1, 11-2R)

tóngzhì 同志 comrade (21-2)

tóu 头 head; (noun suffix) (8-2R)

túshūguǎn 图书馆 library (3-1)

W

wài 外 outside (12-21, 2-2R)

wàibian 外边 outside (12-2, 12-2R)

wàiguo 外国 foreign country (18-2)

wàiguo huà 外国话 foreign language (18-2)

wàiguo rén 外国人 foreigner (18-2)

wàiguoyǔ 外国语 foreign language (18-2)

wàijiāobù 外交部 foreign ministry (6-1)

wàimian 外面 outside (12-2, 12-2R)

wàitou 外头 outside (12-2, 12-2R)

wàizǔfù 外祖父 maternal grandfather (15-2)

wàizǔmǔ 外祖母 maternal grandmother (15-2)

wān 湾 bay (2-4R)

wán(r) 玩(儿) play, have a good time (22-2)

wǎn 晚 be late (23-2, 23-2R)

wǎnfàn 晚饭 dinner, evening meal (11-2, 23-2R)

wǎnshang 晚上 in the evening (9-1, 23-2R)

-wàn 万 ten thousand (10-2, 10-2R)

Wáng 王 Wang (1-1R)

wǎng 往 to, toward (18-1, 18-1R)

wàng 忘 forget (15-2, 15-2R)

wéi 喂 "hello" (on the telephone) (18-2)

wèi 位 (polite measure for people) (5-1, 7-1R)

wèi 喂 "hey" (21-2)

wèi 为 for (15-1R)

wèishemme 为什么 why (15-1, 15-1R)

wèizi 位子 seat, place (11-2, 11-2R)

wēn 温 warm, mild (22-1R)

wēndù 温度 temperature (22-1, 22-1R)

Wēnzhōu 温州 (city in Zhejiang) (22-1R)

Wén 文 Wen (1-4R)

wénhuà 文化 culture (9-2)

wèn 问 ask (5-1, 5-1R)

wǒ 我 I, me (3-1, 3-1R)

wǒmen 我们 we, us (4-2)

wū 屋 room (5-2R)

wǔ 五 five (1-1R, 7-1)

Wǔ Dà Hú 五大湖 Great Lakes (2-4R)

wǔfàn 午饭 lunch (11-2)

wǔyuè 五月 May (9-2, 9-2R)

wù 物 thing, matter (20-2R)

wù 雾 fog (23-1)

X

xī 西 west (2-2R, 18-1)

Xī'ān 西安 Xian (2-3R)

xī'àn 西岸 west coast (23-2, 23-2R)

Xībānyá 西班牙 Spain (5-1)

Xībānyáyǔ 西班牙语 Spanish language (16-2)

xīběi 西北 northwest (15-1)

xībiān 西边 in the west (12-1, 12-1R)

xīfāng 西方 west, the West (18-1)

Xīfāng rén 西方人 Westerner (18-1)

xī'nán 西南 southwest (15-1)

xīwàng 希望 hope (21-1)

xíguàn 习惯 be accustomed to (23-2)

xǐ 喜 like, happy, joy (14-1R)

xǐhuan 喜欢 like (14-1, 14-1R)

xià 下 on the bottom, under, below; next (12-2, 12-2R)

xià máomáoyǔ 下毛毛雨 drizzle (23-1, 23-1R)

xiàbān 下班 get off from work (15-1, 19-1R)

xiàbian 下边 on the bottom, below (12-2, 12-2R)

xiàchē 下车 get off a vehicle (21-2)

xiàcì 下次 next time (12-2R)

xiàge yuè 下个月 next month (7-2, 12-2R)

xiàmian 下面 on the bottom, below (12-2, 12-2R)

xiàtiān 夏天 summer (22-2)

xiàtou 下头 on the bottom, below (12-2, 12-2R)

xiàwǔ 下午 afternoon, P.M. (9-1)

xiàxuě 下雪 snow (22-2)

xiàyǔ 下雨 rain (22-1, 23-1R)

xiān 先 first, before someone else (3-2, 4-2R)

xiānsheng 先生 husband, gentleman, Mr. (4-2, 4-2R, 6-1, 6-2)

xiàn 县 county (16-1, 16-1R)

xiàn 现 appear; current (16-1R)

xiān...ránhòu 先……然后 first...then (20-2R)

xiànzài 现在 now (8-2, 16-1R)

xiāng 香 be fragrant, smell good (2-3R, 12-1)

Xiāng Shān 香山 Fragrant Hills (2-3R, 12-1)

Xiānggǎng 香港 Hong Kong (2-3R, 6-1)

xiǎng 想 want to, would like to (11-1)

xiàng 像 resemble (10-2R)

-xiàng 巷 lane (9-2)

xiǎo 小 be small, little, young (1-4R, 4-1)

xiǎodì 小弟 little brother (15-2R)

xiǎohái(r) 小孩(儿) small child, kid (14-2)

xiáojie 小姐 Miss, Ms., young lady (4-2, 4-2R, 6-2)

xiǎomèi 小妹 little sister (15-2, 15-2R)

xiǎoshí 小时 hour (19-1)

xiǎoxīn 小心 be careful (21-2, 21-2R)

xiǎoxué 小学 elementary school (14-1)

xiào 校 school (15-1R)

xiàozhǎng 校长 head of a school (6-1, 15-1R)

xié 鞋 shoe (11-2)

xiéhuì 协会 association, society (15-1)

xiě 写 write (16-2, 16-2R)

xiězì 写字 write characters, write (16-2, 16-2R)

xiè 谢 thank (4-1R, 20-1)

xièxie 谢谢 "thank you," thank (3-2, 4-1R, 4-2)

xīn 心 heart, mind (21-2R)

xīn 新 be new (5-2)

Xīnjiāpō 新加坡 Singapore (5-1)

xīng 星 star (9-1R)

xīngqī 星期 week (9-1, 9-1R)

xīngqī'èr 星期二 Tuesday (9-1, 9-1R)

xīngqījǐ 星期几 which day of the week? (9-1, 9-1R)

xīngqīliù 星期六 Saturday (9-1, 9-1R)

xīngqīrì 星期日 Sunday (9-1, 9-2R)

xīngqīsān 星期三 Wednesday (9-1, 9-1R)

xīngqīsì 星期四 Thursday (9-1, 9-1R)

xīngqītiān 星期天 Sunday (9-1, 9-1R)

xīngqīwǔ 星期五 Friday (9-1, 9-1R)

xīngqīyī 星期一 Monday (9-1, 9-1R)

xíng 行 be all right, be O.K. (3-2, 19-2R)

xíngli 行李 luggage, baggage (19-2, 19-2R)

xìng 兴 interest, excitement (6-1R)

xìng 姓 be surnamed; surname (6-1, 6-1R)

xìngmíng 姓名 first and last name (18-2)

xiōngdì 兄弟 older and younger brothers (15-2)

xiūxi 休息 rest, take time off (9-1)

xū 需 need (19-2R)

xūyào 需要 need (19-2, 19-2R)

xué 学 learn, study (11-2, 11-2R)

xuésheng 学生 student (11-2, 11-2R)

xuéxí 学习 learn, study; studies (4-1, 6-1)

xuéxiào 学校 school (15-1, 15-1R)

xuě 雪 snow (22-2)

Y

yánjiū 研究 research (17-2)

yánjiūshēng 研究生 graduate student (17-2)

yánsè 颜色 color (20-1)

yáng 阳 sun (23-2R)

yǎng 养 raise, keep (20-2)

yàng 样 kind; way, manner (23-1R)

yàngzi 样子 way, appearance (4-1, 23-1R)

yāo 一 one (12-1)

yào 要 want; cost, take; will; should; request; if (8-1, 10-1, 10-1R, 12-2, 19-1, 22-2)

yàoshi 要是 if (11-1)

yě 也 also, too (3-1, 3-1R)

yèli 夜里 at night (10-1)

yī 一 one; a (1-1R, 6-1, 7-1)

yīyuè 一月 January (9-2, 9-2R)

yíbàn(r) 一半(儿) one-half (7-1, 8-2R)

yíbàn yíbàn 一半一半 half and half (8-2R)

yídìng 一定 definitely (22-1, 22-1R)

yíge rén 一个人 by oneself, alone (17-1)

yígòng 一共 in all (7-1, 20-2R)

Yíhéyuán 颐和园 Summer Palace (20-2)

yímín 移民 immigrate, emigrate (15-2)

yíwàn 一万 ten thousand (10-2R)

yíxià(r) 一下（儿）(softens the verb) (5-2, 12-2R)

yǐ 已 already (23-2R)

yǐ 以 take; use; with (11-1R)

yǐhòu 以后 after; in the future (15-2, 17-2, 17-2R)

yǐjīng 已经 already (8-2, 23-2R)

yǐqián 以前 before, formerly, ago (16-2, 17-2, 17-2R)

yǐzi 椅子 chair (11-1)

-yì 亿 hundred million (10-2)

yìbǎiwàn 一百万 one million (10-2R)

yìdiǎnr 一点儿 a little, some (11-2R)

yìhuǐr 一会儿 a while (19-1)

yìqǐ 一起 together (17-1)

yìqiānwàn 一千万 ten million (10-2R)

yìsi 意思 meaning (14-2)

yìzhí 一直 straight (18-1, 20-1R)

yīn 因 because (15-1R)

yīntiān 阴天 cloudy or overcast weather (22-1)

yīnwei 因为 because (15-1, 15-1R)

yīnwei...suóyi 因为······所以 because (15-1R)

yīngdāng 应当 should, ought to (19-2)

yīnggāi 应该 should (5-2)

Yīngguo 英国 England (6-2)

Yīngwén 英文 English language (11-1)

Yīngyǔ 英语 English language (16-2)

yò 哟 "gosh," "wow" (8-1)

yōngjǐ 拥挤 be crowded (19-1)

yònggōng 用功 be hardworking, studious (21-1)

yǒu 友 friend (14-1)

yǒu 有 have; there is, there are (3-2, 7-1, 10-2R)

yǒu yìsi 有意思 be interesting (4-2)

yǒude 有的 some (16-2)

yǒude shíhou 有的时候 sometimes (17-1, 17-1R)

yǒuyì 友谊 friendship (18-2)

yòu 又 again (17-1, 17-1R)

yòu 右 right (12-2, 12-2R)

yòubian 右边 right side, right (12-2, 12-2R)

yòu'éryuán 幼儿园 kindergarten (16-1)

yú 鱼 fish (20-2)

yǔ 雨 rain (22-1, 23-1R)

yǔyán 语言 language (9-1)

yǔyán shíyànshì 语言实验室 language lab (9-1)

yùbào 预报 forecast (22-1)

yuán 园 garden, park (20-2R)

yuán 原 original (16-1R)

yuánlái 原来 originally, formerly (16-1, 16-1R)

yuǎn 远 be far away (17-1, 18-1R)

yuè 月 month (9-2R)

yuè 越 exceed; more (22-1R)

yuè lái yuè 越来越 more and more (22-1, 22-1R)

yuèfen 月份 month (17-1)

Yuènán 越南 Vietnam (22-1R)

yuèpiào 月票 monthly ticket (21-2)

yún 云 cloud (22-1)

yùnqi 运气 luck (23-1)

Z

zài 再 again (8-2)

zài 在 be located in, at, on; be present; progressive aspect (6-1, 11-1, 11-1R, 23-1)

zàijiàn 再见 "good bye" (3-2)

zāng 脏 be dirty (21-1)

zāogāo 糟糕 "darn it"; be a mess (19-2)

zǎo 早 be early; "good morning" (21-2, 21-2R, 22-1)

zǎofàn 早饭 breakfast (11-2, 21-2R)

zǎoshang 早上 in the morning (9-1, 21-2R)

zěmme 怎么 how; why (5-2, 18-1R, 19-1)

zěmme bàn 怎么办 "what should be done?" (11-1)

zěmmeyàng 怎么样 how, in what way (3-2, 23-1R)

zěn 怎 how (18-1R)

zhàn 站 station, stop (20-2, 20-2R)

zhāng 张 (for flat objects) (11-1, 21-1R)

zhǎng 长 grow (14-2, 14-2R)

zhǎngdà 长大 grow up (14-2, 14-2R)

-zháo 着 (action of verb is realized) (21-2R)

zháojí 着急 worry, get excited (19-1)

zhǎo 找 look for; give in change (11-1, 11-1R, 19-2)

zhǎodào 找到 look for and find, find (21-2)

zhǎoqián 找钱 give (someone) change (19-2)

zhǎozháo 找着 look for and find, find (21-2)

zhè 这 this (5-2, 6-2R)

zhèbian 这边 this side, here (12-1, 12-1R)

zhèli 这里 here (14-2)

zhèmme 这么 like this, in this way, so (5-2, 9-2R)

zhèmme shuō 这么说 saying it like this; then (22-2)

zhèyang 这样 this way, like this (23-1R)

zhèyangzi 这样子 this way, like this (23-1R)

-zhe 着 (continuous aspect) (21-2, 21-2R)

zhèi- 这 this (5-1, 5-2, 6-2R)

zhèige 这个 this, this one (6-2R)

zhèiyang 这样 this way, like this (17-2)

zhèiyangzi 这样子 this way, like this (23-1)

zhēn 真 real, really (14-1, 14-1R)

zhěngqí 整齐 be in order, neat (21-1)

zhèng 正 just (22-2, 22-2R)

zhèr 这儿 here (11-1, 11-2R)

zhī 知 know (11-1R)

zhīdao 知道 know (11-1, 11-1R)

zhī 只 (for most animals) (20-2)

zhī 之 (written-style equivalent of 的) (17-2R)

zhīhòu 之后 after (17-2, 17-2R)

zhīqián 之前 before, ago (17-2, 17-2R)

zhí 直 straight (20-1R)

zhǐ 只 only (8-1, 19-2R)

zhǐhǎo 只好 have no choice but (19-2, 19-2R)

zhì'ān 治安 public order, public security (17-2)

zhōng 钟 bell; clock (8-2, 8-2R)

zhōng 中 middle, among (1-4R)

zhōngdiǎn 终点 final or terminal point (20-2)

zhōngdiǎn zhàn 终点站 last station, last stop (20-2)

zhōngfàn 中饭 lunch (11-2, 11-2R)

Zhōngguo 中国 China (5-1, 5-1R)

Zhōngguo huà 中国话 spoken Chinese (16-2)

Zhōng-Měi 中美 Sino-American (6-2)

zhōngtóu 钟头 hour (8-2, 8-2R)

Zhōngwén 中文 written Chinese, Chinese (4-1)

zhōngwǔ 中午 noon (10-1)

zhōngxīn 中心 center (11-2, 21-2R)

zhōngxué 中学 middle school (14-1)

zhòng 重 be heavy (19-2)

zhōu 州 state, district (2-1R)

zhù 住 live (in), stay (in) (10-1, 10-1R)

zhuānjiā 专家 expert (18-2)

zhuānjiā lóu 专家楼 foreign experts building (18-2)

zhuǎn 转 turn (20-1)

zhǔn 准 be accurate (21-2R, 22-1)

zhǔnbèi 准备 prepare, plan (21-2, 21-2R)

zhuōzi 桌子 table (11-1)

zì(r) 字(儿) character, word (5-2R, 16-2)

zìwǒ jièshao 自我介绍 introduce oneself (15-2)

zi 子 (noun suffix) (11-2R)

zǒngjīnglǐ 总经理 general manager (6-2)

zǒu 走 leave, depart, go, walk (3-2, 4-2R, 18-1)

zǒujìnlái 走进来 come walking in (23-1R)

zǒujìnqu 走进去 go walking in (23-1R)

zǒulù 走路 walk (18-1)

zǔfù 祖父 paternal grandfather (15-2)

zǔmǔ 祖母 paternal grandmother (15-2)

zuì 最 most (22-1, 22-1R)

zuì dī wēndù 最低温度 lowest temperature (22-1R)

zuì gāo wēndù 最高温度 highest temperature (22-1R)

zuì dīwēn 最低温 lowest temperature (22-1R)

zuì gāowēn 最高温 highest temperature (22-1R)

zuìhòu 最后 in the end, finally (19-2, 22-1R)

zuìjìn 最近 recently; in the near future (4-1, 22-1R)

zuǒ 左 left (12-2, 12-2R)

zuò 作 do, make (15-1R)

zuò 做 do, make (14-2)

zuò 坐 sit; travel by, take (4-2, 4-2R, 8-2)

zuò mǎimài 做买卖 do or engage in business (16-1)

zuótiān 昨天 yesterday (9-2)

zuǒbian 左边 left side, left (12-2, 12-2R)

zuǒyòu 左右 about, approximately (18-1)